# THEY HURT, THEY SCAR, THEY SHOOT, THEY KILL

# Studies in Young Adult Literature
## Series Editor: Patty Campbell

Studies in Young Adult Literature is intended to continue the body of critical writing established in Twayne's Young Adult Authors series and to expand it beyond single-author studies to explorations of genres, multicultural writing, and controversial issues in young adult (YA) reading. Many of the contributing authors of the series are among the leading scholars and critics of adolescent literature, and some are YA novelists themselves. The series is shaped by its editor, Patty Campbell, who is a renowned authority in the field, with a forty-year background as critic, lecturer, librarian, and teacher of YA literature. Patty Campbell was the 2001 winner of the ALAN Award, given by the Assembly on Literature for Adolescents of the National Council of Teachers of English for distinguished contribution to YA literature. In 1989 she was the winner of the American Library Association's Grolier Award for distinguished service to young adults and reading.

1. *What's So Scary about R. L. Stine?*, by Patrick Jones, 1998.
2. *Ann Rinaldi: Historian and Storyteller*, by Jeanne M. McGlinn, 2000.
3. *Norma Fox Mazer: A Writer's World*, by Arthea J. S. Reed, 2000.
4. *Exploding the Myths: The Truth about Teens and Reading*, by Marc Aronson, 2001.
5. *The Agony and the Eggplant: Daniel Pinkwater's Heroic Struggles in the Name of YA Literature*, by Walter Hogan, 2001.
6. *Caroline Cooney: Faith and Fiction*, by Pamela Sissi Carroll, 2001.
7. *Declarations of Independence: Empowered Girls in Young Adult Literature, 1990–2001*, by Joanne Brown and Nancy St. Clair, 2002.
8. *Lost Masterworks of Young Adult Literature*, by Connie S. Zitlow, 2002.
9. *Beyond the Pale: New Essays for a New Era*, by Marc Aronson, 2003.
10. *Orson Scott Card: Writer of the Terrible Choice*, by Edith S. Tyson, 2003.
11. *Jacqueline Woodson: "The Real Thing,"* by Lois Thomas Stover, 2003.
12. *Virginia Euwer Wolff: Capturing the Music of Young Voices*, by Suzanne Elizabeth Reid, 2003.
13. *More Than a Game: Sports Literature for Young Adults*, by Chris Crowe, 2004.
14. *Humor in Young Adult Literature: A Time to Laugh*, by Walter Hogan, 2005.
15. *Life Is Tough: Guys, Growing Up, and Young Adult Literature*, by Rachelle Lasky Bilz, 2004.
16. *Sarah Dessen: From Burritos to Box Office*, by Wendy J. Glenn, 2005.
17. *American Indian Themes in Young Adult Literature*, by Paulette F. Molin, 2005.
18. *The Heart Has Its Reasons: Young Adult Literature with Gay/Lesbian/Queer Content, 1969–2004*, by Michael Cart and Christine A. Jenkins, 2006.
19. *Karen Hesse*, by Rosemary Oliphant-Ingham, 2005.
20. *Graham Salisbury: Island Boy*, by David Macinnis Gill, 2005.
21. *The Distant Mirror: Reflections on Young Adult Historical Fiction*, by Joanne Brown and Nancy St. Clair, 2006.

# THEY HURT, THEY SCAR, THEY SHOOT, THEY KILL

## Toxic Characters in Young Adult Fiction

### Joni Richards Bodart

ROWMAN & LITTLEFIELD
Lanham • Boulder • New York • London

Published by Rowman & Littlefield
A wholly owned subsidiary of The Rowman & Littlefield Publishing
Group, Inc.
4501 Forbes Boulevard, Suite 200, Lanham, Maryland 20706
www.rowman.com

Unit A, Whitacre Mews, 26-34 Stannary Street, London SE11 4AB

British Library Cataloguing in Publication Information Available

**Library of Congress Cataloging-in-Publication Data**

Names: Bodart, Joni Richards, author.
Title: They hurt, they scar, they shoot, they kill : toxic characters in young adult fiction / Joni
    Richards Bodart.
Description: Lanham, Maryland : Rowman & Littlefield, 2016. | Series: Studies in young
    adult literature ; 52 | Includes bibliographical references and index.
Identifiers: LCCN 2016008890 (print) | LCCN 2016020928 (ebook) | ISBN 9781442230811
    (hardback : alk. paper) | ISBN 9781442230828 (electronic)
Subjects: LCSH: Young adult fiction, American—History and criticism.
Classification: LCC PS374.Y57 B63 2016 (print) | LCC PS374.Y57 (ebook) | DDC 813.009/
    9283—dc23
LC record available at https://lccn.loc.gov/2016008890

∞ ™ The paper used in this publication meets the minimum requirements
of American National Standard for Information Sciences Permanence of
Paper for Printed Library Materials, ANSI/NISO Z39.48-1992.

Printed in the United States of America

*A story helps folks face the world,*
*even when it frightens 'em.*
—*The Night Gardener* by Jonathan Auxier

To the YA authors who know about the darker sides of life, the evil, greed, prejudice, and hatred that exist in our world, and who do not flinch from showing that darkness to their teen readers. They know that teens have to be prepared to face risks, know dangers, and know how to defend themselves physically and emotionally.

These authors are the Wise Ones, the Sages that tell frightening stories that teach so much more than those who hide the truth. This book is dedicated to them, to defend, to honor, and to thank them for their daring, their courage, and their caring. The service that they do to controversial YA literature and the teens who read it is incalculable.

# CONTENTS

# ACKNOWLEDGMENTS

As always, there are multiple people to thank, because books, especially those requiring mountains of research, as this one did, are not written in a vacuum. First and foremost, my very patient editor at Scarecrow, Stephen Ryan, for hanging on with me when I failed to meet my deadlines. Patty Campbell, the series editor, was also patient, but also a bit cranky (in the very best way) when needed. I couldn't have asked for anyone better to work with than the two of you.

I also have to extend my thanks and appreciation to the authors who wrote the books I analyzed, who responded to my e-mails, and gave me their insight about their work. Because of you, this is a better, more thoughtful, and provocative book. I hope it brings more attention to your work, makes it more accessible to teens, and helps librarians defend it in the face of challenges.

Beth Wrenn-Estes, colleague, neighbor, and friend put up with postponed plans and administered reminders and pokes when necessary. Now I'm ready for that long postponed lunch at Horatio's! And going consignment shopping so we can have tofu fries again!

My other colleagues at the SJSU iSchool were great about asking how things were going and helping me stay motivated. Sandy Hirsh, our director, made sure I had a graduate assistant to work with, something that was most helpful and much appreciated.

And finally, Matthew Kirkland, that graduate assistant, who dug up monstrous research, compiled titles into the bibliography, and responded with grace and good humor to all my "DROP EVERY-THING AND DO THIS NOW!!!!" e-mails. He reformatted my citations into the correct style, found all kinds of books and articles to support my theses about the value of difficult and controversial titles with human characters as monsters, worked long hours when inspiration struck and I wrote maniacally, and schlepped his laptop all over the globe to stay in touch even while he was on vacation. And through all this, he kept his sense of humor and of fun, and never stopped reassuring me that he was actually having a good time. This book would not have been written without the years he spent working on it with me. Every writer should have a Matt in their lives.

# INTRODUCTION

## WHY ARE HUMAN MONSTERS SO IMPORTANT IN YOUNG ADULT LITERATURE?

**W**e live in a violent society, and being a teenager today is danger-ous. Mass shootings. Cars used as weapons. Bullying, in person and online. Violence is our national pastime.[1] It is constant: Guns and other weapons are prevalent; alcohol is a part of daily life, and for many, so are drugs. There is violence at home, at school, and in the community. Anyone who is different is singled out for teasing, bul-lying, and worse. Sex, whether consensual or not, is widespread, in spite of what many parents and teachers choose to believe. And monsters with human faces can show up anywhere, anytime.

For adults, much of that violence occurs at work. For teens, work is school, and so much of the violence they see occurs at school. And as the school shootings have increased, so have the YA books about them. *Give a Boy a Gun, Endgame, Shooter, After, Hate List, School Shooter: In His Own Words* are just a few of the titles I pulled up on a quick and dirty search on Amazon. There are many more.

We live in a violent culture, a culture of rage, of fury, of fear. Trying to protect children and teens from the world that they live in now and that will help shape them in the future, is not only futile, it is dangerous. They have to know how to survive the perils that may wait for them, no matter their ethnicity, their social class, their economic status, or their status among their peers. It's essential they know when to flee, when to fight, and how to do both most effectively and efficiently.

And the increase in violence isn't unique to the United States—it covers the rest of the world as well. Wars are fought by multiple countries, or in the case of civil war, by multiple groups within one country. Humans are addicted to violence,[2] and if we do not make stopping it a priority, the future may be as dark and bleak a place as the worlds of the dystopian novels now so popular with teens.

Violence has always existed, but not at the level at which we see it today. And the youngest members of society are having to deal with it at earlier and earlier ages, even when they are at home, where they should be able to feel safe. A stray bullet flies through a wall, killing or wounding a sleeping child. Family members demonstrate violence to the next generation—parent to parent; parent to child; and, less frequently, child to parent.

Why has this happened? People have proposed a variety of causes. The dissolution of the family is often blamed as a primary cause. The family is no longer the cohesive and secure container in which children can be raised and nurtured and taught values and ethics,[3] and as it has fractured and split apart, it leaves the most vulnerable members of society in the greatest danger. Ethics and mores are not passed down to future generations, while mistrust, violence, and rage are most of what they will inherit.

Teens today are a disconnected generation, unable to access the support and wisdom previous generations got from their families, both nuclear and extended. They are essentially raising themselves, apart from adult input. And when they make decisions, they don't always have an adult to go to for advice. I wonder if this is perhaps the reason why teen librarians are seeing an increase in the number of teens who come to them for not only information but also advice.

Weapons of all sorts, especially guns, have become increasingly available, and easier and easier to acquire. And it is also easier and easier to use them to act upon sudden and violent urges. We are also seeing more collateral damage: the person shot or hit by a car while walking the family dog, or bystanders shot by mistake, in the wrong place at the wrong time. More and more often, these shootings involve assault rifles that can be set to automatic firing—guns designed for and used by the military around the world. They are designed to kill people, and to kill quickly and easily.[4] Yet today, although assault rifles are not intended for civilian use, they have been used in many of the recent examples of mass shootings. And semiautomatic weapons, that are nearly as destructive, are available legally. Finding out how to obtain both automatic and semiautomatic weapons illegally, or how to adapt your legal weapon to fire automatically, is available online, on a variety of sites.[5] In fact, information on creating all kinds of bombs and weapons is widely available online as well, information used with catastrophic results by the brothers who devastated the entire country when they set off bombs at the Boston Marathon in April 2013.

Both movies and television have become more realistic and detailed in the depiction of violence, and NC17 ratings are more often given for depictions of sex than for images of violence. There is little that teens have not experienced/read/watched/heard by the time they enter high school, and middle schoolers are becoming more and more aware of problems and situations that previously have been the domain of older teens and adults. As a result, we have become increasingly accustomed to, and perhaps inured to, the ever-increasing levels of violence that we see around us on a daily basis. Psychological numbness to the violence, desensitizing ourselves to it, seems to be an almost inevitable consequence.[6] Just as soldiers are trained with replicas of humans as targets rather than bull's-eyes, to prepare them to be able to shoot at another person, we are taught to shrug off the violence that surrounds us, so we can endure higher and higher levels of it. That numbness allows us to regard it more casually, accept it more easily, even when we ourselves are more violent.

The emotions that lead to violence are anger and rage. While our culture has been described as a culture of fear,[7] it can also be described as a culture of rage. We are an angry people, made up of angry individuals.[8] It's not hard to find examples of anger every day—road rage brought on by overcrowded streets and freeways, anger from presumed discourtesy or offense from next-door neighbors, restaurant waitstaff, people in service positions of all kinds, employers or employees who are angry with each other for a myriad of reasons. The anger, rage, and violence created by our anxiety and fear that we dare not show publicly, are negative emotions that we suppress because they have been demonized by society and are seen as evil or dangerous. As therapists have told us for years, suppressed anger is more dangerous than anger expressed, because it builds up pressure over the years and can explode into psychopathic actions and emotions or turn inward into depression and self-violence. Mass murderers are not born, they are created.[9] Anger that is appropriately expressed is a healthy and positive thing. But when it is suppressed over time, it becomes darker and more twisted, more intense, more difficult to deal with, and more likely to be out of control when finally expressed. Today, anger, rage, and the violence that follows them have become all but ubiquitous in society, and so we are faced with an epidemic of violence on a cultural level, as well as on an individual level.[10]

Books are a source of education that is safer than the streets, safer than tales told by peers, and far, far safer than ignorance. In books, teens can learn by example what can happen in dangerous situations, how to respond to violence, to drugs, to bullying and rumors and shredded reputations. They can learn what actions work in which situations, and which don't. They can learn the ways that monsters with human faces can be outwitted or overcome. They can learn that they are not alone, they are not without choices or options, and survival is possible and achievable. They can see what happens when someone makes a mistake and decide that they will choose not to make the same or similar mistakes. They can learn that some adults are trustworthy; that they can understand and empathize with difficult situations, and even find ways to elude or escape them. Adults can be monsters, but they can also be heroes, rescuing teens in peril and pointing out the right way to go to find success.

But books are also dangerous and scary to adults who try to protect teens from our world, unwilling to understand that today's teens have been soaked in violence their entire lives. Perhaps from their first days of consciousness, and certainly by the time they toddle off to kindergarten, today's children are aware of the dangers in the world around them—through TV, through movies, on the Internet, through what they see on the streets and playgrounds, and sometimes, what they see at home. They learn early, from their parents' actions and messages, that there are some things parents just don't tell them. Parents protect their children, but children also keep their secrets. By the time they are teens, they are one person at home, another in their classrooms, and yet another with their peers. And they are probably far less naive than the adults around them believe them to be. That's not to say they have the answers—they believe they do, but they don't. Not all of them. And they are fortunate that learning, according to social learning theorists, isn't always based on actual personal experience, and can happen due to vicarious experiences, such as those found in books.

This epidemic, I believe, has led to the increasing levels of violence in literature for teens and even preteens. *The Hunger Games* trilogy horrified parents and other adults when the first volume was published in 2008—children forced to kill children, until only one survivor remains, the most violent person of the group. Yet only four years later, after the trilogy was complete, a movie about that book premiered. Its development had begun in 2009, only a year after the first book in the trilogy was published. The trilogy is also a crossover title, with as many or more adult fans as teens, for whom it was written.

It's long been known that teens want books that reflect their world: the sights, situations, and people that they see every day. The more violence they see in their daily lives, the more likely they will want to see that violence and those who perpetuate it in their books. Chris Crutcher is a young adult novelist who has always had a reputation for honest, hard-hitting books, that pull no punches, and speak in the language that teens themselves use daily. His books have been widely banned, but are wildly popular with teens, who see themselves reflected in their pages.

Crutcher has told a story about a presentation he gave at a Houston, Texas, high school. One girl waited until they were alone to approach him. "I don't have a question or anything, I just wanted you to know that when I read *Chinese Handcuffs*, I thought you knew me." One of the girls in the book had been sexually abused by both her father and her stepfather, and because of that depiction, the girl in Texas realized she was not the only one who was being abused, and was consequently able to talk about it and get help. She and Crutcher's other readers are why he refuses to back down from the in-your-face content of his novels.[11]

Crutcher's books are also used in therapy, both with individuals and groups. One group, discussing his novel *Staying Fat for Sarah Byrnes*, talked about how being stabbed (like the main character in the book) doesn't hurt at first, because of the shock. One of the girls in the group knew that firsthand and showed the scars from the stabbing that had taught her that grisly fact. Even the kids who haven't been stabbed by their mother can experience the loss and pain such an experience produces. They can feel the violence, darkness, and fear, but in a safe or controlled place, where they can close the cover and stop reading if it becomes more than they can handle. Real life isn't so easy.[12]

YA authors are well aware of the risks in publishing titles that include controversial and violent topics. Alexandra Flinn, author of *Breathing Underwater*, in which a boy is abused by his father and then abuses his girlfriend, has faced criticism and challenges. She wonders at parents who will let their children go to NC17 movies in middle school, yet object to realistic language and situations in the books they read. Realistic fiction shows the world as it truly is, and most teens who read, read at least some realistic fiction, and others read only that.[13]

That means that the authors of these books can teach lessons about life without the reader having to go through the situation in reality. But it also means that some characters have to be flawed, because perfect people don't have any problems to force them to

grow. Flawed characters are frequently unlikable, and they sometimes say or do dangerous or inappropriate things that teens recognize from their own experience but that adults may object to.[14] But
it is their flaws that force them to change. It is their flaws that make
them valuable to the reader, because the reader is able to see the
character in the book change and grow, and can apply that wisdom
to his or her own life and situations. This is why Alex Flinn wrote
*Breathing Underwater* from Nick's point of view—he was the only
one who was able to see that perspective, and how he went from
thinking he had done nothing wrong, to understanding what he did
and why it was wrong, and finally to changing his thinking and his
actions.[15]

Gail Giles explores the darker side of adolescence, how and why
people go wrong. *Dark Song*, her most recent novel, is about a girl
who falls for an older boy she meets online, and goes from being a
perfect daughter to a wild child, drinking, having sex, using drugs,
and not keeping her grades up. Finally her parents forbid her to see
him again, and the couple then murders the girl's parents. In doing
research on teen couples who kill or try to kill the girl's parents,
Giles found more than twenty cases, and notes that there have probably been others since she finished that research.[16]

Giles wrote her novel *Right Behind You* to examine the question
of how our past influences our future. It was inspired by a story she
saw on Court TV, about a twelve-year-old boy from a severely
abusive home who was sent to live with his grandparents. But they
didn't provide a safe place any more than his parents had, and so he
killed them. The trial didn't take place for three years; by that time
the boy looked and acted significantly different from the way he had
at twelve. It took the jury only three hours to sentence him to life
without parole. He was, essentially, thrown away. Giles began to
consider how we let our past sabotage our future by not dealing with
it, not forgiving ourselves for what we did, and not forgiving those
who harmed us. What if the crime is major or overwhelming? Could
it be so bad that it wouldn't be possible to move beyond it?[17]

Adults may be aware of the power of forgiveness, but few teens
have matured mentally enough to understand it. Their frontal lobes

do not finish developing until the early twenties. This area of the brain is the location of reason, where decisions are made logically rather than emotionally, once development of that area of the brain is complete. Giles's work allows teens the chance to question ideas they may not have previously considered from a rational standpoint. Her courage in looking at what other authors do not opens a door for the teens who read her books—they can look at someone else's dark side and better understand their own. [18]

When asked why she writes dark and edgy books, Giles responded that it is because teens need it. Lack of development of the frontal lobes means that they can't see the possible consequences of their actions. It is this that differentiates them from adults, who are able to see the future situations their current actions may create. Giles sees her books, and those of other authors who write equally dark and difficult books, as being like the Brothers Grimm's fairy tales, showing the dark places, the dangerous places, in hope that their readers will decide not to go there in real life. They show the consequences that teens are not able to see by themselves.

Teens love taking risks, daring themselves, believing that they are safe from any consequences because they can't see into the possible future, as adults can. So Giles wants her readers to go to those dangerous places on paper, to peer over the cliff into the abyss below, without the danger of falling into it accidentally. Books can be a safety valve, allowing their readers to learn about the dark side of life without actually having to experience it, to see that consequences happen to characters, and learn vicariously that such things can happen to them as well. [19]

Anger rules the teen years, and few glide through them smoothly. For most, it is a struggle, because not only do most adults not understand teens, they also don't understand themselves or their actions. Anger is the fuel for teens' journey to adulthood, because they have to figure out how to become an independent individual. And that involves divorcing their parents, at least for a little while, and sometimes that process is acrimonious. Anger can help teens get through it. It can be a constructive process, like surviving boot camp, discovering how strong you are, but too many times it is destructive, as it almost always is in dysfunctional families. It is supposed to be a time to learn how to survive, how to take care of yourself and your friends, and to practice making your own way in the adult world. But it's also a time when teens begin to realize that they've been lied to, and life isn't as easy as they've been told. This means that there is a sense of betrayal by parents or adults, and the result is teen rage. Boys act out on the street or at home. Girls act out against themselves, cutting or hurting themselves, turning against close friends who might help them, and getting into dangerous situations, primarily risky sexual situations, up to and including prostitution. They are in a push/pull tug of war, not a child any longer, but also not yet an adult. They want to be treated like an adult, but they also fear it and its responsibilities.[20]

But the anger teens experience is important, and helps them understand the uses of anger and the consequences as well. It can help them be strong, and understand that strength, but it can also hurt and damage the individual as well as the one it is aimed at. Anger turned inward can lead some to depression, or, depending on the individual and the situation, to psychopathic and criminal behavior. Learning how to use it and channel it is one of the most important lessons of the teen years. And one of the best ways of learning is from others who have experienced the same things—authors don't pull their punches or hide their truths. As Gail Giles puts it,

> If in our YA literature we ignore this teen rage, ignore the adolescent darkness of the heart we tell the traveler that he's alone. He is the only one that feels this way, and he can't understand that he must suffer Shakespeare's slings and arrows. Some books need be his companion, his fellow traveler.
>
> A story has a reader. The reader will seek the story he needs when he needs it. And the literature . . . says, "your feelings are valid. I have felt them too. Read on. This is what happened to me."[21]

But before we go on to a discussion of the dangers, violence, and monsters that teens meet both in real life and between the pages of a book, it's important to put some facts and stats together. According to the Centers for Disease Control, more than sixteen thousand teenagers (ages twelve to nineteen) have died each year since 1999. Most of those deaths were accidents, involving unintentional injuries, and more than one-third of those accidents involved cars. Homicide is the leading cause of death for black males—94.1 deaths per 100,000. In all other ethnic groups, accidents are the leading cause. Males are more likely to die than females, and older teens are more likely to die than younger ones—statistics that fit with the common perceptions about teen deaths.[22]

In addition, according to the ChildHelp website, more than six million children are reported as abused every year, about one every ten seconds. More than 90 percent of sexual abuse victims know the person abusing them. Thirty percent of abused and neglected children will abuse their own children. About 80 percent of twenty-one-year-olds who reported being abused as children met the criteria for at least one psychological disorder.[23] Abuse and violence statistics are spread across all social, class, ethnic, religious, economic, and educational backgrounds. One in four women and one in nine men experience domestic violence at some time in their lives, either as children or adults.[24] Those who experience it as children are also likely to experience it as adults. One in five high school girls reported physical or sexual violence from their dating partner. One in three know someone who has been physically hurt or damaged by their partners.[25] One-third of American adolescents experience some kind of physical, sexual, or emotional abuse from their dating partners, and only 33 percent of them reported the abuse or discussed it with friends. More than 80 percent of parents with dating teens don't think abuse is a problem for their children.[26] These are likely to be some of the parents who object most loudly to novels involving abusive situations of various kinds.

According to the CDC, homicide is the second leading cause of death of those between fifteen and twenty-four. Thirteen of that age group die each day. Males make up 86 percent of that group. Almost 83 percent of that group were killed with a firearm of some sort. More than 40 percent of males were in a fight within the last twelve months, and almost 25 percent of the females. They don't feel safe on the streets or in school, so they frequently carry weapons—almost 17 percent had carried a weapon of some sort within the thirty days previous to the survey. During that time, 12 percent were in a physical fight on school property, and almost 6 percent said they didn't go to school at least one of the previous thirty days because they didn't feel safe at school or on the way to or from school.[27]

Bullying happens daily. In 2010, more than 20 percent of teens reported being bullied on school property, and more than 16 percent reported that they had been bullied electronically. More than 20 percent of the teens bullied online were female, as opposed to 10.8 percent who were male. In 2011, 20 percent of high school students reported being bullied on school property and 16 percent were bullied online, while a 2009–2010 school-year survey reported that more middle school students than high school students reported being bullied on a daily and weekly basis. In 2012, 12 percent of both males and females reported bullying their peers.[28] Homophobic teasing/bullying of their peers was reported by 20 percent of the females and 34 percent of the males. Homophobic teasing/bullying of a friend was reported by 26 percent of the males and 24 percent of the females. Almost 30 percent to 40 percent of both boys and girls reported calling others either gay or lesbian.[29]

Bullying has results, suicide among them. Almost 16 percent of teens have seriously considered suicide, and almost 8 percent have attempted suicide, although reasons for these attempts were not specified. Overall, suicide is the third leading cause of death in people ages fifteen to twenty-four. This means that more teenagers and younger adults die from suicide than from cancer, heart disease, AIDS, birth defects, stroke, pneumonia, influenza and chronic lung disease combined.[30] Bullying, both in person and online, is responsible for enormous amounts of pain and trauma, and even self-injury and suicide. Bullying victims are two to nine times more likely to report suicidal thoughts and behaviors,[31] and bullies themselves are also at increased risk, as many become bullies because they were bullied.

An example of this is the case of Rebecca Sedwick, who killed herself after being relentlessly bullied by girls at school and online. Guadalupe Shaw, the main perpetrator, posted a chilling note on her Facebook page, gloating over the death.[32] She and Rebecca both came from difficult family situations. Neither Rebecca nor her sister had beds to sleep in; their father was not a part of the family, and their mother was unable to adequately take care of them. Guadalupe's mother was arrested for child abuse shortly before her daughter's arrest, and the whole family was characterized as totally out of control, with a "survival of the fittest mentality." Guadalupe seems to have just followed the examples set for her by her family when she began to bully Rebecca. Had Rebecca been stronger, or had Guadalupe's behavior sent up red flags, the ending might have been very different.[33]

Gay, lesbian, bisexual, and transgendered teens are bullied and discriminated against far more than straight teens. In 2009, a study of more than seven thousand LGBTQ teens reported that eight of ten students had been verbally harassed at school, four of ten had been physically harassed at school, six of ten felt that they were in danger while at school, and two of ten had been physically assaulted at school.[34] They were more likely than straight teens to report high levels of bullying and substance abuse. Students who were questioning their sexual orientation reported more bullying, drug use, depression, and suicidal behaviors than either heterosexual or homosexual teens did.[35] Regardless of sexual orientation, students do best (exhibit the lowest levels of depression and suicidal behavior) when they are in a positive school environment and not experiencing homophobic teasing or bullying.

But students' home environment also has a huge effect on how well LGBTQ teens are able to cope. Because parents can sometimes react to their children's decision that they are homosexual or transgendered by rejecting the child from the home, homosexual and transgendered teens have a much higher percentage of homelessness than straight teens.[36] And predictably, teens whose parents reject them also have significantly higher levels of both physical and mental health issues. When compared to LGBTQ teens who did not experience rejection, teens whose parents reacted negatively to their sexual orientation were almost six times more likely to have high levels of depression, were eight times more likely to attempt suicide, and three times more likely to use illegal drugs and engage in risky sexual behavior.[37]

Alcohol and drug abuse may be caused by a variety of reasons, including bullying, social situations at home or school, curiosity, or peer pressure, not to mention the influence of commercials and the actions of adults teens know or see. Most (70.8 percent) students have had at least one drink in their lives, 38 percent drink currently, and 21.9 percent of students have had five or more drinks in a row, or within a couple of hours. Almost 40 percent of teens have tried marijuana at least once, and 23.1 percent use it currently or regularly. Other drugs teens have tried or use regularly include cocaine (6.8 percent), glue/aerosol sniffing (11.4 percent), heroin (2.9 percent), steroids or prescription medications without prescriptions (3.6 percent or 20.7 percent). And 25.6 percent of students report being offered, given, or sold an illegal drug of some kind when on school property.[38]

Gangs and violence are also omnipresent in the lives of teens, with 36 percent of students in urban schools reporting gang violence in 2005, compared to 21 percent in suburban and 16 percent in rural schools.[39] Some of the reasons for the upswing of gang membership may be due to the increasing number of teens who are forced by absent parents to bring up themselves. Parents who work more than one job each are likely not to have free time to spend with their children. This is even more likely in one-parent families, where one person must do the job of both parents. In 2012, McDaniel showed that teens who had more "protective influences" in their lives were less likely to participate in gangs. Twenty-six percent of those who had only up to three of these influences reported gang participation, but only 1.6 percent of teens with seven or more of these influences were involved with gangs. These influences included parental monitoring, control, and warmth; strong social and coping skills; connections with religion or religious organizations; peer support; and support from adults at school.[40] Other studies on resilience in teens have shown that the consistent and positive support of at least one adult can increase a teen's resilience and help that individual overcome the most overwhelming odds. [41]

Statistics get even more startling when you examine the number of teens who die annually. Almost fifty out of every one hundred thousand teens die each year, figures that have been stable and consistent for decades. [42] More males than females die as teens, and death rates go up the older teens get. For males, the death rate goes up 32 percent every year between ages twelve and nineteen, and for females, the rate increases 19.5 percent every year. When these figures are broken down by ethnicity, black males have a death rate of more than ninety four deaths per one hundred thousand, Hispanic males, sixty-eight per on hundred thousand, and white males, sixty-two per one hundred thousand. The rates for females are, respectively, six, two, and one. [43] It's little wonder that kids surrounded by violence and death in real life would also look for the same themes in the books they read.

Whether the issue is sexual orientation, mental, physical, or emotional abuse, or simply surviving in a world where violence is a frequent option, teens need to know that they are not alone, not the only person who has ever had to deal with similar problems and situations, and that there are options and alternatives available to them. And while they are daunting to read and uncomfortable to think about, young adult fiction that presents scenarios that feel real to abused or marginalized teens must continue to be available, to give hope, and to illuminate choices.

## BAD PEOPLE COME FROM BAD SITUATIONS: THE QUESTION OF EVIL FROM A SOCIAL PSYCHOLOGY PERSPECTIVE

"Evil" can be a sloppy word, an impediment to understanding. It means "bad" plus "unidentified metaphysical stuff." Saying something is evil is often a way of ending a conversation, stopping further analysis, letting ourselves be satisfied with thought-

dulling mystery. "Evil" can also be a dangerous word. To say
something is evil is to say it can't be understood; it can only be
hated. We use the word "evil" when we need to prepare ourselves to do violence. Evil is the ultimate "other."[44]

What is evil, and where does it come from? Does it begin with an
individual's own genetics and chemistry, or is it something in the
situation or environment that causes someone to act in ways others
define as evil? It has been described as a lack of empathy, treating
others as objects rather than people, enjoyment of hurting others, or
allowing the situation to set the parameters for one's own actions.
But how do those characteristics develop?

Is evil something that we are born with, some kind of brain
weakness or defect, impossible to overcome? Or does it come from
the environment, the toxic or difficult situation that we live in—the
bad basket that spoils all the apples? Or is it a combination of the
two—bad nature plus bad nurture equals evil, when a combination
of good and bad results in a less-than-evil person, who may be
flawed but not beyond redemption?

Philosophers, psychologists, and religious/spiritual experts from
cultures across the world have debated the question for centuries,
and while some individuals' questions have been answered, there
doesn't seem to be one definitive answer. In addition, there is also
the question of transformation—can evil become good, or at least,
no longer evil? And the reverse, can good become evil? The answer
depends on whom you ask.

According to social psychologists, the meaning of an act depends
on the "eye of the beholder." There are at least two major perspectives: that of the perpetrator (the person doing the act) and the
victim (the person to whom the act was done). There are also other
perspectives involved: observers, who may be involved or uninvolved; family members; friends of either or both parties; and the
behavioral specialists who interpret and analyze the behavior to
determine its meaning.[45]

In addition, the term "evil" can also be said to involve some level
of escalation, as the behavior moves from small or even trivial ac-

tions to those greater and more intense actions affecting a larger group of people on a deeper and more profoundly negative level. In other words, according to Baumeister, studying people who break promises with impunity can tell us something about serial killers.[46]

Evil can also come from a lack of action—doing nothing in a situation requiring action. The classic example of this is the case of Kitty Genovese, who was attacked, stabbed, and raped in an alley behind her apartment building, purportedly while thirty-eight neighbors watched and listened, but did nothing. In fact, it was later shown that some of the "witnesses" had not heard the attack, which began at about 3:15 AM, because they were asleep and were not awakened by the noise. New York City in March is generally not yet warm enough for residents to leave windows open at night, so windows were closed. Not all the observers heard the whole attack, and many interpreted it as being a domestic quarrel or drunken brawl. Nevertheless, it did prompt investigation by social scientists into the bystander effect and the diffusion of responsibility. When there are many witnesses to an act, the responsibility to act is diffused among them, and so individuals are less likely to take action to assist the victim or stop the action of the perpetrator.[47] Diffusion of responsibility can be seen in several different kinds of situations. When a group of people allow events to occur that they would not have allowed had they been alone, it is referred to as "groupthink." The group can also lose motivation and feel less responsibility to the group's job or task, so that either the task is not accomplished or takes longer to accomplish, a process known as "social loafing." Finally, in a hierarchical organization, members claim no responsibility for their actions, because they were simply following orders, or because they gave the orders, but did not take any other action. The Nazis during World War II are an example of this latter form of diffusion.[48] This is commonly known as "passing the buck."

It is also important to remember that each observer in a situation has a different interpretation of it, so that what might be seen by one observer as positive action could be seen as negative action by another. Many people do harmful and cruel things, but yet do not define themselves as evil.[49] Perpetrators do not see their actions as being important, nor extremely detrimental to the victim. The victim, on the other hand, sees the perpetrator's actions as extremely harmful and damaging. The victim plays up the horror, while the perpetrator plays it down. The perpetrators look at only the action itself, in the present, while victims place the event in a timeframe, including both the past and the projected future in their stories. [50]

The causality of the action is also varied. Perpetrators tend to blame the victim for "making me do it," while victims assign no self-blame at all—they think they are completely innocent, and the perpetrator acted without a reason. [51]

Baumeister, in *Evil: Inside Human Violence and Cruelty*, says that those who do what is considered to be evil may not believe that their actions are evil—it is the victim of those actions who defines them as evil, by asking why did this happen, and why did it happen to me? Pain and suffering create a search for their meaning—people have never been content to define suffering as random happenstance. Those who suffer want to assign a reason, a rationale for their suffering, and evil is one reason. Most people have a set of positive beliefs—the world is mostly a good place, and they are mostly good people, and life is mostly fair. When those beliefs are torn apart, it can resonate down to the bedrock of their belief system. While the physical scars of rape, or robbery, or an attack fade over time, the psychological scars can last a lifetime, especially if the individual is unable to work on recovering from those scars in a therapeutic setting. [52]

It is also important to consider why an event is defined as evil. Not everyone defines either people or actions as evil in exactly the same way. So, how to define evil, how to explain what is evil and what is not? It is a slippery proposition. Baumeister demonstrates this with a story of a woman in an airport: she's hungry, and stops at a restaurant and orders a bag of chips and a drink. There are no empty tables, so she sits at one occupied by a middle-aged man in a suit, reading a newspaper. She is a little nervous about sitting with a stranger, so she unwraps her straw and has several sips of her drink. Then she takes a chip. When he hears the crunch, the man glares at her. He looks at the bag of chips and back to her. He says nothing and continues to read his paper. The woman eats a chip every so often, and the man's glare gets increasingly cold and dangerous, making the woman even more afraid. Then the man takes a chip for himself and eats it, looking at her hard as he does so. Neither speaks, but they continue to take turns eating chips, until the bag is almost empty. By this time the woman is truly afraid—why would someone eat food belonging to someone else? Her heart is pounding, her hands shake, but she continues eating until her drink is almost gone, and the bag is almost empty. She can't stand it any longer, so she gets up, nods to the man, and leaves. She is still frightened when she gets to her gate, and she just sits there wondering what just happened. What kind of a person would boldly reach over and take someone else's food and then glare at them so menacingly? She feels as if she has had a narrow escape from such an angry, selfish person. Then her flight is called, and she opens her purse to get out her ticket, and there in it is her bag of chips. *She* is the person who has eaten someone else's food! Certainly, the man was feeling all the same things she had been feeling, but about her!

We all do evil at times—take actions that are considered by someone else to be evil—without ever realizing that what we do is evil. Part of evil involves one person inflicting harm on someone else. (The man ate the chips the woman had paid for.) Another part is the chaos that evil causes. (The woman was less upset about losing a few chips than she was about the rules of her world being violated.) Evil is outside the rules, and evil breaks the rules about "the way things are supposed to be," creating confusion and chaos.[53]

But evil is rarely found in an individual's self-image—it is found in the opinion of others about what that individual has done.[54] The most common form of evil is violence, but evil is also part of oppression and petty or meaningless cruelty. Those actions that are deliberately taken, knowing that they will harm other people, either physically, emotionally, or psychologically, because that harm is desired and intentional, those actions are evil.[55] Ego is also a part of evil—people who are criticized, insulted, or humiliated, can respond with evil—the deliberate attempt to harm someone else in retaliation for the harm done to them.[56] Violence and anger and chaos are all too prevalent in our society. You don't have to give someone a reason to be violent—there are reasons all around us every day. All that is necessary for evil to erupt into the world is to take away someone's need for restraint. Just a small weakening of self-control can be enough to produce an increase in violent and chaotic actions, creating evil that is all too eager to burst upon the scene and stir things up.[57]

All that said, there is still the question of nature vs. nurture—why do some people do evil things when others in similar situations do not? The individual's ethics, morality, and social environment will have a large role in whether or not he or she will or will not respond with violence.[58] I also think that age plays a major role—remember, earlier I said teens have partially undeveloped brains, and are unable to make the kinds of rational and considered decisions that adults can make. They are far more likely to take an immediate and impulsive action that is more a *reaction* than an action. Many parents ask their teens, "What were you thinking?" after finding out about some risky behavior. The answer is, they weren't thinking—they don't really know how to yet—they were just reacting.

Miller identifies four roots of evil—the reasons why people do evil things. First of all, it is a *means to an end*, and results in the perpetrator getting something he/she wants. The means can be evil, while the end is not, or both can be evil, resulting in some sort of material gain by the perpetrator. Second, evil behavior can occur because the perpetrator's ego has been attacked or threatened. Violence can come from that threat when the perpetrator seeks to counter or defend against it.[59] Occasionally, evil can be motivated by idealism—doing evil allows the perpetrator to reach a desired good. In this situation, the perpetrator believes that the end justifies the means.[60] The child who is continually physically punished for doing wrong is one example of this—if the observer sees the punishment as evil, but the end of inappropriate behavior as good. It is important to note that this is not the only example of the end justifying the means, and many are more intense or extreme. Finally, sadism, or the enjoyment of inflicting hurt on someone else, is an attribution frequently seen in victims' accounts, but infrequently in perpetrators'.[61] If inhibitions are worn down or justifications are given for the need to inflict pain, it can result in either of these two last types of behavior.

Two experiments show how easily we can be tricked into doing something that most people would characterize as evil: Philip Zimbardo's Stanford Prison Experiment and Stanley Milgram's Obedience Experiment, done while he was a professor at Yale. While they took place in 1963 and 1971, the implications still resonate throughout the world of social psychology, and experiments similar to them are still being done today. (As a result of regulations protecting the safety of human participants in research experiments put in place since these experiments, they can no longer be exactly duplicated. More information on the American Psychological Association's Code of Conduct is available on their website, http://www.apa.org/ethics/code/.)

Milgram's experiments were done at the beginning of his career, when he was an assistant professor.[62] This series of experiments, begun in 1963, has had a huge impact on the understanding of why people do bad things. The results have been statistically unchanged in the many experiments around the world that duplicated his work.[63] His experiments demonstrated, with no doubt whatsoever, that ordinary individuals could be persuaded to act destructively against another human being, even without physical punishment, and that even average, "off the street" people could do things to another person that were immoral and inhumane. Most people believe that when confronted with a problem demanding a moral response, they would "do the right thing" according to their own definition of right. Milgram's experiments proved dramatically and clearly that this is not always the case. When a situation involves strong social pressure, our morality can be left in the dust.[64] And this willingness to do evil, or to do nothing, crosses boundaries of age, social class, and cultures. The unseen parts of social interaction, social rules and norms, have a far greater impact on our actions than we believe they do.[65]

Three roles were involved in the experiment. The researcher, the student, and the teacher. Unknown to the teacher, who was a volunteer, the student was in collaboration with the researcher. The teacher was to help the student learn a series of paired words, giving the students electrical shocks for every incorrect answer. Milgram designed an impressive-looking machine with switches on it labeled with various shock levels, such as "slight shock," "moderate shock," "danger: extreme shock." The last two switches were labelled only "XXX." The teacher was told that the shock levels went from 30 to 450 volts, increasing 15 volts at a time. The researcher and the teacher were in one room, and the student was in the next room, but could communicate with the teacher. The student would react as if shocked, but would receive no shocks at all. Both the student and the researcher had scripts to work from, ensuring that both did and said the same things with each teacher. The student would complain about the pain and tell the teacher of a heart condition. When the 300-volt level was reached, the student banged on the wall and demanded to be released. After this point the student said nothing at all, and the teacher was instructed to treat silence as an incorrect answer. Most teachers objected to continuing at some point, and when they did, the researcher had a series of increasingly forceful comments, requiring that the teacher continue. These included: "Please continue"; "The experiment requires that you continue"; "It is absolutely essential that you must continue"; and finally, "You have no other choice, you must go on." The experiment concluded when either the 450 mark was reached three consecutive times or the teacher refused to participate any longer.

Milgram had surveyed some of his colleagues, senior university students majoring in psychology and psychiatrists teaching at a medical school, and all had anticipated that only a very small number of teachers would give the maximum shocks, and most would not pass beyond using the switch labeled as "very strong."[66] In reality, 65 percent, twenty-six out of the forty participants, were willing to administer the most extreme shock, even though they didn't want to do it, were uncomfortable about doing it, stopped and questioned the researcher about the experiment, and asked to stop the experiment, offering to give back the minimal amount they had been paid—$4.50 in 1961. They exhibited various signs of stress and tension—elevated breathing, sweating, shaking, groaning, among others. But when asked to continue, all but fourteen did so.[67] They became distraught and angry at the researcher, yet they continued to shock the students.[68]

Miller gives several reasons for this obedience to authority over personal preference or ethics. There was a believable cover story, one that gave the teachers a specific role to play, with specific actions for specific behaviors from the students. The researcher gave verbal requests for the teachers to continue, confirming that continuing to shock students was the desired behavior. The rules for the teacher to follow were clear and specific. The shocks were defined as "helping" the students learn, not "punishing" them for their errors. The shocks started at a very minimal level and built up gradually, letting the teacher get used to shocking the student before reaching the "dangerous" levels of shocks. Then the researcher made the cost of ending the experiment very high with his verbal feedback to the teacher about the necessity of continuing. The levels of intensity and aggression were raised gradually, so the teacher was less likely to notice it,[69] like the story of the frog dropped into a cool pot of water, in which the temperature is raised gradually until the frog is cooked, without its ever trying to jump out of the water. A frog dropped into a pot of hot water will refuse to stay there, but gradually raising the temperature allows the frog to adjust to it, just as the teachers adjusted to a slowly increasing level of intensity and aggression. However, in later experiments, Milgram learned that when peers were present and refused to go along with the researcher's orders, teachers also refused to participate, and thirty-six out of forty refused to give the maximum shock.[70]

However, in more recent years, a California social psychologist, Jerry M. Burger, of Santa Clara University, partially duplicated Milgram's experiment, making adjustments in it that allowed it to pass the university's institutional review board for research using human subjects. Even with these changes making it a more ethical procedure, the results were essentially the same. The majority of participants were willing to continue until told to stop. There were no gender differences, even though Burger thought that there might be. In addition, there was no significant difference between the actions of the participants when they acted alone or with the presence of a peer who refused to continue with the experiment. The influence of the situation and the influence of the individual were seen to be equal to a great extent, giving more power to the situation than had been seen previously. The reactions of the participants had not changed significantly in spite of the almost fifty years separating the two experiments. [71]

In the second experiment, the participants were not being taught something, but were playing the roles of guards and prisoners in a jail constructed in the basement of the psychology building on the Stanford campus. Phillip Zimbardo, a Stanford faculty member since 1968, [72] was the lead investigator and creator of the Stanford Prison Experiment (SPE), which took place at Stanford during August 1971. [73] Originally it was intended to last for two weeks, but was terminated after only six days because of the unexpected changes in the behavior of both guards and prisoners. [74] It is one of the best known experiments on the effects of prison guard behavior on the prisoners they guard.

Twenty-four males were selected to fill roles of either "prisoner" or "guard." They were a deliberately homogenous group, all mentally and physically healthy, and were aware of the roles that they would be expected to play. Half of them were randomly assigned to each group. [75] As Zimbardo noted later, "At the start of this experiment, there were no differences between the two groups; less than a week later, there were no similarities between them." [76] All of them had been completely transformed by their roles in only six days. The guards used psychological abuse, because physical abuse was not allowed. [77] The prisoners either learned how to cope with the situation or broke under the pressure. They were all punished when one of them didn't obey orders, and so were frequently united against the outlier, who was abused by them as well as by the guards. [78] The guards became enforcers of the rules, and the prisoners became their victims. When the prisoners revolted, whether they used passive-aggressive or aggressive-aggressive tactics, they were punished. With some of the guards, they were punished for no reason at all, other than the other guards' amusement.[79]

Zimbardo's girlfriend and later wife, Christina Maslach, confronted Zimbardo and was able to show him how caught up in it even he had become, transforming from an easy-going university professor to a prison superintendent whose first priority was keeping prisoners in line, and so allowing the abuse to continue.[80]

Zimbardo learned from the experiment that bad situations can make good people do evil things. It's not that one bad apple spoils the basket, but that one bad basket can spoil all the apples. Situations where hurtful actions are praised and condoned are much more likely to create evil actions than ones that condemn them. While most people are good most of the time, they can be seduced into committing acts that are antisocial or destructive. Any discussion of evil must involve three things: what the individuals bring into the setting, what the situational forces bring out in those actors, and how the system forces create and maintain those situations.[81] Good people will do evil in bad situations. The power of the situation far outweighs the power of the individuals in that situation.[82] In the Stanford Prison Experiment, Zimbardo created a situation that was far more powerful than anyone, even he, had expected. It was so powerful that although the experiment was cut short, those who participated in it, no matter what roles they played, were utterly changed for the rest of their lives.

Zimbardo takes three psychological truths from his work at Stanford. First, both evil and good exist in the world—they always have and they always will. Second, the barrier between good and evil is permeable, thus, the third truth—angels can become devils, and although it is more difficult, devils can become angels. In one lifetime, an individual can be both an angel and a devil.[83] Given the right situation and motivation, anyone can commit evil deeds. We fear evil but are fascinated by it, drawn to the Otherness of it, the wrongness of how it doesn't fit into our world. Based on these three truths, Zimbardo defines evil similarly to the way Baumeister did: "evil consists of intentionally behaving in ways that harm, abuse, demean, dehumanize, or destroy innocent others—or using one's authority and systemic power to encourage or permit others to do so on your behalf." Evil is knowing better and still doing worse.[84]

Most people choose to believe that there is an unbridgeable chasm between good people and bad people. This makes evil a quality that exists in some people and not in others. That takes the responsibility off the good people. They don't have to worry about being a part of anything evil. Evil is Other to them.[85] However, some people subscribe, like Zimbardo, to an incremental view of evil—anyone can do evil, depending on the circumstances. Our human nature can be changed by the situation, either toward more good, or toward more evil. We can become more evil regardless of our genetics, personality, or family dynamics and heritage.[86] This is a far less comfortable perspective, since it requires the individual to be aware continually of his/her actions, thoughts, motives, and emotions in every situation. It focuses on the situation, rather than the individual.

To some extent, the situation determines the individual. You are not the same person all the time. You are not the same person working alone or working with a group. You are not the same person with close friends and with acquaintances. You are not the same person in a romantic setting and in an educational setting. In one setting, you might be a good person, in another, not so much. We all exist within overlapping systems of power, and it is those systems that control the situations, and ultimately the individual. This is the essence of Zimbardo's definition of evil—it exists, and it exists everywhere, so constant vigilance is essential.

The SPE quickly became notorious and was widely criticized for the way students had been treated, although the Stanford Human Subjects Research Committee had approved the project. No one had imagined that the guards' treatment of the prisoners would become that extreme that quickly. In 1973, an inquiry by the American Psychological Association revealed that the study had indeed complied with the professional guidelines at the time. However, since that time, those guidelines have been changed to prevent similar research protocols being done in the United States.[87]

In 2002, a documentary series was produced by the BBC that replicated the SPE, but which included various controls to prevent unethical treatments of those who participated in it. These measures included screening and continuous observation of the participants by clinical psychologists, medics, security personnel, and a six-person ethics committee, which had the power to stop the experiment. During this series, the guards did not get so deeply into their roles as the SPE guards, and the prisoners generated a shared sense of community, leading them to resist the guards' demands, eventually leading to a prison breakout that effectively ended the experiment two days earlier than expected. However, its goal was examining tyranny and resistance, and how setting up a social network among the prisoners could help foster the latter, as contrasted to Zimbardo's investigation into prisoner-guard interactions.[88]

Yet another social control/social psychology experiment took place at Cubbersley High School in Palo Alto, California, during the spring of 1967, when first-year history teacher Ron Jones decided to teach his students about the Holocaust by re-creating it in his classroom. When students asked him how the German people could just go along with all the things the Nazis did, he couldn't give them an answer, so he decided to show them, inventing a movement he named the Third Wave.

The next day, when sophomores in his three classes of Contemporary World walked into class, they were greeted by *Strength through Discipline* written on the board, and a new way to act in class that would help them learn. Then the mottos *Strength through Community* and *Strength through Action* advanced the idea that working together and taking action as a group could give students power and energy. The Third Wave quickly spread throughout the school, with dozens of students cutting classes to go to Jones's classes. There were membership cards, armbands, banners, and a salute. The social positions of students were changing, and suddenly everyone was part of the group—or wanted to be. There was a martial air about the Third Wavers, and they were rigid about who was a part of the Wave and who wasn't. Members who didn't obey the rules of the Third Wave were reported to Jones for disciplinary action or were bullied into submission.

By Thursday, the fourth day, Jones knew he had to stop what was happening. The next day, there was a rally for Third Wave members in the auditorium. The members were from all of the cliques and social classes in the school, the jocks, the populars, the nerds, the druggies, even some of the loners and the losers. Jones revealed to them how they had been manipulated, and why they had become the Nazis of their school. Then he played a film about the Holocaust that ended with stark words on the screen—"Everyone must accept the blame. No one can claim that they didn't in some way take part."

Jones then explained how they would all make good fascists, because fascism doesn't exist just in history, but in the present day as well. They too would have looked the other way; they too would have made "good Germans."[89] And perhaps in the same situation, so would we.

There are times and there are situations when good people do bad things, letting the situation have power over their ethics and their morals. Perhaps they will be able to revert to being good people when freed from that situation and that setting, learning how to recover and live without damaging themselves or others. Or perhaps not, and they will carry that situation with them throughout life, continuing do bad things, to do evil, and to damage others and themselves. Perhaps they are monsters, or perhaps they are just broken and unable to recover. Either way, their deeds and actions can be monstrous and can hurt and scar and shoot and kill. They are the ones we need to know how to confront and vanquish, in one way or another. Confronting the monster is not easy, especially when we realize that the monster is within us, but it is necessary.

# Part I

# Mass Murderers: Serial Killers and School Shootings

These days the news is full of mass deaths—in schools, in malls, on streets and highways, in places once considered safe, that no longer are. Reading or watching the news is frequently no fun at all. And as always, what is happening in the world teens live in is reflected in the books they read.

Recently, one of the most visible monsters in teen fiction has been the serial killer. Famous serial killers from the past have been cloned in *The Cain Project*, by Geoffrey Girard, who also published the same story from an adult point of view in *Cain's Blood*. A teen girl is fixated on a serial killer in Robert Cormier's *Tenderness*. Barry Lyga's protagonist in *I Hunt Killers* and *The Game*, is the son of the world's worst serial killer, who has taught him everything he knows. Fortunately, Jazz has decided to take what he learned and hunt killers, rather than becoming one. The Cordelle sisters, daughters of a serial killer, decide to follow in his footsteps in Dia Reeves's *Slice of Cherry*. Serial killers have even invaded graphic novels, with *My Friend Dahmer*, by Derf Backderf, which has won three awards from YALSA, and introduces the adolescent Dahmer, as seen by Backderf, who went to school with him. It is the chilling unraveling of a troubled boy, with multiple demons pulling at him, and ends with his first murder, when he went from being (in Backderf's mind) a human being to a monster.[1] In Todd Strasser's *Wish You Were Dead*, death is as easy as writing someone's name in a blog. This is one blog you definitely want to avoid. John Halliday's *Shooting Monarchs* traces the development of a serial killer from "cradle to courthouse"[2] revealing a childhood with little hope and few options that led to dropping out of school, stealing, kidnapping, and finally murder, while still in his teens.[3] *In the Path of Falling Objects*, by Andrew Smith, follows two brothers on a road trip from hell, and includes one of the most violent and creepy serial killers/ psychopaths I have ever seen in young adult literature. Graham McNamee's *Acceleration* is about how Duncan's summer job at a lost-and-found office of a subway station leads him to the journal of a serial killer, a madman stalking his prey on the subway trains.

Jack the Ripper is featured in several titles, including *The Name of the Star* and *The Madness Underneath*, by Maureen Johnson, as well as the Shades of London series; the Ripper trilogy by Amy Carol Reeves, including *Ripper*, *Renegade*, and *Resurrection*; and *Ripper*, by Stefan Petrucha.

School shootings may involve only one incident, but there are always multiple victims. *Hate List* by Jennifer Brown, *Endgame*, by Nancy Garden, *Quad*, by Carrie Gordon, *Give a Boy a Gun*, by Todd Strasser, *The Last Domino*, by Adam Meyer, and *Shooter*, by Walter Dean Meyers, are only a few of the many titles published on this topic. After Columbine, Chris Crutcher trashed his book on a school shooting, and all that remains of it is a short story, "Guns for Geeks," in Don Gallo's anthology on outsiders, *On the Fringe*. (This story is discussed starting on p. 77.) He wrote about it in *School Library Journal*, in August, 2001.

> [I] got it in the mail about two weeks before I was to make a presentation to the Texas Library Association. I arrived in Dallas, took a cab to my hotel, unpacked my clothes, and flipped on the television set, only to be astonished with the rest of the

nation by the now familiar images of students hurrying out of Columbine with their hands on their heads, past the police and SWAT teams. When I recovered from the initial shock, the obvious became just that, and I called Susan Hirschman, then my editor at Greenwillow Books. She said, "We've been waiting for your call." I asked if my manuscript was on her desk and she said yes.

"Is your garbage can next to your desk?"

She said yes, and I said, "Do it."

She said, "Thank you."

There was no way that novel could have been published without being seen as exploitative, no way my intent would break through. Absent that, Columbine still reduced the events in my story to a footnote, our collective consciousness regarding guns in schools forever changed.[4]

Crutcher had based his story on a shooting in Moses Lake, Washington, in 1996. Barry Loukaitis, fourteen years old, had been bullied and tormented for years, came to school dressed as an old western gunfighter with a long black coat, a rifle, a revolver, and 78 rounds of ammunition and shot two boys in his algebra class, wounded a girl, and killed the teacher. One of the coaches heard the shots, and came into the classroom and was able to stop him.

Why the demand for books about kids who kill, or who might kill, or who will kill? Serial killers are featured on TV shows such as *Criminal Minds*, *NCIS*, *Dexter*, and many others. School shootings may not be a part of entertainment television, but they are certainly part of the national news programs on a disturbingly regular basis. Why wouldn't they show up in books as well?

And it's important to point out that not all teen protagonists in these titles are killers. Some hunt the killers. In *The Cain Project*, the narrator isn't a killer, but just has the genes of a killer—the potential of a killer. They look at the genesis of a killer, how someone first learned to kill, and then learned to enjoy the process. They explain the killer, and resolve some of the mystery that surrounds him, allowing readers to see commonalities between the characters in the book and the people in their own lives. Information allows understanding, and understanding can help reduce fear and rejection.

These books confront the question of good and evil, what they are and why they exist. Understanding the difference is just one of the life lessons of adolescence, and teens can find at least some of the answers by learning about killers and why they decide on such drastic and radical actions. Evil is frightening, and learning more about it helps teens gain some control over their fear.

And it is important to remember that it is adults who do most of the objecting to books about mass murderers. Teens take from them what they want and need, and skip over the parts that are too difficult for them to deal with.

But one question none of the fiction on mass murderers can answer is "Why?" Sure, some kids who are bullied become killers, but many more don't. Even psychologists have not come up with a definitive answer. Until recently, in fact, psychologists have not really examined the question, because they explained it in one of three different ways: Killing four or more people at one time could be explained using the same theories that are used to explain single victim crimes; mass murders were caused by psychopathy, severe mental disorders that were most appropriately treated by psychiatry; or such events were considered rare aberrations, and therefore not worthy of research. In addition, it has been hard to study the mass murderer because of the paucity of primary material: mass murderers are usually deceased, inaccessible for legal reasons, or simply not inclined to cooperate and participate in research studies. Because of the lack of research, much of the material on the question of causality has been based on myth, misunderstanding, and speculation.

Murderers do not snap and suddenly kill indiscriminately without planning. In actuality, they have planned for weeks, months, or years to kill, and where, when, how, and whom to kill. They are methodical, careful, and detailed. This careful preparation can help explain their relaxed demeanor while killing many people, one after the other. Motives for mass killing center around five different themes: revenge (the most frequent cause for action), power, loyalty, terror, and profit. And the assassins know exactly what they are doing and why.[5]

Another myth is that mass shootings are on the rise, although FBI data on them indicates that there have not been significant changes in the number of mass shootings since 1976,[6] nor has the number of victims per incident increased,[7] in spite of rumors and even research asserting the opposite. It is an emotional and contentious issue for several reasons. First, there are political motivations on both sides, and, as with many other issues, the loudest voices are frequently the most extreme. Secondly, there is no clear and precise definition of what "mass killing/murder" really means—the precise number of people killed, their relationship to the murderer, and so on, making it easy to find reputable studies supporting either position in this argument. The FBI statistics are commonly cited in many of the related studies, but the issue lies in how the data is massaged. While some studies, such as the highly publicized one put out by *Mother Jones* in 2013[8] show a rise in mass shootings over the last few decades, they do so partly by using a somewhat arbitrary set of criteria for defining "mass shootings," leaving out gang-related violence and only including events where "killings were carried out by a lone shooter" where at least four people were killed.

These limitations distort the data set to a certain extent—for instance, a study put out by Texas State University[9] found that the median number of people killed during "active shooter events" was two, meaning that many of the incidents that law enforcement would define as "mass shootings" were left out. This discrepancy is pointed out in a 2013 editorial by James Alan Fox, a professor of criminology at Northeastern University who has published multiple books on serial and mass murder, in which he notes that "*Mother Jones* also eliminated massacres involving family members, even though they too can involve large body counts, such as the massacre of 14 relatives and two others by R. Gene Simmons of Russellville, Arkansas, in 1987. Other massive shootings, like the execution-style slaughter of 13 in a Seattle club in 1983, were ignored because of their relation to gang activity or some criminal enterprise. Particularly mystifying is the decision not to include cases involving multiple perpetrators yet to waive this condition for two school shootings."[10] Not only is it hard to defend the statistics published by *Mother Jones* because of the criteria used to disqualify certain cases, those criteria were not applied consistently and unilaterally. It would seem to indicate that *Mother Jones* cherry-picked the data to give the results they wanted to find.[11]

However, the FBI figures are based on information from those reported to them by local law enforcement as part of the routine collection statistics. The FBI figures exclude only incidents in which fewer than four victims (other than the shooter) were killed, incidents that did not include the use of a firearm of some kind, and ones that occurred in areas where statistics were not reported to the FBI.[12]

It is also important to remember that the public's perceptions are more strongly influenced by recent events than by those in the more distant past, especially with the blitz of media attention mass shootings now attract, and our increasing use of a variety of media formats to keep up to date with the latest statistics.[13]

Given that any data set can prove anything, based on how the individual figures are manipulated, it seems logical that the FBI figures, which are the most inclusive, with the fewest number of restricting criteria, should be given precedence over other figures that have been more narrowly interpreted.

And while many connect violent entertainment, especially video games, to mass shooters, no such link has been found, although violent people are attracted to violent entertainment, including video games.[14] A Canadian study in 2011 found that there were no significant differences in the emotional response to violent or negative images between groups of violent video game players and groups of non–game players. The game players had not become desensitized to the negative images despite their playing violent games.[15] In addition, a *Time* editorial published just after the Newtown shooting cited several research studies, including the Ryerson one, that were not able to link playing video games with subsequent violence. Exposure to violent video games neither increased aggressive behavior nor decreased prosocial behavior. Viewing violence on the screen did not decrease gamers' empathy for victims of real crimes.[16]

In 2002, Brooks Brown, who was a friend of Dylan Klebold and Eric Harris, the shooters at Columbine High School in 1999, wrote *No Easy Answers: The Truth behind Death at Columbine,* to share his perspective on the event. Although both Klebold and Harris enjoyed violent music and video games, Brown states that he does not believe that these influenced the two to take action. He states that hundreds of kids play violent video games, watch violent television shows and listen to violent music, yet do not commit violence.[17] The answers to the question "why?" are far more complex, although it is far easier "to say *Doom* and *South Park* are ruining our kids than to think we may have had something to do with it."[18]

Brown also comments of the isolation of adolescent culture, since parents are both working, sometimes at more than one job; have their own lives; and leave the upbringing of their children to school personnel, who are neither tasked with nor prepared for that responsibility. As a result, teens today are an example of "the blind leading the blind," getting their morals and values not from caring adults, but from schoolyard bullies and teachers who prefer the popular kids to the outsiders who intimidate them, and of whom they are afraid.[19] Kids learn that might means right; that beauty, popularity, and approval always win; that there is a virtually unmovable hierarchy in schools; and that those who do not fit in for some reason are at the bottom, scorned and even attacked by all, including the school personnel assigned to protect them. Bullies demand whatever they choose from these outsiders, who are taught the message that life is not fair, and that "Because I said so" is a reason powerful enough to enforce almost any edict.[20]

While some teens learn how to survive years of jeers, sneers, and attacks, some do not and develop a deep-seated darker side, steeped in rage, and determined to achieve revenge. Did the video games, the movies and TV, the music, the bullies, or the unseeing adults create that dark side? Why are some kids affected and others not? Is it a genetic difference enhanced by a societal one? There are no definitive answers in spite of the massive amount of research that has been done on the "nature vs. nurture" argument. Brown notes that, to prevent future escalation the toxic atmosphere of many schools must be changed. Teachers must want to be there and enjoy their interactions with the students, and teachers and administrations must remain sensitive toward negative behaviors, staying aware of their own prejudices and biases and working to reduce them. They need to become aware of those students who are isolated and invisible or hazed and hassled, and to work actively to change the school culture and society that these teens have to live in. It is not a comfortable process, and perhaps it shouldn't be, since change almost always brings discomfort, but according to Brown it is the only way to prevent Columbine from happening all over again.

In 2011, a study in the journal *Psychology of Violence* found that the primary factor that predicted a short-term increase in aggression was not violent content but competition. Participants in the study played both a violent, noncompetitive game and a completely nonviolent competitive game, and found that "video game violence was not sufficient to elevate aggressive behavior compared with a nonviolent video game, and that more competitive games produced greater levels of aggressive behavior, irrespective of the amount of violence in the games."[21]

Some earlier studies found a statistically minor connection between video game violence and antisocial behavior, for instance, the 2005 study by Williams and Skoric.[22] Christopher Ferguson points out that there were significant flaws in the experiment.[23] A number of factors were not controlled, including the backgrounds of the participants as well as the level of competition in the game itself, and the outcome measures were more relevant for mild, non-serious aggression; intentions to commit physical assaults were not measured. In his more recent study, which looked to remedy these oversights, Ferguson found that "Results indicated that current levels of depressive symptoms were a strong predictor of serious aggression and violence across most outcome measures. Depressive symptoms also interacted with antisocial traits so that antisocial individuals with depressive symptoms were most inclined toward youth violence. Neither video game violence exposure, nor television violence exposure, were prospective predictors of serious acts of youth aggression or violence."[24] Finally, in 2012, the Swedish government joined the U.S. Supreme Court and the Australian government in affirming that there is little connection between video violence and actual violence, and that the research in the field is both inconsistent and flawed.[25]

It may be that it is not that the entertainment industry is so powerful, but that other institutions and organizations that used to help children grow into adults have become so much weaker.[26] According to many family psychologists and researchers, the majority of children and teens in the United States are bringing up themselves, with little parental or family involvement. Parents work multiple jobs to make ends meet, and they lack the time and energy to focus on their children. While some teachers reach out to their students, many don't, from fear of censure or needing to maintain a certain distance from their students. Churches and youth organizations have far less influence than they used to have on previous generations. Kids are teaching each other how to grow up.[27]

And while it is tempting to think that paying more attention to "warning signs," will effect a change, research indicates that current commonalities among mass murderers (male, Caucasian, usually at least twenty years old, depressed, resentful, isolated, tending to blame others for their own problems, interested in violence and in guns) are so frequently seen in the general population that there is no reliable way to sort out the killers from the rest of us, without a tremendous number of "false positives."[28] Anyone of us could become a monster in the right situation.

However, other researchers have found that there are three overarching characteristics of school shooters: They tend to obsess about others who have wronged them in some way and against whom they want revenge; they suffer from depression or psychosis; and they have longstanding antisocial personality traits, first seen when they were in their teens, such as lying, stealing, truancy, aggressive or violent behavior, no respect for the truth, and recklessness.[29] And they are overwhelmingly male. All of the worst mass murderers in U.S. history have been male; from Charles Whitman in the University of Texas Tower shooting in 1966 to the Arapahoe High School shooting in 2013, all the shooters have been men.

Many mental health professionals have said that increased mental health services would reduce the number of mass killers, because they would have access to treatment. While this would certainly be helpful, there is no guarantee that greater access to these services would make them more used. In general, mass killers see others as the ones needing help, needing to be fixed, and would reject the suggestion that they themselves would profit from any kind of therapy—*they* aren't the ones who need help![30] In fact, research shows that only 4 percent of violent crimes overall are committed by people with mental health disorders. Among mass murderers the number increases to about 20 percent.[31] However, many killers were never evaluated for mental illness before their shooting spree, and then committed suicide or were killed by police before they could be evaluated afterward.

Increased gun control may not be the answer either, since most mass murderers don't have criminal records, and could easily purchase a gun legally. Even those who look or act strangely cannot be deprived of their Second Amendment rights. And if they cannot purchase a gun legally, there are many other ways to get them— from family and friends, theft, or even borrowing.[32] It's important to remember that Adam Lanza, the Newtown shooter, used guns his mother had purchased legally and had in her home. Even banning assault weapons might not make much difference, since weapons are so easy to get illegally, and many legal guns can be made into assault weapons, from instructions available online.

Chris Crutcher has another viewpoint on why school shootings happen: isolation and bullying. While this may not be part of all school shootings, it is certainly a part of the majority of them, the ones with shooters who are eighteen and younger. Crutcher points out the dangers of isolation and the power of community. Shooters are those who feel themselves marginalized, outsiders, bullied, and humiliated.[33] They are left alone to stew in their own unhappiness, their resentment and rage building up inside them. As Crutcher points out, when an individual's self-worth drops below a certain point, nothing matters any longer. [34] He is not going to reach out for help, because he doesn't believe anyone can help him. He is where no one can reach him, where nothing matters any longer—and that means that anything can happen, and sometimes does. Sometimes being noticed is more important than what you are noticed for—as in the case of the man on death row who said, "I'd rather be wanted for murder than not wanted at all." [35] Teens are resilient, they can come back from the edge, but they need one positive and supportive relationship with one adult, who can mentor them, listen to them, talk to them, and remove them from the isolation and otherness that tells them no one cares. And if that adult can't be found in real life, perhaps a substitute can be found in a book, and in the person with the courage to write that book that makes some people uncomfortable, but to those lonely and isolated teens, it's a world where they can see people just like them, and feel less alone.

Several titles stand out from among the list of titles about school shootings, many of them written after the Columbine High School shooting. Todd Strasser, Nancy Garden, and Walter Dean Myers are all well-known names in YA literature, and each has a different perspective on the topic. *Quad*, by Carrie Gordon, which is sadly out of print, but still available in many libraries, tells the story from six different perspectives, when six students from different cliques are trapped inside the campus store while a shooter roams the school quad outside. *Hate List*, by Jennifer Brown, is about two high school students who make a list of the people they want dead, and in Adam Meyer's *The Last Domino*, the narrator and shooter isn't the monster; the boy who manipulated him into believing that a gun was the solution is the monster.

# I

## *I WISH YOU WERE DEAD*
## BY TODD STRASSER

The novel is framed by posts on an anonymous blog by Str-S-d and the responses to her posts. She feels like she is being bullied at school and is letting off steam in her blog, promising to be honest about the way she's treated. Several girls send supportive messages, but when she takes one's advice, things get much worse. After that, she reveals that what she really wants is for the teens who torture her to die.

> I just wish they would die. . . . The more I try to rid myself of these thoughts, the stronger they grow. So forget trying to be nice. Forget trying to pretend. Those people have made my life miserable. I want them to die.
> I'll begin with Lucy. She is definitely first on the list.[1]

There are responses from some of the previous posters, and also the first post from IaMnEmEsEs, who writes, "Perhaps your wish will come true." And it does. Lucy vanishes that night, and eventually two other students, Adam and Courtney, also vanish after Str-S-d wishes they would also die, Adam because he embarrassed her in class, Courtney because she sucks up to the popular kids and can't be bothered to even notice Str-S-d. Madison, Lucy's best friend and a close friend of Adam's, works with Tyler, a new kid in town that she's very attracted to, to see if they can figure out what happened.

While this might be a run-of-the mill bullying story, Strasser has added several details that make it unique. First of all, the serial killer turns out to be a woman, one of the high school teachers. She also sponsors the Safe Rides, a group of students who give drunk kids a ride home if they call and ask to be picked up. All of the major characters in the book are affiliated with the group in one way or another, and when an animal tranquilizer is connected to the disappearances, it should be fairly easy for the reader to connect the dots and come up with the chemistry teacher. However, the fact that about 90 percent of serial killers are male may fool the reader into looking for someone who is male.

A 2013 article in the *Journal of Investigative Psychology and Offender Profiling* describes the research on female serial killers in detail, and presents several characteristics of female serial killers that are different from their male counterpoints, which are reflected in Strasser's novel *Wish You Were Dead*, although it was written in 2009, showing that he did his research when creating the character. According to this comprehensive research article, women serial killers tend to be more reactive than predatory; they tend to kill using poison or some other nonviolent method; their murders are linked to prior victimization; and they are most likely to be white, to begin killing in their thirties, to not work as part of a killing team, and generally to not have previous criminal records.[2] While most women tend to find their victims in their homes or workplaces, and become localized killers, others move from one state or country to another in order to find new territory for their victims.[3] These characteristics all fit Strasser's killer.

The whole novel covers just two and a half weeks, and after Lucy is kidnapped about 3 AM Sunday morning, Strasser keeps the reader up-to-date on how the missing teens are doing by inserting brief transcripts of one-sided conversations between the killer and the teens, starting when Lucy has been gone just a few hours, and then more or less every twenty-four hours after that. The killer is the only one speaking, and refers to herself as "us" or "we" never "I."

Through these inserts, we watch Lucy gradually die of thirst and dehydration, because she is given no food or water after she is captured, despite begging for them, and promising to change her behavior. In addition, she is being held either outdoors or in an unheated area, because she is very cold, and has no blanket or other covering to keep her warm. The tone of the killer's voice is chilling, as the reader gradually realizes just how much she is enjoying watching her captives suffer and die for the way they treated their classmates. She truly believes that they deserve this sadistic treatment, and treats them as little more than animals, penning them in dog runs with no shelter or bathroom facilities.

When the killer's lair is found, she reveals that she was bullied as a teen and, as an adult, tried to remake herself with plastic surgery, dyed hair, and designer clothes. But she was still the same person on the inside, and people didn't really change the way that they responded to her. She feels betrayed all over again, and becomes angry, resentful, bitter, and vindictive, determined to take revenge on those who wronged her. But there's no way she can do that directly. So instead, she seeks out places where there are teens like the ones who tortured her, and uses them for her revenge.

After her capture, we learn that she has killed seven teens in five states, all "popular kids" in safe, wealthy suburbs just like Soundview, but Strasser doesn't reveal her final destiny. She is obviously mentally ill, but preparing to slaughter her captives and go on to another state to start over when the police arrive.

Str-S-d's blog posts, eleven in all, are also inserted into the story, as she is at first angry and defiant, then guilty, afraid, and feeling to blame for the kidnappings. No matter who responds to her posts, trying either to help her or to diss her for what she's said, she never connects with any of them. Even when Madison realizes who she is and tries to talk to her, Str-S-d refuses to open up. At the end of the novel, she and her family are rumored to be leaving town, hoping for a new start. Sadly, by this time the reader knows full well that this is impossible, since she will be carrying her guilt and her rejection of herself and of others with her.

The various kinds of social networking technology definitely support the story and further the plot, but they are not the totality of the story. Their different formats make them stand out from the text itself, drawing the reader's attention to the different perspectives they represent.

Madison narrates the story itself, beginning with the night Lucy disappears and ending just a few days after the mystery is resolved and the survivors rescued. The novel is written in first person, but the occasional foreshadowing could give the canny reader hints about what is going on before she actually knows it. She is occasionally distracted from her search by a cyberstalker who has been e-mailing her for about a year, sneering at her choices and activities. "I bet you'd never go out with someone like me," he says in the first e-mail included in the book. "How come you only hang out with people in the most popular clique?" Madison knows it's one of the kids from school, but has never felt threatened by him, so she's never told her parents about him. Then as the situation continues to escalate, she suddenly realizes who he is and why he is e-mailing her, and understands that he isn't the threat, and has nothing to do with the kidnappings.

But someone is following her—she hears footsteps on the dock late at night when after returning home with her father from a yacht race, she realizes she has forgotten her backpack of schoolwork, and goes back to the boat alone to retrieve it. Later she is locked into the stables where her horse is kept, and when she's released, her car's tires have been slashed. Notes appear in her car and at the guard stand to the gated community she and her wealthy parents live in— in the largest and most luxurious house.

With a few exceptions, all the people in the town of Soundview and its gated community Premium Point are extremely wealthy. Madison's parents gave her an Audi for her sixteenth birthday, and her father travels all over the world for the investment firm he owns. The whole town has an air of entitlement—the residents feel that they deserve their trendy, chic, and materialistic lifestyle, and so do their kids. But as the disappearances continue, parents begin to pay more attention to where their kids are and why—perhaps their town is not as safe as they thought it was. These parents may be wealthy, but they immediately circle the wagons when their children are perceived to be in danger. The exception is Courtney, whose father travels extensively on business, and whose mother has moved back to India to care for her ill mother. Courtney's older sister is supposed to supervise her sister, but infrequently spends time at home, so Courtney is often alone in the huge mansion her family lives in. Oddly, there are no housekeepers, cooks, chauffeurs, or anyone to buy food or otherwise take care of the house, and Courtney frequently comes to school hungry, devouring the unimpressive school lunches because she's had nothing to eat. This is an odd detail that doesn't seem to fit in with the rest of her life—she seems to have money for clothes and for her personal appearance—why doesn't she ask Madison to take her grocery shopping or out to eat?

Strasser created the novel in order to confront a serious social issue in our society—bullying and cyberbullying. He says his previous books were ones that were about contemporary social issues that used thriller elements to move the plot along, but that this one is a thriller that addressed the issues of bullying, stereotyping, and popularity. The plotting is much more intricate than his previous books, and he compares it to "a very tough Sudoku," where all the pieces have to be in exactly the right place to make everything work.[4]

# 2

# THE FORENSIC MYSTERY SERIES BY ALANE FERGUSON

The Forensic Mystery series by Alane Ferguson begins with *The Christopher Killer*, which introduces Cameryn Mahoney, seventeen years old, daughter of the town coroner in the small mountain town of Silverton, Colorado, which actually exists, as it does in the series, off the beaten path in the Colorado Rockies, an old mining town that caters to the tourist trade in the summer, and to skiers and hikers in the winter. Cameryn is fascinated by forensics, planning to major in it in college, and persuades her father to hire her as his assistant, over the objections of the sheriff and the medical examiner. It turns out that she has a gift for detail and observation and is able to help solve the first murder the town has had in years—the fourth victim of "the Christopher Killer," nicknamed for the small St. Christopher medal that he leaves with each body. She is keenly aware that all the bodies she studies in her forensic pathology textbooks have one thing in common—they have no voice. There is no one to tell their story, and the science geek in her wants to do that, wants to discover the stories those bodies can tell, and solve the mysteries of their deaths. Her father warns her that she has to learn to detach, to stay objective and focus on the job at hand—this is the last line of defense for the dead, the last chance to bring the criminal to justice. The process is made more difficult by the fact that she knows the victim: Rachel worked with her as a waitress at one of the town's restaurants.

The killer turns out to be the major suspect, although several red herrings have drawn attention away from him, and he fits the general characteristics of the male serial killer—an organized, methodical killer whose crimes are committed to help enhance his reputation and financial gains. Ferguson does extensive research for this series, so it is no surprise that she's able to create an authentic picture of a serial killer. She was drawn to the idea of forensics after the "horrific death" of her best friend's murder, and found it cathartic to funnel everything through the writing process, to help her flush out her psyche.[1] It also helps her control the uncontrollable things in her life. She enjoys writing for teens because she is a teen on the inside—a fourteen-to-sixteen-year-old girl—and loves their energy, and that they have the world ahead of them, because they haven't chosen their path yet. Writing about them allows her to live vicariously through them. One thread that runs through all the books in her forensic mysteries series is the importance Cameryn places on telling the story of the victim of the crime, helping the body give up its secrets, because it is the last story it will be able to tell, the last chance to name the assailant.

But the world of forensics is a dark one, that is both difficult for Ferguson to enter and to leave behind. It is essential that she create the pain that killers impose on their victims and those who love them, so sometimes she sits writing with a box of Kleenex right at hand, in case she breaks down in tears. She has to live in the mind of a serial killer when she writes, and counteracts that darkness by surrounding herself with peace and light in her own life. Her books are not entertainment centered on violence, but about stopping the evil by using science to catch the killer. The violence takes place offstage, while the focus is on stopping the violence by resolving the crime.[2] Her focus is on justice rather than violence. Today's teens are somewhat cynical about the justice system, both in real life and how it is portrayed on television and in movies, but they still know the difference between right and wrong, and want Ferguson to bring in the bad guy rather than letting him get away. But she wants to limit the violence she shows in her books—and she wants to show that someone's death leaves a hole in the lives of loved ones left behind. While there is recovery, the pain and the loss go on and on. You can recover relatively easily from losing your stuff. It's not fun to do without or to replace, but the pain of losing a friend is a loss that one may never really recover from.[3] It is the ultimate loss, and when it happens violently, deliberately, it impacts the individual at a far deeper level. It is a sudden, unexpected death that is far different from a death that has been expected, based on age or illness. And reading about it can help teens prepare for the day when they will face similar, even if not deadly, losses.

Ferguson has written four books in the Forensic Mystery series, and she loves to hear from her readers. She originally thought the series would center around forensics and the puzzles that murders create. But her readers are just as interested in the romance angle of the stories and the relationship between Justin and Cameryn. They objected forcefully when Ferguson tried to pull them apart, even though she was doing it for dramatic tension. They wanted a love story to go with the mystery, and so they got it.[4] However, she still includes authentic details about the work of a coroner and the various kinds of autopsies that are necessary, so the forensic aspects are examined in detail. Teens who enjoy these details in television shows will respond to them as well as to the romance.

# 3

# *ACCELERATION*
# BY GRAHAM MCNAMEE

Graham McNamee wrote *Acceleration* because he enjoys sus-
penseful novels and thought it would be fun to write one about boys
like him and his friends when they were teens, slacker guys, giving
them the impossible task of finding a serial killer. He describes it as
"What I Did on My Summer Vacation" meets *Silence of the Lambs*.
He knew the ending before he knew the beginning—he'd played in
the Toronto subway tunnels when he was a teen, and commuted
downtown by subway as an adult, so it was familiar territory. He
also set the story in a part of town that he was very familiar with—
The Jungle, a collection of apartment buildings on the edge of an
industrial area, home to blue-collar workers of all kinds. He remembers it as a great place to grow up—an urban wilderness for the
adventuresome—and writing the book was like going back home
and waking up all the ghosts.

Because he writes in first person, McNamee takes on the personality of his protagonists, and for *Acceleration*, that involved not only
getting into Duncan's head so he could narrate the book, but also
into the head of the serial killer Duncan is looking for, as Duncan
reads his diary chronicling his various crimes, including animal mu-
tilations and arsons, and his hunt for his first human victim, a murder that takes place on the subway. After McNamee finished writing

the book, it was a relief to leave the dark story and the mind of
Roach behind him. He felt it was almost like an exorcism, because,
especially as a vegetarian, creating a character that enjoyed torturing
and killing small furry animals was extremely unpleasant. [1]

However, it is to his credit that he created Roach carefully and
methodically, doing research on the psychology of serial killers, so
the character would be authentic. Reading the diary excerpts draws
the reader into Roach's world—dark, twisted, and thoroughly repulsive. Particularly creepy are the scenes set in Roach's house, in the
basement room where he performed his revolting experiments on
animals. There had to be a reason for Roach's proclivities, and
McNamee chose to create a horrific childhood for him, living with a
grandmother who regularly tortured and punished him, locking him
into a cell in the basement for days, sometimes convincing him that
she had forgotten him. It was this abuse that taught him how to be
abusive himself, first setting small fires, experimenting on small
animals, then gradually building up to more intense experiences.
But gradually, he begins to realize that everything he's done is just
"kid stuff," and that what he needs is a human target. He chooses
three women he sees on the subway and stalks them methodically,
learning their habits, tracking them to their homes, even sitting next
to them on the subway. He is about to make a choice when he loses
his journal on the subway and it is turned in to the subway lost and
found, where Duncan is working. About ten days later, Duncan
finds it when looking for something to read. At first he is repulsed
and then fascinated by it, determined to figure out who the writer is
and stop him before he makes his choice about who his first victim
will be.

McNamee worked in a library when he was writing the book,
and he frequently spent half his shift doing research. He generally
does many drafts of his novels, which come together slowly, piece
by piece of dialogue, detail by detail of character. [2] In order to create
Roach, McNamee says, "I had to read a bunch of ugly stuff about
these grotesque personalities . . . [and go] into the dark places
twisted people go to feed their deviant desires." He compares creating Roach to a blind guy building a house, and when the book was

over, he had to kill the Roach walking around in his head before he was overwhelmed by him. He also noted, "That kind of stuff leaves a stain on your soul. You know, once you see something you can't un-see it." He had to explore the darkest parts of the human heart and mind, the reptilian core of the brain, where he believes the animal capacity for violence lives.[3] It must have been a relief to leave all that behind after the book was over and the characters were flushed from his mind, so he could walk in the sun again.

Duncan has his own demons haunting him. The previous summer, a girl drowned in a nearby lake because he could not save her, even though he is a powerful swimmer and tried to find her as hard as he could. The tragedy broke him in many ways—he has dreams of the incident, and for months afterward was unable to sleep at all. Generally, he averages about two hours a night. His mother has taken him to doctors and psychiatrists, but they haven't been able to help. He even considered suicide at one point. His best friends, Vinny and Wayne, have stuck by him, helping him cope as much as they can, but his focus on his failure has driven away his girlfriend, who didn't want to be drawn into the dark world Duncan now inhabits.

When Duncan tells Vinny about the journal, Vinny tells him to take it to the police, but Duncan refuses for two reasons: First, he doesn't think they will buy into the need to find the killer, who is not named and who has committed no crime; second, he and Wayne got caught in a harebrained scheme to make money by stealing fancy toilets from a new apartment house so they could resell them, and he has a police record as a result. (Wayne's character provides much of the comic relief in the novel. Duncan describes him as a perpetual seven-year-old, who will never grow up, and never stop getting in trouble for his inept attempts to make money.) Nevertheless, when Vinny pressures him, Duncan does take the journal to the police. Two officers, both busy with other things, glance through it, and grudgingly agree to look into it. But Duncan knows it will most likely never happen, and he takes back the journal, making a commitment to find the person he has come to call "the Roach," and enlisting Vinny's help in researching his crimes. He has decided that it is his destiny to find the criminal and, in capturing him, somehow make up for the girl he was unable to save. His focus and determination sharpen, and gradually, he and Vinny begin to make strides toward finding the Roach. His life and that of the Roach are now inextricably linked, with death as the only possible result.

Heroes aren't always heroic, and while Duncan is able to stop the Roach, it takes a terrible toll on him, leaving him close to dead himself. Even though he is questioned over and over by the police, he decides to leave the real story of what happened hidden, known only to him, Vinny, and Wayne, who agree not to tell it. As McNamee had to expunge the Roach from inside his head, the three boys, and particularly Duncan, had to do the same. Finally redeemed from his guilt, he reaches out to Kim, and once again finds peace at the bottom of a swimming pool. The ghosts have vanished, and he can get on with his life, just as his creator did.

Why is this book important, and why does it continue to resonate after the last page is turned? It lets the reader know that there are terrible people in the world, people who have been broken by life, flawed by their genes, and they do terrible things as a result. But they can be stopped, with effort and with determination. It also demonstrates that guilt is self-inflicted to some extent, even when there is no justification for it. Bad things happen to bad people, and it makes them worse. But bad things happen to good people as well, and those people must learn how to figure out a way to get through it and to go on with their lives.

# 4

# *IN THE PATH OF FALLING OBJECTS*
# BY ANDREW SMITH

Andrew Smith never wanted to be a published author. Although writing was something he'd always done—poetry, short stories, plays—he never considered sharing it with anyone. He wrote for himself, and for a few close friends.[1] After he got out of college, he tried writing for newspapers or radio stations, but he quickly discovered that it really wasn't for him.[2] So he spent several years wandering around the world, working at this and that, but always writing—for himself. In about 2004, a friend he'd known since high school who was a published author herself, Kelly Milner Halls, started nagging him about publishing what he wrote, and finally he told her he was working on a novel and promised to try to get it published when he finished it. He freely admits that had it not been for Kelly, he would still be writing for himself and his hard drive.[3]

But the origin of *In the Path of Falling Objects* comes years before that, when he was in college, and wrote a short story with a character like Mitch, *Path*'s serial killer, and two boys whose older brother was serving in Vietnam. His professor liked it, and tried to persuade Smith to submit it somewhere. Smith refused, but because of the man's praise, he never threw it away. When he found it years later, while digging through an old roll-top desk stored in the garage, he realized that he was ready to expand the story into a novel.[4]

It is the story of a road trip, set in the 1970s, during the Vietnam War, and is partly built on the letters he got from his older brother when he was on tour in Vietnam. He and his brother were very close, and had always shared a bedroom. It was incredibly traumatic for Smith when his eighteen-year-old brother went to Vietnam, and for months he didn't sleep much and had nightmares when he did. He and his brother wrote back and forth constantly, but at that time letters were the only form of communication between home and the field, and they could take weeks to get back and forth—assuming they arrived at all, since deliveries to soldiers were not always reliable. Families and loved ones saw only body counts and snippets of news on the television and in newspapers. Not knowing what was happening, or learning about it weeks after it had happened, made the separation more painful and more frightening, leaving those left at home to feel lost and isolated.[5]

Also, he took a road trip through the Southwest with two of his friends, sitting in the back seat beside a life-sized metal statue of Don Quixote. The car wasn't a Lincoln, like the one in the book; rather the Lincoln entered the story because Smith's father-in-law bought a 1940 Cabriolet before he died and Smith always intended to put the "amazing vehicle" in a book someday. It was perfect for a road trip with a serial killer, and the elegant car and its camp art passenger made Mitch's bizarre and puzzling actions and choices even more arresting.[6]

Smith created Mitch based upon a kid who liked to hitchhike to the airport to watch planes take off and land, and the sexual predator who picked him up. He gave Mitch his own obsessive-compulsive disorder, counting numbers and other ritualistic behaviors, and a fascination with religious imagery—although he is quick to point out that Mitch's OCD is far more extreme than his own, and that he is *not* a serial killer.[7]

Jonah, sixteen, and Simon, fourteen, have nothing left. Their older brother, Matthew, is serving in Vietnam, and after he left, their mother fell apart. One day, she just wasn't there. She went off to Georgia or Texas or someplace with one of her man friends, leaving her two younger sons in the crumbling shack they called a home.

When the electricity was cut off, and there was no food left, they had no choice but to leave. Their father was a heroin addict, in jail in Arizona, and Jonah thought they should be there when he got out.

After walking for miles, exhausted and starving, a 1940 Lincoln Cabriolet convertible catches up with them. The driver is short, with dark hair and a beard, and he looks older to Jonah, maybe about twenty. His passenger is a tall, slender, blonde girl with faded jeans and a tight pink T-shirt, who looks about Jonah's age. Jonah's reaction to them is instantaneous—he's repelled by the man—there's something wrong, something "off" about him, but he is fascinated by the girl. He hasn't seen many girls, and she is more than attractive. Jonah wants to keep walking, but when they offer the boys a ride, Simon accepts before Jonah can turn them down. They end up in the back seat with the life-size metal statue of Don Quixote that Mitch and Lilly picked up in Mexico. And so the brothers' road trip from hell begins.

The suspense builds as it becomes obvious that all four of them have secrets that they aren't willing to share that will change the ways they interact. Simon is always looking for trouble, trying to push Jonah's buttons any way he can. He knew Jonah didn't want to go with Mitch, but he was tired of walking, and the old car was cool. Jonah knows how much Simon likes to bug him, and does his best to keep his temper. Lilly and Mitch have some history together, but Lilly still seems almost afraid of him. Mitch is the one that pushes all their buttons, and pulls all their strings, without caring what happens when he does. His cruelty is first seen when he deliberately runs over a scrawny, tattered-looking coyote, then stops to admire his handiwork. Jonah is horrified, Simon is excited, and Lilly is resigned—she had made him mad, and killing is the way he blows off steam. Mitch saws off the coyote's tail with a nail file and attaches it to Don Quixote's helmet, rather like Davy Crockett's coonskin hat. It is out in the open now—there is something wrong with Mitch, and he is leading them further and further down his own twisted path.

When they stop at Tucumcari, Mitch sees the map that Jonah is drawing to record their trip, and the expression on his face as he looks at the sketches of the car, himself, and Lilly, makes Jonah feel a little sick. Mitch has just sealed the brothers' death warrant. When they get back to the car, Mitch puts the plates Simon stole on the car, and when Jonah realizes who stole them, his temper explodes, and he beats Simon within an inch of his life and then refuses to get back in the car. Mitch has to threaten to kill Simon before he changes his mind.

The incident changes everything, ensuring that Mitch is in complete control of the other three and their immediate and even future destinies. They are his unwilling puppets, forced to dance at his command. When they stop at a motel, Lilly waits till everyone is asleep, then persuades Jonah to have sex with her. In the morning, Simon and Mitch are united against them, and Mitch becomes even more out of control.

Later that day, while stopping at a roadhouse for a beer, Mitch once again "blows off steam" by killing, but this time it is the bartender, whom he shoots point-blank, for no reason, while Simon, who came in to drink with him, is in the restroom. Meanwhile, Lilly and Jonah wait in the car, and she tells him what happened to her and Mitch before they met the brothers. She is pregnant and needs to get to Mexico so she can get an abortion, and she asked Mitch to take her. Mitch then killed his father and stole his car, and they took off to Mexico. But Lilly was too scared to go through with it, and asked Mitch to take her to California instead. On their way out of the country, Mitch stopped to buy a full-sized scrap-metal statue of Don Quixote, and killed the man who created him. This seems to be the first time he dealt with his anger by killing for no reason at all.

But Mitch's anger about Lilly's betrayal has not waned, and he tells Simon he's going to shoot his brother, so the three of them can continue alone. Even though Simon is incredibly angry at Jonah, he doesn't want him dead, so he shoves him into the river before Mitch can shoot him. It is at this point that Smith's story splits in two, as Jonah narrates his own story and also that of his brother, which he fills in on the map and journal he has been keeping after he learns about it at the end of their journey.

After he crawls out of the river and walks back to the bridge where Simon shoved him in, Jonah meets Dalton, a boy his own age who lives in the desert with his parents and younger sister. Dalton, who is amazingly self-assured for his age, introduces Jonah to his hippie parents. With the parents' blessing, Jonah and Dalton set off to find Simon in an old camper truck.

Meanwhile, Mitch has refused to go back and look for Jonah, and to convince Simon, he's told him that he shot the bartender. Simon realizes that Mitch is insane, and decides not to follow his lead any longer. Not long after that, the Lincoln dies and burns up, leaving just enough time for them to grab a few things from the trunk. The fire attracts the attention of an old Indian, Walker, who comes to find out what's happening, but then goes back to his own camp. In the middle of the night, Simon and Lilly sneak off, desperate to escape Mitch, and run into Walker again, who takes them to his camp. Along the way, Lilly confesses she is the one who talked Mitch into picking up the boys—she wanted some company.

When Mitch wakes up the next morning, he is alone, and his insanity rapidly takes over, obscuring everything but the need to find Simon and Lilly, and get Lilly back. He covers himself with soot from the Lincoln, cuts himself all over his body, and rubs the blood and soot into a paste, calling himself Black Simon, and plotting his revenge. His manic actions and speech clearly show that he is no longer in touch with reality except in the most superficial way. His determination to find and punish Simon and Lilly is in no way diminished.

Walker's home is a tiny trailer with two mud houses nearby. By the time they get there, Lilly, who has been getting sicker and sicker with a pain in her side, collapses, and Simon decides to run to town for help. He runs into Jonah and Dalton, and when they all go back to get Lilly to a hospital, Mitch attacks, throwing boulders down on the trailer from the mesa above. He stops only when Simon comes out and screams at him that Lilly died before they got back to the trailer, and is beyond his reach now. But Mitch only pauses in his attack, then sets the trailer on fire and eventually shoots Walker and attacks the brothers. Simon is able to get hold of the loaded gun that

Jonah has been hiding the whole trip, and fires at Mitch until he runs out of bullets, killing him. The three survivors shove Mitch's and Walker's bodies into the trailer and hope that the fire will cover all the evidence.

Jonah had brought only a few things with him on the journey—a few clothes for each of them, his journal and map, and a packet of letters his brother had Matt sent from Vietnam, recording the horrors that he found there and his increasing inability to deal with them. It gradually becomes obvious through these letters, which are interspersed throughout the book, that there is no happy ending and reunion awaiting the brothers. After Matt's best friend, Scotty, is brutally shot by his comrades, Matt gives up. He sends a final letter to Scotty's mother, hoping that Jonah will go there to see if she has any information on him and learn what finally happened. Jonah gets the letter after Dalton takes him and Simon to Flagstaff to find Scotty's mother. Knowing what he has been through, Jonah realizes that there are "some things in life that there's no coming back from."[8] and that the horrors that both he and Matt went through will haunt him forever. Unfortunately, Matt was alone when the worst came and was not able to survive it. Jonah has Dalton and Simon, now a band of brothers, to help him survive, and the promise of a new family with Dalton's parents. He will be able to survive, eventually, and he has his map to remind him of where he came from, and how strong he had to learn to be to put that past behind him and go on with his life.

It is interesting to consider each of the main characters from a perspective of motivation, since they all, at one time or another, were motivated by self interest and selfishness. Lilly persuaded Mitch to help her, because she was desperate for an abortion. She forced him to stop for Jonah and Simon because she didn't trust Mitch and no longer wanted to be alone with him. She knew he was sexually interested in her, and she needed a buffer to keep him at a distance.

Simon wanted to get out from under his big brother's thumb, and saw a cool car with a cool couple in it, and asked for a ride when he knew Jonah didn't want to. Pushing his brother's buttons even more by stealing, drinking, and smoking both pot and cigarettes, was another way to assert his own independence.

Jonah feels responsible for keeping his brother safe, and frantically denies the reality that Matt is gone and won't be returning from Vietnam. He is frustrated and angry because he feels powerless, and flashes out of control when he realizes that Mitch can manipulate Simon better than he can. He fights Simon's smoking during the whole trip, only to see at the end that he can't control his brother, and must allow him to make his own mistakes—which is what Simon wanted all along.

Mitch is one of the most purely evil characters in young adult literature. He lives to make people fear him, to control them, and to manipulate them to satisfy his own twisted desires. He manipulates everyone around him to get what he wants, no matter the cost. He is able to cope with reality and function in the real world most of the time, but at the cost of committing savage, meaningless murders, in order to quiet his rage. When he discovers he is alone in the desert after Simon and Lilly sneak off, his ability to stay in control and function is completely shattered. He has lost his car, his transportation, and his two followers and is unable to survive alone. Getting his disciples back is the only way he can see to regain his power. His OCD immediately almost takes over his thinking processes. He changes his appearance, so he is not himself any longer—after rubbing soot all over his body, he is Black Simon. Then he carefully traces his skeleton on his chest and arms—ribs, breastbone, collarbones, the bones in his arms and legs. The soot and blood make a paste that covers his skin completely, making him almost unrecognizable. His focus is on Simon and Lilly and how to kill them or bring them back under his power. Clinging to that bit of reality allows him to make plans and to follow through with them. Had Simon not killed him, he would have been able to create even more havoc than he did.

Dalton is the only one of the main characters who isn't in it for himself, and his serenity and acceptance are in stark contrast to the "me first" attitude of the others. He's willing to do whatever he can to help Jonah, and his Zen-like attitude almost never falters. He is ready to accept anyone at face value, but he isn't naïve, and realizes right away how dangerous Mitch is. His openness and peacefulness are just what the brothers need to help them overcome their horrific background. He and his parents are the light characters that make the darker ones, like Mitch, stand out in contrast.

It is also important to note that all of these characters are necessary to stand up against Mitch—fighting this monster needs an ensemble, not an individual. In addition, Smith decided to take Lilly out of the equation at the last minute, allowing the males to fight Mitch alone. And it is this final battle that allows them to see how much they have changed and grown since this "road trip to hell" began just a few days ago. Change happens most quickly to those who are under the most pressure to survive in the most harrowing circumstances, something Smith likes to do with his characters to force them to change.[9] The brothers have to work together and eliminate the wedge that Mitch placed between them in order to overcome him.

While the ending does not resolve every problem, there are hints that Jonah, Simon, and Dalton will be able to recover and move beyond what they suffered at Mitch's hands. He stashed his stolen money in their truck, so Jonah and Simon are no longer empty handed. They have a place to stay as long as they want it, and the determination to let nothing separate them the way Mitch was able to do. They also have Jonah's map to remind them of what they have accomplished and overcome. They have turned from the past to the future, from the darkness that enveloped their lives from the beginning, to the promise of a new dawn.

# 5

# *I HUNT KILLERS* SERIES
# BY BARRY LYGA

Barry Lyga didn't intend to write a book about serial killers. It was a misunderstanding that got the ball rolling. He was talking to his agent and described the protagonist in his next book as "a real killer," and she thought he'd said "serial killer." That discussion led him to consider what serial killers might be like[1]—but it felt wrong to make a teen a serial killer, sensationalistic and odd.[2] Then Lyga started thinking about the families of serial killers, and it came to him—what if your father was a serial killer? What if your father wasn't just a serial killer, but the worst, most notorious serial killer in the world? And what if he'd trained you to be a serial killer as well? Lyga knew he had to write it, and Jazz Dent and his father Billy were born.[3]

Lyga had always known he was born to be a writer, something he decided when he was about eight. He wrote short stories all through middle school, high school, and college, but not much ever came of them. But when he switched over to novels, everything changed. "I think I'm 'built' to write novels."[4] He has never shied away from violent or controversial content, noting that we live in a violent "post Columbine" world, but he also states that not all kids pick up a gun and use it to retaliate against someone. In his first novel, *Fanboy and Goth Girl*, Fanboy keeps a list of bullies who have tormented him, that he wants revenge on, and carries a single bullet in his pocket.[5] But he never uses it. Lyga also points out that it's important to remember that kids have fewer pressure-release valves than teens had in the past. They are watched and monitored closely, and in many places "zero tolerance" is enforced.[6] Ways of blowing off steam that might have been available to teens twenty years ago are now forbidden. It is this idea of "impotent rage" that helps him create his characters[7]—how do they deal with it, and what do they use as pressure-release valves?

Lyga admits to a fascination with serial killers because no one has ever proved conclusively what makes someone a serial killer.[8] Many theories have been proposed, some of which have already been discussed, but no absolute proof exists of causality. Supernatural villains are one thing, but they can't leap off a movie screen or the pages of a book. Serial killers are disturbingly real. They exist, and they can look like anyone—they carry no sign or mark. And research shows that there are likely to be thirty-five to fifty serial murderers active in the United States at any given time.[9] They are not necessarily easy to pick out of a crowd, nor are they isolated loners or evil geniuses.[10] In fact, one of them could be, Lyga says, a neighbor or friend, and anyone could fit his fantasy of death.[11] Serial killers look like everyone else—and that's what makes them so scary—until they act, they don't look like serial killers at all. John Wayne Gacy entertained at parties as a clown. Ted Bundy worked at a rape crisis center,[12] and others have been pillars of their communities—until they weren't. No one knows why some psychopaths become serial killers and some don't. It's a complex combination of psychological, genetic, and situational factors, which thankfully rarely exists.[13] Serial killers are the twenty-first century's boogeyman, which is why Lyga was intrigued enough to create one.[14]

Before he started writing, Lyga spent about three months doing research. He admits that he immersed himself in the world of the serial killer, and occasionally worried about what people around him might think about him, because he was carrying around books about serial killers and their pathology, the history of serial murder, serial killer case studies, and forensic science,[15] and once Googled "how to get away with murder," marking his digital profile forever. [16] But his research was time well-spent, since it allowed him to create Billy Dent, a twisted, evil, vile person who fooled everyone, even when the bodies piled up, and taught his son everything he knew about killing and getting away with it, over and over and over again.

Lyga calls Billy an "evolved" and "self-actuated" serial killer, one who actually likes what he does, and studies the mistakes that other killers have made so he doesn't make them. He is always striving to get better and better, including changing his MO (modus operandi or method of operation) often enough to elude police. He knew what would lead to his capture, and he avoided doing it. Killing is the central focus of his life. Perhaps that's why the urge to kill again, after all those years, was too strong to resist. [17]

Billy might have been evil, but he was also smart, the antithesis of the stereotypical "dumb criminal," and when he moved to Lobo's Nod, a sleepy little town where everyone knew everyone else, and violent crime never happened, he took care to set up a personality that would eliminate him from suspicion, and became a pathologist. [18] He also became the town's leading solid citizen, a good ol' boy, always ready to help a friend—even G. William Tanner, the local sheriff. Unfortunately, Billy let his arrogance get the better of him, and when Jazz was thirteen, Billy went back to killing, forgetting the advice he'd given Jazz—"Don't crap where you eat." [19] Killing where you live, especially when it's a small town, is not smart. Even though he'd killed hundreds of people, and gotten away with it, he couldn't stop himself. It was only two girls, but Billy went back to his old patterns, and even though G. William didn't have a clue about who was responsible for either of the deaths until he typed the details of the crimes into the FBI's criminal database, he came up with a match. Billy was convicted of over 120 murders, and went to prison, which is where he stayed for four years, until Jazz was seventeen.

But by the time he went to prison, Billy had had thirteen years to teach Jazz everything he knew about killing and getting away with it. His parenting was more like brainwashing, and left Jazz with phobias he can't control. For instance, seeing a knife in the sink terrifies Jazz, and brings back the smell of blood and the sight of it running down and circling around the drain, making him shiver and tremble. Knives can't be left in the sink—they must be cleaned and put away immediately. Jazz has had his father's voice in his head for years, reminding him about all the details "Dear Old Dad" taught him. Jazz knew everything he needed to know to be a serial killer, which is why he kept a close eye on himself, always afraid that it would be all too easy to follow in his father's footsteps. Fortunately for Lobo's Nod, and the rest of the country, Jazz decided to use his knowledge to hunt killers, rather than become one.[20]

As the books progress, layer after layer of the manipulation and abuse that Billy heaped on his son are revealed: on his seventh birthday, Jazz waited in the car while Billy killed his thirty-ninth victim and used the crime scene to teach Jazz about cleaning up the evidence so no clues were left. On his ninth birthday, Billy taught him how to dissolve parts of a human body using quicklime. Jazz's bedtime stories were Billy's descriptions of his kills, and Jazz found human teeth left from one of those kills when he was seven. When he was eight, he watched as Billy tortured and killed his dog Rusty, whom he'd loved and played with his whole life. "You don't gotta help, but you gotta watch," Billy told his son, and Jazz watched in tears while his father destroyed the animal he loved with all his heart. He cried and cried, and Billy let him, even encouraged him to cry. Finally, when he was through, long after Rusty was finally dead, when Jazz finally ran out of tears, Billy showed his son that his tears had changed nothing—Rusty was still dead, still just two piles of meat, fur, and internal organs. Jazz never cried again—as his father had demonstrated so horribly, it didn't do any good. Billy had started torturing and killing animals when he was only eight and enjoyed their pain and fear. Jazz hadn't begun to exhibit the same tendencies, and Billy thought it was time for him to get started. But Billy miscalculated. He didn't know his son as well as he thought he did—Jazz has never killed a living thing. Miraculously, Jazz has been little tainted by his father's lessons and twisted mind.

Jazz remembers little of his childhood with any clarity—Billy's lessons, flickers of memories of his mother, before she left—or before Billy killed her—the day he met Howie, who became his best friend, and a few other snapshots—but mainly it's a fog of bits and pieces that are hard to fit together. Jazz's fear of knives comes from some of those bits and pieces—Billy is teaching him to dismember something with a huge knife—a human body? There is someone else is the room, but Jazz can't tell who it is. Or maybe it wasn't a body—was Billy showing him how to cut up a chicken instead?

In addition, because of Billy's teachings, Jazz is very good at reading people—their facial expressions, body language, their eyes and their voices. He may never have seen his father kill anyone, but he certainly saw the aftermath, and one of his jobs was to organize his father's trophies in the hidden room where they were stored.[21] He understands his father, and he understands other killers as well. He spent his childhood obeying his father, and when G. William had found him in the trophy room after he'd tied up Billy, Jazz felt himself come alive in a way he never had before, free of his father, and able to make decisions on his own. One of the first decisions he made was not to be like Billy. But even four years later there are two things Jazz is afraid of: first, that everyone thought he was predestined to become a serial killer, because of genetics and up-bringing; and second, that they were right, and Jazz's destiny is out of his hands. That's one of the reasons he's never let himself get too close to anyone, but Howie is an exception to that rule. They've been friends since they were about ten, and Jazz caught a bunch of older boys tormenting Howie. Even though Jazz was smaller and younger than they were, he already knew how to fight dirty when the situation called for it, and this one did. Howie was a Type A hemophiliac, which meant that he could bleed to death if someone looked at him too hard, and could bruise immediately if he was poked too hard. Jazz's swift administration of justice had earned him a bloody nose and a friend for life. Jazz needs Howie—needs the reminder that life is fragile, and people are all too easy to kill. Howie connects him, grounds him, and helps him control himself, which is why, when Jazz is going to do something risky or possible illegal, he always has Howie with him. It wasn't something Lyga intended when he introduced Howie, but it evolved as he wrote the first book. Howie is one of the constants in Jazz's life—even after Billy was arrested and convicted, and everyone else turned their backs on him, Howie's loyalty never faltered. He helps Jazz remember his mantra to differentiate himself from his father—"People matter. People are real." Even when they're dead, they are still people, never objects. [22]

Jazz's other touchstone is his girlfriend, Connie. She is beautiful, black, and accepts him like no one else but Howie does, more than he accepts himself, and unlike his relationships with other women, he allows her to accept him, to get close to him. Connie is no pushover—she is able to stand up to him, and call him on it when he feels too guilty or sorry for himself. For Jazz, Connie is safe—Billy didn't stick to one type when he chose people to kill, but he never killed anyone African American, so Jazz doesn't have to worry about flipping out and hurting Connie, and she makes him believe that with her, he just might be able to have a normal life.

But other than G. William, Howie, and Connie, no one sees the real Jazz. They see a boy who looks like his father, who was trained to act like his father, a bomb with a timer ticking down, a carbon copy of a monster. Jazz isn't even sure who the real Jazz is, and is watching himself as carefully as the people around him, waiting for him to turn into Billy. The families of Billy's victims pester Jazz, wanting absolution, wanting closure. But Jazz isn't his father, and can't give them what they want and need.

Jazz also lives with a huge burden of guilt. He never tried to stop his father, even though he knew what Billy was doing was wrong. He didn't help his mother, who was the one bright spot in his childhood, until she disappeared. He loves his grandmother, but also knows that most of her mind is gone, and she is cruelly manipulative, physically abusive, and delights in stoking Jazz's anger and pushes his buttons. He doesn't really want to kill her, but at times, it feels like maybe he does, and this deepens his guilt. Killing is okay, his father taught him, when it's one of the two of them doing the killing, so maybe if Jazz was able to catch one of the killers, it will mean he isn't a killer after all.

*I Hunt Killers*, the first volume in the trilogy, was set in Lobo's Nod, and featured a new string of murders. In *Game*, the second volume, the action moved to New York City, and a series of murders called the Hat-Dog Killings, after "signatures" left at the crime scenes. Jazz, haunted and frustrated by his father's impact on his life and his voice in Jazz's head, went to New York to work with the NYPD and the FBI. *Game* also provided multiple points of view in addition to Jazz's—Howie, Connie, and even Billy's. [23] The stakes have gotten higher, as has the body count. Not everyone survives, and some deaths will surprise the reader. [24] *Blood of My Blood*, the third volume, brings the story to a close. Lyga has always known how the story would end and enjoyed writing the last scenes. [25] The story opened in New York City, where Jazz has been shot and left to die, and Billy has finally captured Connie, but in the Nod, Howie was bleeding to death in Jazz's home. The three of them must find a way to rise above the horror that has become their lives and conquer Billy once and for all. But when Jazz crossed a line he had never crossed before, everyone began to wonder if "like father, like son" was really true.

Lyga also created three prequels to the series that fill in some of the gaps about how Jazz got his nickname and how he and Connie met and fell in love, and tell the story of Billy's capture four years before the trilogy began. In "Career Day," Howie decides that his best friend needs a nickname, and comes up with Jazz, over Jasper's protests that he doesn't need a nickname. Lyga also gives more information about Howie's appearance than he did in the first two books, where he is described as being "NBA sized" with big hands and feet, very thin and gangly, Lyga reveals that he is also 6'7" tall, another characteristic, along with his hemophilia, that makes him stand out in a crowd. The short story also described how Jazz and Howie met Connie soon after she moved to town, and how her self confidence intrigued Jazz. Going out with her was almost too easy, and he worried about how it might turn out.

"Neutral Mask" takes place two or three weeks after "Career Day," and is written from Connie's perspective, describing her family and how they ended up on Lobo's Nod, and her parents' reactions to her dating a white boy. Connie also found out about Billy and how horrific Jazz's life had been when he was younger. She researches him online and also checked with one of her new friends at school, who warned her to stay away from Jazz. But Connie was still attracted to Jazz, and persuaded him to join the drama club with her, discovering in his first performance that he had a unique ability to pretend to be someone else. His ability to demonstrate such passion, such emotion, such awareness of being alive and loving life convinced her he could never be the soulless killer his father was. Like children of alcoholics who never drink, Jazz will spend his life avoiding the slightest chance of hurting anyone, for fear of turning into his father. It is also revealed that while Jazz looks exactly and sounds exactly like his father—physically they are carbon copies—Billy's attempt to make them psychological duplicates failed.

"Lucky Day" is a novella that takes place four years before the trilogy, and tells the story of G. Williams Tanner, the sheriff of Lobo's Nod and a grieving widower running for reelection, and how he figured out almost by accident who was the killer of two girls from town, and then managed to take down Billy Dent. It's a story that Lyga is particularly fond of, because it gives so much background for G. William and his relationships with both Billy and Jazz.

# 6

## *PROJECT CAIN*
## BY GEOFFREY GIRARD

The two Cain books developed both simultaneously and individually. Geoffrey Girard is head of the English Department at a private boys' school in Ohio, and his students inspired both books. A discussion about serial killers got started in one of his classes, and when a student found a trivia site on serial killers (just Google serial killers trivia—there are lots to choose from) and started asking questions, Girard was able to answer many of them, because he had been studying serial killers for years, reading books and watching biographical movies about them. Since his students seemed interested, he began thinking about how he could share his interest with them in a fictional format. He wrote an experimental novel for teens based on a story for adults he had written in 2007 and sent it to his agents, but they said they'd like to see a novel for adults on the same scenario, so he wrote *Cain's Blood*. When they saw it, they suggested doing something for teens based on Jeff Jacobson's character. The result was *Project Cain*, and Simon and Schuster was interested in publishing them simultaneously, for two different audiences, or perhaps one audience with two different preferences in the books they read.[1]

*Cain's Blood* is a traditional thriller, written from multiple points of view, but primarily narrated by Shawn Castillo, former black ops expert, who is sent in to clean up the mess when a group of serial killer clones in their late teens kills twelve of their creators and captors and escape the laboratory where they were created and lived, and go on a cross-country murder spree, looking for other clones and killing them and their families.[2] Each clone eerily resembles the original killer in the way he talks, interacts, thinks, and prefers to kill. They know who they were cloned from, and are enthusiastic about "following in their footsteps." But they are not the only clones, and the others make them look like very small potatoes. Through the various points of view, the reader is able to see the whole plot, and how frighteningly plausible it is.

*Project Cain* is a more personal story, narrated only by Jeff Jacobson, who is told the day that the story opens that he is the clone of Jeffrey Dahmer, and the man he has always known as his father is, in fact, the person in charge of the whole serial killer cloning operation, and works for the federal government, trying to create clones who can become perfect killers. There are things in *Cain's Blood* that Jeff doesn't know about or finds out about only as the story progresses. Shawn tells him some of what is going on, but not all. Jeff also chooses not to share some of his own knowledge, saying frankly in the beginning of the book, that he's not going to go into all the gory details, and if readers want to know what happened in more detail, they should do some online research themselves.

Girard wanted to make sure that if there were people who read both of the books, they would be able to get something unique from each one, although there are scenes that are common to both. One gives the big picture, including the points of view of the good guys, the bad guys, the heroes, the victims, and the *really* bad guys, and includes lots of information that would surprise Jeff, because he has only a limited amount of information about what is going on.[3] He was a very small part (although it turns out, a very important part) of the whole project. He has his own journey, which includes incidents that aren't a part of the larger picture. He is a teen who's just found out he has a potential monster inside him and has to figure out how to control it.[4]

Cloning humans is not illegal in the United States, and since 1996, when Dolly the sheep was cloned, great advances have been made. Many species have been cloned, including dogs, cats, monkeys, goats, pigs, and cows, among others.[5] Girard thinks it is likely that unreported human clones have already been created. A monkey was cloned only three years after Dolly, fourteen years ago, and science has moved rapidly since then. One of the scientists who worked on Dolly said it was impossible to prevent human cloning.[6] What advances have been made in the seventeen years since then that have been kept from public knowledge by the label "Classified Top Secret"? It is a truly chilling question.

Girard has stated in several interviews that the science in both of the Cain books is completely real, that he created nothing, and only reported what he found from reputable sources. "I made up not one word of the experiments conducted by the U.S. on its (and other) citizens. Most every one of these has been 100 percent admitted to by our government, damages paid, apologies made. Cloned serial killers are made-up fiction, but anything else, I invite and encourage anyone to look into it."[7]

One of the things that Girard enjoyed most about writing the two books was the in-depth research he had to do on several topics he had long been interested in, in addition to serial killers: how genetics influence violence, crime statistics, military science, PTSD (posttraumatic stress disorder), adolescent genetics, development and psychology, cloning capabilities and laws, military testing of all kinds and the cover-ups that followed it as well as the human right violations it involved.[8] Girard had studied serial killers for years, but in doing research for these two books, he focused on the early lives of serial killers—what were they like as children, as adolescents, and as young men? How did their early lives inform or enhance their violent tendencies?

However, the information he discovered on what the government has done to its citizens and others was what disturbed him the most.[9] Trillions of dollars have been spent in secret, from black budgets none of us know about, with no regulation or public accountability.[10] Apologies have been issued for years of secret testing on everyone from mental patients and prisoners to children and entire cities. Blame has been admitted, murders and other acts confessed to in the name of military science, in defense of our country.[11] Overall, America spends more money researching weapons than it does on medicine, agriculture, manufacturing, education, and transportation combined.[12]

The most important question Girard wants people to consider when reading the books is "Why?" Why this one person, and not another? What are the influences of nature vs. nurture? If Jeffrey Dahmer, John Wayne Gacy, Ted Bundy, or others, had been brought up in a loving, supportive, healthy family with positive psychological habits and beliefs, would they still have turned out to be serial killers?[13] Most of the serial killers who have been caught or studied seem to be physiologically different from other people in chemical makeup and brain functioning and formation, which speaks to the nature side of the question. But they also have had horrible, violent childhoods, involving psychological, physical, or sexual abuse that changed the way they see themselves and others.[14] Could a serial killer growing up in a stable, supportive environment still enjoy killing? Perhaps, but the more critical question may be can a normal person without the genetics of a killer be taught to enjoy killing and violence?[15] Girard believes both are possible, because nature and nurture have equally powerful roles.[16]

Serial killers have been romanticized to some extent, the way gangsters and criminals were in the 1920s and 1930s.[17] They are one of the bogeyman of the twenty-first century—monsters with human faces. Statistics estimate that about 2 percent of Americans are violent sociopaths—maybe forty thousand of them.[18] And one of them could be the man you passed on the street, or the person who starts honking just seconds after the light turns green. He could be a hitchhiker, a neighbor, and perhaps even a friend. Serial killers are con artists, able to fake emotions, and can be quite charming fellows.[19] The idea that you could meet them anywhere—home, school, at the mall—and have no idea how dangerous they might be, makes them incredibly dangerous, and also incredibly fascinating.[20]

Another reason serial killers are fascinating is simple morbid curiosity—our fascination with someone else's injury or death. It's why we slow down for car wrecks and scenes of violence and chaos, why slasher/horror movies are so popular,[21] why we watch the aftermath of violent events almost obsessively. Perhaps watching the dead and dying helps us come to grips with the reality of our own demise and, for most of us, its unexpected and unheralded arrival.

Girard thinks of serial killers as the vampires of the modern world. Dracula was the result of fifty years of Victorian behavior control, and today, in a different century, what we say and do is similarly controlled by the PC police, until we don't even know how to greet people during December! And here again is a monster/vampire who lives by his own rules, doesn't care about what is right or proper or politically correct, and knows enough to fool the average person into thinking he's a good guy, until the weapon is revealed or the hands close around a vulnerable neck, and death is eminent. And when that is translated to fiction, when no one *really* gets hurt, you have a hero/villain that could stick around for years.[22]

*Project Cain* opens with the scene during which Jeff discovers that he is not at all who he has always been told he was. His entire life, his entire biology, has been one gigantic and overwhelming lie. The man he's always thought of as his father hands him a manila folder and tells him to read it. He then goes downstairs and drives away from the house where he and Jeff have always lived.

Jeff is a clone, a duplicate of the infamous serial killer Jeffery Dahmer. And he isn't the only one—many of the boys who live at the laboratory complex where his father works are also clones. The next day, while he watches from the neighbor's bushes, men from DSTI, his father's lab, come and take all his father's computers and files, and everything that had to do with Jeff—photos, clothes from his closet and dirty clothes from the laundry room, books, soccer equipment, computer, school assignments, his toothbrush, his movie posters, even his pet bearded dragon. There was nothing left in the house that had anything to do with him. It was as if he had vanished.

The next night, Shawn Castillo appeared. Ex-ranger, Department of Defense employee, he had seven medals and twenty-three con-

firmed kills from his years as part of Delta Force. When he was
hired to find out what was going on at DSTI and why twelve people
who worked there had been killed, and six male teens had escaped,
he didn't know about or expect Jeff. Still, after talking to him for a
while, Shawn decided to ask Jeff to help him find those six kids and
see if they could find out what had happened to his father. That was
the beginning of a road trip the likes of which Jeff had never imagined. They were not only chasing the six teens who were clones of
the worst serial killers—Albert Fish, Jeffrey Dahmer, Henry Lee
Lucas, Ted Bundy, Dennis Rader, and David Berkowitz; but once
they realized that the six killers had an agenda of their own, Shawn
and Jeff were also after other clones, secret clones, who'd been
created and adopted by families across the United States. Those
families had been paid to adopt the clones, although they didn't
know they were clones. All the families knew was that they were
paid to abuse them in certain horrible and specific ways, or else to
give them a loving, stable home to grow up in. All so that Jeff's
"father" could find out which was stronger, nature or nurture.

In order to create these two characters that would have slightly
different roles, and reveal slightly different parts of themselves in
the two novels, Girard had to do a great deal of research. He read
everything he could find on Jeffery Dahmer, and paid serious attention to his father's autobiography and a graphic novel written by one
of his high school friends, *My Friend Dahmer*, by Derf Backderf.
(The latter is discussed in depth in the next chapter.) He wanted to
know what Dahmer was like when he was a kid, before all the
killings started, before he became a monster, which is the same goal
Backderf had for this graphic novel. He watched hours of taped
interviews that Dahmer gave from prison, and studied his voice, his
body language, his expressions. How would all of those things have
been expressed at sixteen? He even kept a photograph of the young
Dahmer on his laptop wallpaper for a while. Who was that kid?[23]
What did he do? What did he think? What would he have been like
before it all went so wrong? Girard filled his head with Jeff as a kid,
who he was, and what he was like, until he came to life, and there
was no stopping him.[24]

The process by which he created Shawn was similar. Girard had to do a lot of research, because he had never been in the military, can't throw a proper punch, and doesn't know what PTSD is like, which is an important part of Shawn's character, since he lives with it daily. He read books on the military, on PTSD, and interviewed veterans about their experiences overseas and after coming home. He looked at the latest information he could find on the kinds of treatment our veterans are getting or not getting, and the most effective ways to recover. And just as he did with Jeff, Girard brought the real qualities of the people he met into Shawn's character, using the specifics they told him to bring the person of Shawn Castillo to life.[25]

But while Girard answers the question why, he allows the reader to answer the question of who. Who is the monster in this book? Is it the clones, fated to live out the lives of the serial killers they were made from? There's no doubt that some of these kids are evil incarnate, and their actions can make the most phlegmatic reader's skin crawl, but what of the serial killer brought up in a loving and supportive family? Is he a monster as well? And what about Gregory Jacobson, Jeff's "father," who came up with the cloning project when the DOD asked him to create the ultimate weapon, and gave him billions of dollars every year to find the answer? Isn't he a monster? He paid some families to abuse their adopted boys in specific ways that mimicked the way their cloned "father" had been brought up—these boys were sexually and physically abused, made to feel unworthy and insignificant, just to see what they would do. Could they overcome both nature *and* nurture? The others that worked for and with Jacobson at DSTI and knew exactly what was going on—were they not monsters as well? The scientists who created the Dark Man clone, with his incredible and formidable powers—were they not monsters? And what of those who struggle to keep the monster at bay? Shawn, with his twenty-three kills and his nightmares about them and other horrors he committed and witnessed—is he a monster? Jeff, who always thought he was normal, until he found out he wasn't, that he had the genetics of a serial killer who was also a cannibal and who tried to resist his homosexuality until it helped drive him to violence—is he a monster? And what of the men and women who funded the research, who asked for more of it, who wanted to take it further and further and further until it turned back on them—aren't they the real monsters? These are questions that the reader must answer, must decide, and perhaps, re-decide. The answers are in your own heart, and mind, and soul. May you live easily with them.

Another take on this theme is Gordon Korman's new series on clones of criminal masterminds, written for middle school grades (five to eight), so the focus is much lighter and less complex than Girard's books, which is appropriate. Projected as a trilogy, it looks at the same dark questions as Girard does. What is the difference between nature and nurture, and are the monsters the cloned children, or the scientists keeping the eleven thirteen-year-olds imprisoned in a tiny desert compound? Is a sociological experiment worth such manipulation?

Serenity has fewer than two hundred residents, and all information and news—print, television, and Internet—is sanitized. These children know only peace and harmony, and when a newspaper from outside accidently slips through, the girl who finds it has to go to her parents for a definition of a word she's never seen or heard—*murder*. When one of the boys tries to leave the city limits, he discovers that he cannot because of the inexplicable and severe pain and nausea that attack him when he tries. Some kids can leave the town, others can't. Why? This question fuels the search for the answer, as five of the eleven begin to work together secretly, learning that the town and its residents, including their "parents," are all part of an elaborate charade, aimed at finding out whether they will follow their genetic nature or their structured nurture.

While reviews have been excellent, it is worthwhile to consider the question of how quickly the trickle-down effect has occurred: Girard's books came out in September 2013, and Korman's *Masterminds* came out in February 2015, not even two years later. It is somewhat disconcerting to see books for preteens emulating those for older teens and adults so quickly. It will be interesting to see how Korman develops his storyline over the next two volumes, and how dark and difficult they become.

# 7

# *MY FRIEND DAHMER*
# BY DERF BACKDERF

**D**erf Backderf (only his mother calls him by his given name, John) knew he had to write the story of how he knew Jeff Dahmer shortly after he got the news about Dahmer's death. The news media identified him as one of Dahmer's boyhood friends, and they descended in droves—calling until he stopped answering his phone, living with TV crews camped out on the lawn, knocking on the door, and trying desperately to get a glimpse of the monster's friend. But the only media outlet he talked to was the *Akron Beacon Journal*, where his wife worked, and he was a part-time member of the art department.[1] All the other media that covered the story got their information from the *Beacon*, because it was virtually the only source covering Dahmer's childhood and adolescence.[2] So, directly or indirectly, most, if not all, of the information about Dahmer before he started killing came from Backderf.[3] But about a month later, the media circus faded away, and other events took over the headlines. In August 1991, Backderf met with two of his high school friends, Mike and Neal, who'd also been members of the Jeff Dahmer Fan Club, to talk about what they remembered, and how Jeff had turned out. They met at Neal's house, which was just about two hundred yards from the Dahmer home, surrounded by yellow crime scene tape. They each shared stories of their strange friend, some old, and some

they'd never told before, because they seemed random and irrele-
vant. But now that they knew what Dahmer had done after high
school graduation, all the bits and pieces of information that they
had about him had new significance and chilling redefinitions. As
the three of them talked, Backderf took out a small sketchbook and
began to sketch out the stories as he heard them, eventually filling
about fifteen pages. It was his usual way to "take notes." As he
sketched out the scene of Jeff and Neal going fishing, a lightbulb
went off in his head, and he realized that this was the biggest story
of his life, and he had to share it with the world.[4] But it took him
twenty years to set it down in its final form, and several parts of it
were published in different formats before it reached its final itera-
tion.

After that, Backderf continued to collect stories and other material about Dahmer, and between 1995 and 1997, he wrote several
short stories about him. In 1998, he wrote a hundred-page graphic
novel, that he shopped around to various publishers for four years,
but without success. In 2002, Backderf self-published a twenty-
four-page graphic novel, including three of the stories he wrote in
1995–1997. He hoped a publisher would be interested in seeing a
longer version after seeing this publication, but again, he met with
no success. However, the book did become a cult classic,[5] and it
was nominated for an Eisner Award, which is given for creative
achievement in comic books. It is frequently described as the Oscar
of the comic industry.[6]

The next year, Backderf decided to set aside everything he'd
collected so far, which depicts Dahmer from a very personal point
of view, and write instead of a memoir, a biography of Jeff Dahmer
that would include everything about his life, crimes, arrest, trial,
incarceration, and death. He began to interview people who had
known Dahmer and read everything he could find on him, including
news stories and FBI reports.[7] If two people could corroborate each
other's stories, he took it as fact.[8] His primary sources were transcripts of FBI interviews (the entire Dahmer FBI file, including
more than ten thousand documents, is now in the public domain,
and freely available); several documentaries by *Dateline NBC*, in-

cluding the only television interview done by Dahmer, or by his mother, who was interviewed separately; his father's biography, *A Father's Story*; and newspaper stories from the *Akron Beacon Journal*, *Milwaukee Journal*, and *Milwaukee Sentinal*. He felt that these three local papers got more of the detail correct than the ones from the national media did.[9] In 2009, after completing two other graphic novels (*Trashed* and *Punk Rock and Trailer Parks*), Backderf was able to complete the whole project in only a few weeks, because he had spent so much time researching and thinking about what he wanted to say and how he wanted to present Jeff Dahmer.[10] He had also been hauling around a lot of baggage about Dahmer and had to take time to sort through that before starting to write. He also had other stories that he wanted to tell, and he needed to learn how to write a graphic novel, which is a very different format from the short stories he'd written previously about Dahmer and from the comic strips and political cartoons he'd written for a variety of publications.[11]

Backderf was also thinking about how he wanted to present Jeff's story, and ultimately decided to give it a focus that would appeal to teens.[12] It is the story before the story everyone expected him to write, before Dahmer killed for the first time, and in Backderf's mind, became a monster.[13] There is little violence in the book, and no swearing, because Backderf wanted it to have "a PG rating." With the exception of one scene,[14] the violence, including Dahmer's first murder, takes place offstage, with only the buildup to it and the results of it included in the story itself. Backderf includes themes of how teens treat each other, how they are bullied or form friendships, and how oblivious the adult world is to the world of adolescents.[15]

He knew he was taking a chance presenting Dahmer as a troubled kid rather than a monster, but that was the Dahmer he knew. He never knew the monster. But in addition, Backderf points out that if we allow people to be labeled as monsters, then there is a certain inevitability to that designation—and no chance for them to become anything else—no hope for any level of salvation. He doesn't agree with that, and states over and over in both the book and interviews about it, that there is a chance that Dahmer could have been saved had any adults voiced their concerns, or been more aware that cause for concern existed.[16] And, of course, Dahmer himself could have chosen to speak up, to talk to someone about his thoughts and urges, but he also remained silent. At one point, Dahmer was a person, a deeply troubled child and adolescent, coping with the monsters in his life the best way he could. But when he chose to kill, and then did not choose to confess, but to kill again and again, the monster from the headlines won out over the person inside. Backderf has no sympathy for the monster Dahmer became, reserving that sympathy only for the boy and the teen that monster came from. And although Backderf asks the question "What if?" he knows that the time for answering that question is long gone.

Backderf was determined to make his story as close to reality as possible, and the e-book version of *MFD* includes sketches of the location of Dahmer's clubhouse, the interior of the Dahmer house, and sketches of interior mall scenes. Backderf's blog and some of his interviews also include additional photos and sketches of the Dahmers' property, which is currently for sale. He even described why he originally located the clubhouse Dahmer used for his road-kill experiments in the wrong place, and explored the property until he was able to locate where the actual clubhouse had been. His research on what high schools and malls looked like in the seventies was meticulous, and he carefully explains what he did and why.[17]

Backderf first met Dahmer when he was twelve and they were entering junior high together. Both were fairly clueless and occupied one of the lowest rungs on the status ladder. Backderf knew Dahmer didn't have any friends, and described him as "the loneliest kid I'd ever seen."[18] But at the same time, he was strange enough that Backderf didn't try to make friends with him either. And soon enough, he had proof of that strangeness, as rumors about Dahmer's roadkill and his clubhouse began to spread. This became one of the opening scenes of the book, and even though Backderf later learned that he had located it in the wrong place,[19] the kids who had actually taken part in that scene assured him that he had gotten everything else right. Dahmer didn't begin to change until he started high school as a sophomore (junior high included ninth grade). All through junior high, he didn't stand out at all, in spite of the constant bullying he was subjected to. His sophomore year, he began having fake fits and ticks and loud outbursts with slurred words, like someone who had cerebral palsy.[20] Both he and Backderf were band nerds, and Dahmer fascinated and amused Backderf and his band nerd friends, who soon became the Jeff Dahmer Fan Club. They encouraged his outbursts, and became the only friends he had—although he was so strange that "friends" was a somewhat relative term. He was more of a mascot than anything, but definitely the center of attention for Backderf and his friends, about twelve or so kids in all, which he reduced to three plus himself to make the book easier to write. The three he includes were the major players of the group, men he is still in touch with on a regular basis.

It was also about this time that their hormones kicked in full time. Backderf was fascinated by girls, while Dahmer was horrified to realize that he was attracted to men. In the 1970s, coming out was out of the question, and homosexuality was something to be hidden and ashamed of. But it was worse for Dahmer, who wasn't just attracted to men, but to dead men, men he could control and fondle. He didn't know where the urges came from, but there was no way he could confess to them, and soon, no way he could control them without the oblivion of alcohol.

During this time, school was definitely an escape for Dahmer—he was around other boys who were his friends, who kept his mind from his constant urges and from the horror that was his home life. His parents fought viciously and loudly, and in the small house where they lived, there was no way for Dahmer to escape the conflict. His parents were absorbed in themselves and in their battle, ignoring their sons, not realizing or caring about the damage they were inflicting on Dahmer.

By the time his junior year started, Dahmer had discovered his own way to escape his life—he began drinking as soon as he left home in the morning, and didn't stop till he got home at night. The cluelessness of the adults to what was happening with him is the source of the question that Backderf poses over and over again—

how the adults around Dahmer, especially the teachers and school employees he saw every day, did not notice that there was something horribly, terribly wrong with him, when he was drunk all the time, early morning to late evening.[21] Backderf notes that every kid who got near him could smell alcohol on his breath, but no adults ever noticed. Dahmer had the ability to become invisible to adults whenever he wanted or needed to, and when school personnel were interviewed by Backderf while researching this book, most of their responses indicated that they didn't remember him at all.[22]

September 1976 was the tipping point, when he began to drink heavily on a daily basis, and in a few short weeks went from being merely strange to dark and scary.[23] He carried a Styrofoam cup around at school (there is a picture of him with his cup on page 8 of *MFD*), filled with dark liquid that adults assumed was coffee, but it was really hard liquor, bourbon or scotch. If anyone said anything about it, he could just chug it and toss the cup in the nearest garbage can—but no one ever did, even though he reeked of booze all day, and stashed extra booze outside the school in various places to make sure he didn't run out.[24] He was confronted about drinking only once during the four years he was in high school. A brief account of it is included in Backderf's notes for *MFD*,[25] but the complete incident described below is included only in the e-book version of *My Friend Dahmer*, because Backderf didn't hear the details about it until the print version had already gone to press.

When one of the coaches saw Dahmer drinking in the school parking lot, he took him to the assistant principal for punishment. Dahmer was given a choice—either call his parents and confess, or take ten licks (ten hard strikes on the buttocks with a wooden paddle). Dahmer chose the licks. He later told Neil, a member of the Jeff Dahmer Fan Club he considered a friend, how much it had hurt. The principal was very muscular, and he didn't hold back. The paddle he used, as Backderf depicted it in the scene, is a long, thick, sturdy wooden paddle, which certainly must have left bruises for days.[26] (During this time period, getting licks was a common punishment for both boys and girls in junior and senior high schools, and was considered an appropriate punishment, rather than corporal punishment or child abuse.) After this incident, Dahmer was even more careful to hide his drinking from school personnel.

In interviews after he was arrested, Dahmer confessed that he knew his urges and thoughts were sick and twisted, and filled him with revulsion. But no matter how he tried, he couldn't make them stop. But if he was sick and twisted, he was also clever and charming, and on a trip to Washington, D.C., during his junior year, he was able to persuade a White House aide to give him and a few other students a tour of Vice President Mondale's office, where he met not only Mondale but also columnist Art Buchwald. He was smart and charming and willing to try anything—what might he have accomplished had that person been allowed to live? As Backderf puts it, "What a waste."[27]

During their senior year, Backderf says he can't recall having a normal conversation with Dahmer—he was either in character, twitching and jerking, or he was drunk and oblivious. His personality was entirely gone, obliterated by his role or by alcohol, or both.[28] But the Jeff Dahmer Fan Club was going strong, and Backderf thought of all kinds of pranks they could use Dahmer to pull—like sneaking him into every picture of every club in the yearbook. And while Dahmer seldom attended class, none of the teachers ever called him on it. He was a senior, and soon he'd be someone else's problem—and he was.

Things at home were getting worse and worse. His father had finally moved out, and the acrimonious divorce had begun, with battles that escalated beyond belief. Dahmer had continued his fascination with roadkill, but now he went deep in the woods, where no one could see him dismembering animals with only a knife. It helped to quiet his urges.

Even his final and most outrageous scene with the Jeff Dahmer Fan Club, which took place sometime in March 1978[29] at the Summit Mall and lasted for several hours, seemed to cause no concern and was more or less ignored by adults.[30] It was that morning, when Derf and Kent went to pick up Dahmer, that Derf finally realized how truly scary Dahmer had become. Dahmer chugged a six pack of beer before they'd finished the ten-minute trip from his home to the mall. He didn't drink for enjoyment—he drank for numbness, the numbness that silenced the horrific voices and pictures his brain churned out continually[31]—and it was obvious from the casual way he worked his way through six cans of beer that it wasn't an unusual occurrence for him. It seemed to Derf no more difficult than some-one taking several prescription drugs to deal with some inconven-ient but chronic condition. Alcohol was Dahmer's drug of choice, and he used it to self-medicate as necessary.[32]

Even given the fact that it was the 1970s, before the time of school security and zero tolerance,[33] it seems appalling that his peers knew he was drunk at school[34] but the adults around him never noticed,[35] and none of the students ever reported him—no one would ever "narc" on another kid—it was a guarantee of instant and complete rejection.[36]

The Jeff Dahmer Fan Club disbanded after the day at Summit Mall. It had become obvious that Dahmer was too strange and even dangerous to be around. While there was no formal dissolution, that day marked the end of the club, and from then on, all the former members excluded Dahmer from all their activities.[37] Dahmer was alone with the voices, the thoughts, and the urges he could no longer escape. He had tried so hard to keep from being alone, but by the middle of June, not only had school ended, his father had moved out months before, and finally his mother and his little brother, David, moved out of the house and left him alone. It was a solitude that was reinforced by his mother's demand that he not tell his father that they left, because leaving the state was in violation of the Dahmer's custody agreement. This left him by himself and gave him the de-serted setting he needed to commit his first murder and dismember-ment.[38] By July 22, 1978, Jeff Dahmer, the troubled kid, was gone. In his place was Jeffrey Dahmer, the most notorious serial killer since Jack the Ripper. The monster had been born. Backderf notes in *MFD* and in his blog that while he could feel sympathy for Dahmer prior to his first murder, that event crossed the line, and made him into a monster. Every subsequent murder just com-pounded that result.

# 8

## *GIVE A BOY A GUN*
## BY TODD STRASSER

*Give a Boy a Gun* has been said to have been written in response to the Columbine High School shooting, but in actuality, Strasser started researching school shootings before Columbine. His own kids were going into middle school, and "it felt very strange to have to be worried about whether they'd be killed there."[1] However, it was the first book on a school shooting published after Columbine happened in April 1999, coming out on September 1, 2000, just a year and a half later. While the shootings happen in the school gym, not the library, and one shooter survives in a coma after being beaten by other students, it is still reminiscent of the Columbine shooting. In addition, facts and figures about school shootings, gun violence, and gun ownership are featured at the bottom of most of the pages, in a different font. The frame for the novel is based on interviews of those involved, done by a college journalism student who returns to town, "determined not to leave again until I understood what happened there." It is not until the last page of the book that the reader discovers why she is so passionate about finding out what happened and why.

When the book was published, the reviews of it were mixed, *Publisher's Weekly* describing it as heavy-handed, pompous, and disconnected. The multiple viewpoints were distracting, as were the facts and figures at the bottom of the pages.[2]

Others commented on the lack of curse words, represented by various symbols (%^&*#$*), seeing it as both a positive and a negative. However, anyone familiar with the language teens use among themselves, will be able to translate the symbols into letters with ease.[3]

The large cast of characters and the brevity of most of their comments does make the book seem choppy, and it could potentially be confusing. However, Strasser's goal seems to have been to introduce the main characters from the widest variety of perspectives, so they are seen both by their friends and their detractors, their classmates and adults inside and out of school, which make Brendan and Gary much more rounded and complete characters. And the adult characters' perspectives are important because they provide a different view of the teen characters that isn't present in the comments from their peers. In addition, the novel is brief, only 188 pages (2002 mass market paperback) without the appended information afterwards which makes it easier to keep track of the characters.

In contrast, the *Booklist* review said it was haunting, harrowing, deeply moving, disturbing, and compared the flow of facts and figures that enhance the story to a device used by John Dos Passos. It was described as "deserving of a wide readership, discussion and debate."[4]

It was popular with YA librarians and readers, and when the title list for the first Radical Reads book was being finalized, three YA literature specialists working with me to compile the title list told me that if I didn't put this title in, everyone would ask me why I didn't. It had to be in the book. That's why the RR books have 101 titles, rather than the more standard 100. I include it here because it was the first of the school shooting books published after Columbine, which changed this country's schools—and especially middle and high schools—forever, and forced school shootings to the forefront of our country's psyche. In addition, I believe it had a major influence on YA authors and YA literature in general, because it showed the transformation of two bullied boys into monsters, reinforcing the idea that anyone can be a monster when forced to live in a monstrous situation for long enough.

Strasser found this key point in an in-depth article about Columbine in *Rolling Stone*. In it, a boy who knew them said, "Every day being teased and picked on, pushed up against lockers—just the general feeling of fear in school. And you either respond to a fear by having fear, or you take action and have hate."[5] That was the point he wanted to make—that sometimes bullying and teasing can lead to violence. He also notes that he has gotten e-mails from bullies, thanking him for writing the book, because before reading it, they had never thought about what their bullying was doing to their victims.[6]

Strasser researched school shootings and gun violence in general, and Columbine in particular, before writing his book, and it shows in both his plot and characters, who are similar to Harris and Klebold (the Columbine shooters), as well as in the informational "footnotes" at the bottom of most of the pages. These are made up of snippets of information, quotations, and statistics that form a factual "background" for the novel. Strasser is a gun control advocate, and his perspective comes through clearly in these "footnotes," as well as in the story. However, it is important to note that this book is fourteen years old, and the statistics are out of date, although current statistics are equally dramatic.

Almost half the book (pages 118–84, 2002 mass market paperback edition) is devoted to what happened the evening of the dance, with more than fifty pages on the shooting itself. However, it is important to note that Strasser also details the violence that came after the shooting was over, when a group of boys began beating Brendan, continuing even after he was unconsciousness, and characterizing their actions as "equally inexcusable and evil."[7] Brendan's mother muses on the different signs she has seen: "Drug-Free Zone," "Gun-Free Zone," and notes that by the time bullied teens are thinking about guns, it's too late. The sign should read "Teasing/Bullying-Free Zone."[8] Strasser is not saying that gun control is the answer, but that creating safe spaces for *all* teens, especially at school, including the ones who are outsiders and easy to attack, is the answer.

The book opens with an introduction from the interviewer and consists of snippets of interviews given by family, friends, teachers, and townspeople describing Gary and Brendan and reflecting on the gradual changes in them over the years as they endured bullying, teasing, and hazing from the varsity football players and their entourages. Finally, they realized that no adults were going to do anything even if they witnessed what the jocks did, that none of their peers would help, and that they were on their own. If any action was going to be taken, they would have to take it themselves. When Brendan saw the World War II semiautomatic handgun his father bought for his gun collection, it was as if the last piece fell into place. From then on, the shooting seemed inevitable.

But it is also important to note that, like Harris and Klebold, the protagonists made sure the friends they cared about would not be at the dance, and when Gary realizes that Allison is actually in the gym despite his warning to stay away, everything changes for him. There is no way for her to get out, and no way to protect her inside. He escapes in the only way he can, by shooting himself, and ending the chaos.

Strasser makes it very clear that it is the years of torture that are at the heart of this shooting. Anyone, when cornered and in fear for his life, will turn and fight in the most effective way he knows how to, with whatever weapons he can find, just as any trapped animal will do. But this is not a case of someone suddenly snapping, but a gradual progression, from jokes about retaliation to fantasies of it to realistic planning and, finally, when there is no other alternative, action. Yet even as horrible and inexcusable as the shooting was, it is important to remember that Gary was the only person who killed someone—himself. Other people were wounded, and the chief torturer was deliberately mutilated, but no one other than the perpetrators died. The violence was contained and limited—something that is not the case with other, more recent books about school shootings. This isn't surprising for a first title about a difficult or controversial situation, but I wonder, if Strasser were to write this book today, perhaps about the Arapahoe High School shooting in Centennial (Colorado), how much more graphic and violent it would be.

# 9

# *THE LAST DOMINO*
# BY ADAM MEYER

*The Last Domino* could work equally well in the sections on bullies or manipulators, but the school shooting is the result of both bullying and manipulation. Travis is a shell of a person since his older brother Richie committed suicide several years before. Richie's room is locked, and their parents don't allow any conversation about him. Travis is bullied by the school football hero, P. J., who is also the indulged son of the sheriff. When Travis is caught throwing rocks at cars on the freeway, the sheriff throws the book at him, partly because the only damage Travis did was crack his son's windshield. P. J. forces Travis to pay for the new windshield when his parents won't help him, or even discuss it with him. So Travis gets a job at the local Starbuck's clone so he can pay P. J. But his whole life changes when Daniel moves to town and lands in Travis's English class.

While the reader doesn't realize it at first, Daniel begins to manipulate Travis, first in small ways, then finally separating him from anyone he's been close to—friends, classmates, and even his parents. Friends see what is going on, and try to caution Travis about Daniel, but by the time this happens, Travis is firmly caught in Daniel's spider web, and virtually unable to think for himself. The climax of the book is not the gory shootout when Travis kills his parents, showers, and goes to bed, waking up the next morning with the memory of what he did. He tries and fails to kill himself, and then goes to school to start shooting. He seems at first to know that this is somehow Daniel's fault, because Daniel is supposed to be one of his first targets, but he isn't in the classroom. Neither is the girl he's been crushing on. Travis soon learns that they are in conference with the school counselor (Richie's ex-girlfriend) and the principal. Daniel is once again twisting facts and revealing partial truths and even outright lies to allow him to continue to control Travis, and to convince everyone else that Travis is doing this all by himself without Daniel's help. After killing his teacher and wounding several other students, Travis steps into the chaos that's erupted in the school, and goes to find Daniel. He shoots Daniel, but is not able to kill him. He is captured, and gets away briefly to confront Daniel, who reveals some of his machinations. He wants to kill Daniel, but he's out of bullets. Daniel turns and runs toward the police, who are just arriving, and Travis realizes that he is planning his story even as he runs.

A year later, Travis is in jail and unable to remember anything that happened to him, or answer any of the police or psychologists who ask him "Why?" He knows something terrible happened, that he and Daniel did it, but he is the only one in jail. Unaware that his parents are dead and that he went to their funeral, he thinks it's strange that he's heard nothing from them. It is only when Daniel calls him on Richie's birthday to gloat over the better-than-expected success of his plan to control Travis, to push him as far as possible, that Travis begins to remember what happened and what he did. Although Daniel pushed him and manipulated him, Travis was the one who took all the action. Travis is broken, and may never be able to put himself back together again, and will certainly spend all or most of the rest of his life behind bars. Daniel, however, who is broken or malformed in a much deeper and more serious way, is in college, continuing to manipulate those around him, believing he is untouchable.

This book contains one of the most evil characters I have ever met in YA fiction, and getting to know Daniel was not pleasant.

Daniel is the true monster in the story, the one who sets up two other boys (at least) to fail, to push them to the breaking point, while cleverly avoiding any of the blame. He has a lot of the "classic" signs of the monster, which are gradually revealed throughout the novel, culminating in his last phone call and confession to Travis, knowing that he is safe from any accusation Travis might make. It is important for teens to know that there are physical bullies and there are mental and manipulative bullies, because the latter are much harder to see when someone is scarred and hurting.

Travis is an example of someone who gets into a bad situation, can't get out of it, and finds himself doing monstrous things, almost as if he can't help himself. Finally, he is so horrified at what he's done that he suppresses it and shoves it into "a black hole of my memory." He isn't a monster; in spite of what he does, he is as much a victim as a perpetrator. With Daniel controlling his every move, there was little chance for him to think for himself and see how he was being herded down an increasingly dark path.

As in many YA novels, the adults are less than helpful. Travis's parents have not recovered from Richie's death any better than he has, and when his mother attempts to bring normality back to the family by turning off the TV during dinner and talking about Richie, his father blows up and forbids either of them to mention his name. Both parents die without ever realizing what is going on with their son. In addition, none of the teachers are aware of what is going on under their noses, not the bullying from P. J., nor the manipulation by Daniel. Beth, Richie's former girlfriend, who is now the school counselor, does try to reach out to Travis, but even she is unable to see beyond Travis's grief over his brother's death, and believes the lies and innuendos she hears from Daniel and the students he has influenced.

The violence in the book is detailed, with splashes of blood, falling bodies, blood-slicked floors.[1] Travis's mother tries to reassure her son that she loves him, with her last words and breaths, while his father continues to roar and bluster at his son, until he finally falls and dies. Teachers and students die in blood-spattered rooms with bullet holes in the walls. Yet, after all the accurate shots

Travis made, it is interesting that even though he shot Daniel several times, he was unable to kill him. That might have been partly because Daniel was continuing to talk to him, controlling his thoughts and perhaps his actions, or it may have been because he still saw Daniel as a kind of friend.

Meyer adds complexity to the plot by inserting police detective interviews with various characters, and excerpts from the journal of an ex-football player who likes Travis.[2] And there is no dearth of discussion topics, especially since the use of social psychology is compelling,[3] as the reader begins to understand the various motivations and drives of the characters.

There is little doubt that this is a controversial book, one that parents and teachers may find hard to deal with, since the characters are not positive or supportive ones. However, it does give important information about how easy it is to allow yourself to be manipulated by someone you trust. It also presents two different types of monsters, and a number of flawed and monstrous characters as well. It is not pleasant reading, but it is powerful and valuable, and deserves a place on library shelves.

# 10

## *ENDGAME*
## BY NANCY GARDEN

*Endgame*, by Nancy Garden, came from her need to "do something" after Columbine.[1] But she wondered if a book about a school shooting would persuade kids to copy the shooter in her book. It wasn't until she went to Chatfield High School, where the Columbine students went after the shooting, to talk to a class of teens who were interested in writing, that she changed her mind. At a dinner that night, she shared her interest in writing a book based on a school shooting, and also her hesitancy about it with that class's teacher, Jan McClain. The teacher said, "No, you've got to do it. You must write it." Garden thought of those words often while she was writing *Endgame*.[2] She also noticed that even though most school shootings involved kids who were bullied, that it was given little attention, and the prevailing attitude seemed to be boys will be boys. But Garden disagreed with that attitude, and she decided to make bullying a major part of the book. She was bullied as a child, and so had personal experience about how that felt. She and her partner also were friends with twins from a dysfunctional family just up the street, and while the girl was at their house frequently, they saw the boy less often. Yet, after Columbine, he wrote a letter to them, saying that if it hadn't been for his music and basketball and people like them, he might have done the same thing. He is not a character in the book, but this story and the specifics of his being bullied inspired Garden when she created her main character, Gray.[3]

Garden was also careful not to make Gray too much of a victim, because in the first drafts of the novel, editors objected, saying no one would like him.[4] Oddly, a reviewer who reviewed it right after Newtown felt Gray was too sympathetically drawn, and said that reading the book felt like a betrayal of the Newtown victims. She said she steeled herself against feeling any sympathy for Gray, and this colored her experience of the book. But she admits that Garden did take a balanced approach when creating Gray's character, and presents the bullying and lack of teacher and parental support he had to endure, as well as the awful decisions he made and the price he had to pay for them.[5] She also had him use various strategies to stop the bullying: enduring, becoming resistant to it, and finally, confronting the perpetrators with a level of violence that exceeded theirs.[6]

As in *The Last Domino*, *Endgame* allows the reader to see the progression of the killer's thoughts, getting closer and closer to deciding that using a gun is the best solution. Garden frames the story as a series of interviews between Gray and his defense attorney, with brief interludes that let the reader know what life is like for Gray in prison. After nine months of constant bullying, including name calling; physical harassment; and abuse of Gray and of his best friend, Ross, Gray decides to act on his plan to kill his torturers. He sees no other way out, after the bullies have taken away his music, the girl he has a crush on, his dog, and finally, his best friend. In addition to being beaten up on a regular basis, giving him a black eye and multiple bruises, Zorro and Johnson have humiliated him in every way possible, usually with the jeering chorus of the rest of the varsity football players and/or the other boys in his and Ross's PE class. They also forced him to drink paint because Zorro thought Gray had talked to someone at school about Zorro trashing his drums, and finally, stripped him and Ross naked and tried to get Gray to perform oral sex on Ross, resulting in a fight between the two boys and the loss of their friendship, which had no chance of overcoming this ultimate humiliation. The latter two incidents seemed to push Gray over the edge. He knew his father had purchased a semiautomatic hand gun, and Gray had shot it once, getting multiple bullseyes. The plan that had been mostly fantasy became real. Gray knew no one was going to help him—teachers and school administrators turned a blind eye, and those that did take notice could not get Gray to talk for fear of reprisals, so they chose to not follow up on the rumors and accusations from other students. And since the paint incident was the result of the school counselor putting two and two together in spite of Gray's silence, and questioning Zorro and Johnson about destroying Gray's expensive drum set, Gray seems to have been correct about paybacks from the bullies. The counselor did not follow up on anything after that. In fact a few days later, Gray commented that everyone (teachers and administration) had decided to let him and Ross alone—and this is when Zorro and Johnson struck again, in the shower room scene, trying to force Gray and Ross to perform oral sex.

In the end, Gray cut himself off from everyone else, and saw no other option than to take the gun to school and kill first his tormentors and then himself. But because his brother tackled him and took the gun away, Gray will spend the rest of his life in prison without the chance of parole, and his torturers will go free, except for Zorro, who was Gray's first victim. Sadly, the others that he killed and wounded included several of the people who had been close to him in one way or another.

The buildup to the shooting follows the descriptions given by psychologists of how serial killers, and especially school shooters, gradually change from outsiders to killers. It also shows how bullies are grown and developed and how they take advantage of their power to trample the kids that they see as different or vulnerable in some way. Zorro and Johnson chose Gray and Ross to persecute and left other nerds and outsiders alone. Because of that, Gray is left to wonder what is wrong with him and why he virtually instantly attracts their unswerving and malevolent attention.

Sadly, it is clear by the newspaper stories and the memorial service for the victims, when Johnson gives a moving speech about Zorro, that no one in that high school has learned anything about how and why the whole scenario came about. Teachers will still say "Boys will be boys," and the counselors will continue to accept the silence of the victims who dare not name their tormentors. They will continue to believe that evil is Other to them, that Gray is to blame for everything, and that the bullies are not really doing anything harmful or dangerous. And sadly, the other students will continue to look away from the bullying so they don't also attract attention. Instead, they give even more adulation to the jocks who run the school than the administration does. I wonder what will happen to Ross now, and who Johnson's next whipping boy will be, and who will become the next Zorro.

Garden's characterizations leave no doubt that she did research into both social psychology and school shootings before she began to write *Endgame*, because they show accurately the various roles that are frequently seen in school shootings: the bullies/jocks who have no one to give them boundaries or tell them no, affording them an unshakable sense of entitlement; the overbearing father who wants his son to be different and devalues his abilities and talents; the ineffective mother who doesn't stand up against her husband and protect her child; the teachers who look away and make excuses for the bullies; the students who also look away or fade into the background, not wanting to attract attention; the one or two students who try to stand up to the bullies, or for the victims, with negative results; and the victims, too frightened to make a scene, knowing that things could only get worse if the bullies are crossed.

It is interesting to note the roles that the fathers of Gray and Zorro play. While Gray's father finally tries to help his son after his dog is killed, and first talks to Zorro's father and then files a lawsuit against him, Zorro's father believes his son without question, and reacts with rage. It seems that Zorro has learned from his father to be a bully. Gray, on the other hand, didn't learn how to be a bully, but rather how to be his father's and then other bullies' victim.

Garden's plot moves swiftly, as the evil begins to grow and intensify, and as one option after another is eliminated. Finally, violence is the only answer, and the ultimate futility. Garden closes the story as the jail doors close on Gray, leaving him inside for the rest of his life, finally and ultimately alone, cut off from friends and family because of his desperate act. I wonder who will survive in prison, the musician and songwriter or the vengeful shooter.

# I I

# "GUNS FOR GEEKS" BY CHRIS CRUTCHER, FROM *ON THE FRINGE* EDITED BY DON GALLO

After Chris Crutcher trashed his novel about a school shooting, based on a 1999 shooting in Moses Lake, Washington, he reused some of the characters and plotlines to create this short story for Don Gallo's anthology on outsiders. Moses Lake was a rural town of about 10,000 when Barry Loukaitis, fourteen years old, who had been bullied and tormented for years, came to school dressed as an old western gunfighter with a long black coat, a rifle, a revolver, a semiautomatic pistol and seventy-eight extra rounds of ammunition. He went into this algebra class at Frontier Middle School, and shot two boys, wounded a girl, and killed the teacher. One of the coaches heard the shots and came into the classroom and was able to stop him.[1]

The morning it happened, the local NBC affiliate asked Crutcher to come in for an interview (he didn't live far from the station), and he watched the live feed from Moses Lake in the studio. Afterward, he was interviewed, and although most of the segment ended up on the cutting room floor, he remembers saying "No, folks, I don't know how we can see this coming, but I've probably got four or five kids on my caseload right now with that kind of rage. . . . That's

77

what we should focus on." Later, he began to think about what he'd
seen, and wondered, "What was it like to be in that room? And how
do you get to be Barry Loukaitis?" It was such a small town that it
would be impossible to avoid his family, because everyone knew
everyone else. What might have happened if Barry's parents ran
into the parents of one of his victims at the town's one supermarket?
At the time, Crutcherthought of it as an anomaly, but as he began to
write, there were more and more school shootings, and finally, Columbine, which changed everything, and made Crutcher's book ob-
solete. He says the second version is better, anyway. [2]

By the time he wrote the story, he was more interested in the
aftermath of the shooting than what caused it. His questions were
more about "What do we do now?" and "How do we go on?" than
"How/why did this happen?" which had been his previous focus.
The story itself and the description of the shooting come straight
from the first book, and eerily reflect the Loukaitis shooting.

The story opens in a high school classroom, where Mr. Beemer,
the basketball coach, is leading a discussion on the Second Amendment and whether the founding fathers would have included it if
they had known that someday guns would exist that could fire
multiple bullets without reloading, or that guns would make the
United States one of the most violent nations in the world. Just
before the bell rings, the door opens and Gene Taylor, one of the
outcasts at the school, stands in the doorway with a rifle, and begins
to shoot. Two students fall immediately, then Beemer, and Carly,
the narrator's girlfriend, and finally another jock. His plan was to
kill everyone in the room, but Sam, the narrator, and his brother T.
J. manage to stop him.

After that, the story does what few school shooting stories do—it
looks at the survivors and how they deal with the abrupt and overwhelming changes in their lives. When Gene shot his last victim, he
had his back to Sam, but Sam was frozen and unable to move. He
feels a terrible sense of guilt about that, because he might have
prevented Johnny from being killed. After he goes to talk to Johnny's father to confess his failure to act, he learns to begin to go on
with his life. On the day the decision is to be made whether to try

Gene as an adult or as a juvenile, Sam goes to see Mr. Waller, Johnny's father, who sums up the whole situation in just a few words. "They're trying to figure out how to punish him. . . . Hell, don't they know guys like Gene Taylor are punished *before* they do their deed?" What Gene did was unthinkable, and Sam hates him for what he did, and what Sam feels as a result, but Sam also remembers the times when Gene came to his house, ravenous for food, and resentful and embarrassed because he didn't have what Sam did—family, love, security, clothes, and a girlfriend. And remembering that, he decides that no one is to blame for what Gene did—and everyone is to blame. Parents don't deliberately set out to mess up their kids, but sometimes that happens. In the end, Sam realizes, when someone is dead, it doesn't really matter whose fault it is. That person is still dead and gone, one way or another.

# 12

# *QUAD*
# BY C. G. WATSON

*Quad* takes place in a high school where there are six major cliques: Jocks, Freaks, Preps, Techies, Gays/Choirboys, and Theater geeks/ Drama Queens. Predictably, the Jocks and Preps are at the top of the pecking order, and the Freaks and Choirboys are at the bottom, the others falling somewhere in between. The book opens on Monday, April 6, as someone starts shooting up the Quad at Muir High. Ranger Ng, one of the Freaks, quickly realizes what's happening, and herds five students into the school store to get them out of the Quad and away from the shooter. Two of them move a freezer chest in front of the door, so the shooter can't get in, and they try to figure out what's going on. There are members of five of the six cliques in the store, and no one is really willing to trust anyone else. All they know is that someone has brought a gun to school, and is using it.

Then a series of flashbacks begins, filling in the backgrounds of the kids in the store and the groups to which they belong. They start about a month before the shooting, and involve at least two people from each group, and sometimes more. Some days involve glimpses of what the kids in all the groups are doing; others have only some of the groups. The last flashbacks take place on Friday, April 3, and include all six groups, centering around a wild party thrown by one of the popular kids when his parents were out of town, involving liquor, drugs, sex, and an attempted rape. The shooting takes place the following Monday afternoon.

There are two couples among the groups—Jocks Ken and Hayley and Techies Theo and Maggie—and several pairs of best friends—Ranger and Rufus are Freaks, Sage and Paisley are Drama Queens, Brittany and Nicole are Preps, and Perry and Christopher are Choirboys. The football Jocks are the largest group, and are also known as the "steroid posse," although Stone and Calvert are into it more than anyone else, and Ken doesn't use them at all. Haley is the star of the volleyball team and is supposed to be Stone's girlfriend.

One of the more unconventional parts of the novel involves who the bullies and the victims are. The football players have it in for everyone except the Preps—especially Stone, who has sudden and intense fits of "roid rage." But the two Techies are hiding secrets that allow them to bully anyone in the school by making their secrets public, either on video or in the underground school paper. The Preps see everyone except the Jocks as below them, and the Drama Queens' devastating prank sets up the climax of the book. No one is truly exempt from bullying and cruel teasing. Each of them could be one of the suspects, each of them had a motive to kill.[1]

As in *Give a Boy a Gun*, the author's goal in writing the book was to show that violence frequently follows when the teen who is different in some way finally has had enough and decides to fight back. Watson is a high school teacher, and she decided to write *Quad* after watching students at her high school mount a campaign of meanness, bullying, teasing, and isolation that could have ended in tragedy. She believes that everyone needs to speak up when they observe or experience that going on. It is never acceptable behavior, and must be stopped.[2]

As the students cower inside the student store, wondering who the shooter is, most of them believe it's Stone—he is out of control and has antagonized many of the characters in the book. The football coach has finally discovered the steroids he's been taking, and he's off the team and has to be tested for drugs. He's found out that Haley may leave him for Ken. His drug stash for Massey's big party has disappeared, and he has no chemical way to chill out and escape losing his increasingly volatile temper. Theo taped the whole out-of-control party, and Stone was recorded attempting to rape Paisley and taking drugs. And his biggest secret, his first name, has just been published in the underground school paper.

But some of the students think the shooter might be Rufus—he has been getting more and more depressed since Stone destroyed his prized longboard, and Rufus has vowed revenge. Even Ranger wonders if his best friend has finally snapped.

However, it is important to note that this shooter doesn't have some of the characteristics that school shooters usually do, in reality and in fiction. There is no planning involved, or at least seen on stage. While there is a long lead-up of teasing and mocking, the author gives the reader no indication that the most recent incident is the one that causes a breakdown. And unlike other school shooters, this shooter is a girl who is portrayed as mentally and emotionally fragile, and we know of only one girl she killed. There were many shots, but only one victim was identified—one of her primary persecutors. The book ends just as the reader learns the identity of the shooter, and there is no resolution or denouement.

This book is notable because it examines the varying perspectives from all of the cliques, and shows how both boys and girls can be bullies, that they can come from any of the student groups, and that when someone is bullied for long enough, even the most cowed of victims may be inspired to fight back. It also shows the high level of mistrust among the different characters, and how that feeds into the bullying that occurs.

# 13

## *HATE LIST*
## BY JENNIFER BROWN

Jennifer Brown didn't want to write a book about a school shooting, a book that would end with bullets flying and people screaming. She wanted to write a book about what happened after the shooting, about recovering from the shooting, learning to live with the pain, picking up the pieces and going on. As many other authors have done, Brown literally dreamed up the story in her sleep, and when she woke up one morning Valerie was in her head, talking to her. She knew she had to tell her story. The soundtrack for that story was the song "If Everyone Cared," by the Canadian group Nickelback. Brown even created scenes that mirrored the first lines of the song, as Nick and Val lie on their backs in the middle of a field, gazing up at the stars and talking about anything and everything, and loving each other so freely and purely. (You can find the official video of the song on YouTube at https://www.youtube.com/watch?v=-IUS-ZyjiYuY.)

Jennifer and Nick met when he moved to town at the beginning of her freshman year. They clicked immediately, even though he was from one of the few low-income parts of town. He had ratty clothes, sometimes too big and never stylish, and an "I don't give a shit" attitude that fit with the way Valerie was feeling about her own life. He was cute, with dark eyes and a shy, lopsided grin, and he just *got* her in a way no one else did.

The Hate List was Valerie's idea, but it was a joke, and a way to vent about the way they were treated by some of the popular kids, and even by some of the teachers. It belonged to her and Nick, and they never told anyone else about it. Valerie had no idea that Nick would use it as a plan to kill the people on it. He never told her, or anyone else, what he planned to do when he got to school that day with a gun. She was left to deal with the aftermath alone.

Brown was deliberate when she created her characters—she wanted contrasts, connections, and conflicts—she wanted to show the good and the bad about them. Valerie was bullied cruelly during the first three years of high school. She was a victim. She created the Hate List. She was a villain. She stopped the shooting, and nearly died doing so. She was a hero.[1] She was also goth, with black eyeliner, dyed black hair, and clothes with holes ripped in them. She was an outcast at school, and that was okay with her. At home, she was also an outcast, watching and listening as her parents' marriage fell apart. She was loved, but she was not accepted, and she just tried to stay out of the way as much as she could.

Jessica was a bully. She was a villain. She was the last person Nick shot before he killed himself, after he had killed several of her friends. She was a victim. She reached out to Valerie when she was the most hated girl in school, supported her, and tried to make Valerie part of her own group. She was a hero.

Nick had a hard life, without any of the advantages Valerie grew up with. He slept on a mattress on the basement floor. He was different, he was Other, an outsider. His attitude hid much of what he thought and felt, and he was constantly and viciously bullied. He was a victim. He loved Valerie, and cherished their time together, showing her who he was behind the attitude. He put up with the bullying, as much as he could, even when there was no reason for it other than meanness. He was a hero. He helped Valerie write the Hate List, and kept it with him part of the time. He brought a gun to school, and deliberately killed people that he believed had wronged him and Valerie. He was a villain. Zimbardo would have called him a good apple ruined by a bad situation, a flawed boy, broken and made desperate by the torment he lived with daily. [2]

In fact, Brown created Nick in two phases. When she began the book, she didn't think she needed to have him be a fully fleshed-out character—he was the monster, the killer, the villain. It wasn't until the editing process began that Brown realized that the reader needed to see the Nick that Valerie fell in love with, the Nick who was her romantic hero, the person she connected with so deeply. And because she romanticized him so much, she was unable to see his rage and how it consumed him, and why she had no idea what he meant to do or that he'd use the Hate List to do it. So Brown wrote Nick's character in two phases—first the villain she created in the first draft, then the hero Nick that Valerie fell for. [3]

Humans are complex, with conflicting emotions, and Brown's characters reflect that. Valerie's parents are horrified about the shooting, worried about a daughter that came so close to death, yet unable to trust her. Would she screw up again? They felt guilt and anger—they hadn't seen it coming, their friends' children had been wounded both mentally and physically, and the conflicts between the two of them had exacerbated the situation. Valerie's father, Ted, was almost out of the house when the shooting occurred, and he ended up staying to make the best of a bad situation, and when the break finally came, it was much worse than he had thought. Jenny, her mother, is afraid for her daughter, and tried to help her by getting her the therapeutic help she needed, but was unable to trust her in any way, and so she created scenes that were destructive and painful for everyone in the family. Brown drew upon her own experience as a parent and as the child of a broken home to create the splintering Leftman family. Brown reports that some readers have seen Jenny and Ted as mean, cold, even cruel. But like most of her other characters, they are deeply flawed and doing the best that they can. Sometimes that's quite a lot, other times, not so much. [4] But it is significant that by the end of the book, Valerie realizes that even she and her parents will reconnect someday—able to forgive, even if they are not able to forget.

One of the more interesting adult characters is also the one who keeps much of himself private and appears almost always in the same setting, his office. Dr. Hieler has experience with teens and violent cases, and sets up a safe place in his office for Valerie to share and listen without fearing his censure. Heiler reveals little of himself because it is appropriate in a therapeutic situation, and Valerie fills in the gap by imaging the life she'd like him to have. Brown's husband is a psychologist, and she based Heiler's character on him, working through therapeutic conversations with him.[5] It is no surprise that his sessions with Valerie are just as accurate and realistic as Chris Crutcher's are, with his many years of therapeutic experience. Readers may learn a lot from Valerie's sessions with Hieler, just as Crutcher's therapist characters share their wisdom in his books. *Ironman* is a perfect portrayal of how an anger management group is run. Heiler pushes Valerie to go beyond the comfort zone, but he never withdraws his support and affirmation of her, encouraging her to look at people and situations as they really are, not how she'd like them to be or fears that they may be. He also tells her to look at herself the same way and to find out just who that self really is. As she sets off on her journey, in their last session he reminds her to stay safe, makes sure she has enough money, and tells her she'll be fine, as Valerie thinks to herself that she's sure she will never call, even just to say hi. In my heart, I hope she changes her mind. I deeply regret a therapist I never talked to after our final session. The *Voice of Youth Advocates*'s review characterizes Hieler as "easily one of best adult characters in YA literature," because he created an "oasis of comfort" and safety for Valerie.[6]

While there are flashbacks in the book that fill in the background, the book is firmly set in the present, the now, not in the past. This is Valerie's story, not Nick's. The recovery, not the crime. It's not about getting back to where they used to be before the shooting. It's about finding a new way to move forward, because the past is over and done with. Too many things have changed too dramatically, and the door to the past is closed. The only way to move is forward, through the door to the future.

And that is where Valerie and the other members of the class of 2009 are headed, some with a destination in mind, others, like Valerie, hoping to find the destination by beginning the trip. Her family and friends are moving on, Heiler has helped her regain her footing, and it is time for her to begin her journey.

This is not an easy book to read, especially all at once, rather than in small increments. The characters are realistic and engaging, and their confusion, their hope, and their pain are easy to see. Many who read it will need to do so with a box of Kleenex nearby. It is complex in its treatment of a variety of issues and settings, and there is much to ponder and discuss. It tells a story other YA titles on school shootings don't—the story of after, of recovery, of going on, and learning to live with the past.

# Part II

# Bullies: In Your Face and on Your Screen

*Fear, you see, is an emotion people like to feel when they know they're safe.*—Alfred Hitchcock [1]

I live about a block from one of the local high schools, and during nine months of the year, I hear the bells, the announcements, the roar of the crowds at various sports events, and the voices of kids who park all along my street to avoid the rules for parking in the school lot. Occasionally I've heard loud voices or seen fights break out as clumps of kids pass by on their way home, and wondered what to do, but only once has it seemed serious enough to warrant calling the police because the two teen boys at the center of the group seemed intent on hurting each other. And that time, an experienced mom with a confrontational teen son, waded into the melee and ended it before the police arrived. She had no fear, and I was in awe. But then summer comes, the street is quiet, with fewer cars, and noise from the campus is far less intrusive. Everyone seems to relax a little bit.

But come September, the noise, the kids, the cars, and the jeering comments will be back, and the tension on the street rises again. The cliques reorganize; those who are in or out are specified, as is what's cool and what's not. Lines are drawn, and the hazing, the hassling, the bullying, the drama, begins again. Some kids are eager to get back to school, to see friends they haven't seen over the summer, to see how people have changed, to trade gossip, to show off new styles they've adopted. But for other kids, September is something to dread, as they know all too well that the bullying they have had to endure during previous school years will start all over again, sometimes the first time they set foot on the school bus or on the campus. Cyberbullying can occur anytime, even during the summer, but the intensity and frequency increases during the school year, when kids see each other daily, and the actors for the three different roles in a bullying situation are always available.

These roles all work together to create the bullying scenario. There is the bully, his or her victim or victims, and the observers that witness the incident between the bully and the victim. However, a specific and detailed definition of what bullying entails has been elusive. Does it involve both verbal and physical acts? What if bullying goes online? Can a single act be defined as bullying, or must it be repetitive? Both state laws and researchers differ on defining bullying, but most state that bullying must involve the intent to hurt or harm someone else. Being rude or insensitive is not necessarily bullying; however, a deliberate attempt to cause someone social, psychological, or physical harm does constitute bullying.[2] Since 1999, forty-nine states have created some kind of law about bullying and how it should be punished, but they vary in their definitions of bullying and their punishments for it.[3]

And bullying is nothing new, but it was seen as a part of growing up and developing a strong character. This makes me wonder if the emphasis we place upon it today, and its increasing frequency, has to do with an increase in the behavior, or an increase in awareness of the behavior. Cyberbullying, of course, is new, dangerous, and increasing.

## FACE-TO-FACE BULLYING

Bullying is about dominance—who has it and who doesn't. And it isn't limited to humans—according to evolutionary anthropologist Christopher Boehm, hierarchically organized animal societies, like apes, monkeys, wolves, or lions, have bullies.[4] It is an adaptive behavior, ensuring that the stronger members of the society get more food and better mates, and thus produce more offspring. Clearly, it could have worked the same way for humans in the distant past, but it has become a maladaptive behavior today. In that distant past, aggression and antagonism against the outsider or the one who was different, who worked against the group, could be a positive thing, keeping the community safe. But it could also be misused when directed against an innocent who is perceived to be different but isn't actually doing any harm. But does that mean that bullying cannot be cured? Maybe, says Boehm. Bullies are created by both nature and nurture. We may be hardwired for bullying in the deeper and more animalistic parts of our brains, but these urges can be controlled by "higher" brain regions in which moral reasoning and rational thought reside. However, this presumes a functional family environment that includes altruism and moral teaching. If this individual's environment is dysfunctional or harsh, the negative behaviors learned at home may be exhibited outside it.[5]

Bullying behaviors can include verbal attacks or harassment about an individual's appearance, disability, race, religion, or sexuality.[6] Essentially, any characteristic that makes someone appear different in some way can be the cause for bullying attacks. It can also involve physicality: shoving, bumping, slapping, or other physical attacks that can vary in intensity. The victim's possessions and clothing are also at risk, and can be stolen, played with, defaced or damaged in some way. But the third kind of bullying, social or relational bullying, is more difficult to pinpoint. This kind of bullying involves isolating the individual, by ignoring, shunning, or excluding him or her. The victim doesn't even have to be present to hear the bullying—the bully shares his/her comments about the victim with friends, and the rumor quickly spreads among all the members of the group, class, grade, or school. "He's just a fag"; "she's slept with the whole football team—don't talk to her, everyone will think you're easy too"; or "look at her clothes—what a loser" are all comments that will have an impact of the person they are about. Social bullying can also be seen in gestures that are used to put down or reject the person they are aimed at, such as eye rolling, shrugs, frowns, sneers, stares of ridicule or hostility, or laughter. In addition, deliberately excluding an individual from games, parties, and events of all kinds is also a type of social bullying.[7] Social bullying can take place either in person or online, and can be even more harmful than physical bullying.

Bullies can frequently also be the most popular or coolest kids on campus, as research done at UCLA in 2012 found out. These bullies did not fit the traditional picture of bullies at all, having a high level of self-esteem, almost of entitlement, that allowed them to persecute those they considered beneath them. When elementary schoolers make the change to middle school, going to separate classes with different people, it can be a confusing and frightening time. Those who are able to adapt most quickly and learn dominance behaviors, or are the biggest, strongest, or most attractive, quickly rise to the top as school leaders, and are seen as popular or cool kids by both their peers and by faculty.[8] These discoveries are not as surprising as they might seem, when one thinks of all the pretty, popular "mean girls," and the jocks and homecoming kings who have little tolerance for those who are smaller or weaker. These are standard stereotypes from countless teen-oriented movies.

But no matter what kind of bullying it is, bullying always includes contempt for the victim or target. The bully wants the victim to feel worthless, inferior, and not entitled to respect. The contempt that the bully feels toward the victim comes from three beliefs held by the bully. First, bullies have a sense of entitlement, which allows them to dominate, control, and abuse verbally or physically another human being. Second, bullies demonstrate a low tolerance for people who are different from them—different means inferior and unworthy of respect. Third, bullies know the pain of exclusion, and do not hesitate to use it against anyone who is different from them, and therefore inferior. These psychological mind-sets or beliefs not only demean others that a bully deems inferior, it also protects the bully by not allowing anyone to see the hurt and damage inside that must always be covered up. Bullies must put others down in order to feel better about themselves.[9] Many bullies are former victims of other bullies. And it can be a generational trait, passed down from parent to child, as the bullied child learns to be a bully from the parent, first bullying other children, and then growing up to bully his or her own children.

An extreme case of this was widely publicized in 2013, when twelve-year-old Rebecca Sedwick killed herself by jumping off the top of a cement factory silo, after months of relentless bullying both at school and online. Guadalupe Shaw, who was the primary bully, was only fourteen. She not only sent Sedwick threatening texts and messages, but she also turned Sedwick's friends against her. The bullying didn't stop even after she began going to another school.[10] Shaw is accused of persuading more than fifteen girls to send Sedwick hate messages encouraging her to commit suicide.[11] One of the policemen involved compared Shaw's family to a *Jerry Springer* episode," saying "the way she [Shaw's mother] treated those kids was just horrendous," and she was later arrested for child abuse after a video of her beating a young boy was discovered.[12]

It is also important to point out that bullying that does not involve physical pain can cause mental pain, activating the same parts of the brain that react to physical pain. Individuals as young as thirteen have been shown to react to social pain the same way they react to physical pain. We as human beings are hardwired to be part of a group; we are social animals, and being ostracized can be no less painful than being beaten physically. In addition, the repetitiveness of bullying also changes the individual's brain patterns, increasing sensitivity to future bullying and altering thinking so that innocuous situations can be seen as threatening.[13]

Bullying dehumanizes its victims and makes it easier for observers to buy into the idea that bullied individuals deserve what they are experiencing. It also creates a sense of terror in the victims, making it less likely that they will tell anyone about what is happening. The victims are made to feel so totally powerless that they will not even fight back or defend themselves in any way.[14] Reduced academic achievement is also a result of bullying, because the individual may be reluctant to go to school, feeling it is not a safe place,[15] and because it is more important to avoid or hide from bullies than it is to pay attention to what is being taught. In fact, a 2012 study showed that only one or two out of ten incidents of bullying are reported. Between 8 and 90 percent go unreported[16]— something that makes the number of reported incidents even more alarming. (See following section "Facts and Statistics.")

Teens are most often targeted for bullying because they are seen as different in some way. Adolescence is a confusing time of life because teens are looking to become individuals separate from their family, making up their own minds. Yet at the same time, they are required to be just like everyone else around them, in their own peer group. It's necessary to fit in, sometimes at any cost. The major task in adolescence, according to developmentalists Havighurst and Erikson, is formulating a self-identity and a positive self-image. Being different should be the norm, yet difference is sometimes not tolerated. Discovering who you are intellectually, socially, and sexually is an important part of adolescence, and realizing that you are different in one of these areas can be the source of doubt and fear and make you an easy target for bullies. Several studies have been done on bullying that involves LGBTQ youth (lesbian, gay, bisexual, transsexual, questioning/queer). In 2009, a national study of more than seven thousand youth ages thirteen to twenty-one was done, and it showed that most teens were bullied at school about their sexual orientation: 80 percent were verbally harassed, 40 percent were physically harassed, 60 percent felt unsafe, and 20 percent had been physically assaulted.[17] Another study done in 2009, also looked at more than seven thousand individuals from the Midwest, and found that among these seventh and eighth graders LGBTQ youth were more likely to report high levels of bullying and substance abuse. Those who were unsure or questioning about their sexual orientation were more likely to be bullied, victimized, more frequently absent from school, using drugs more frequently, depressed, and considering suicide more than either heterosexual or homosexual teens who didn't question their sexuality. The lowest levels of depression and suicidal feelings were reported by LGBTQ students who were not bullied about their sexual preferences and by all students who were in a positive school setting and weren't bullied homophobically.[18]

However, a study done in 2011 showed that the impact of parents and their reaction to finding out that their child is LGBTQ can have an overwhelming effect on the children's current and future mental health.[19] Parents have gone so far as to toss their children out into the street to cope on their own, one reason why there is a high level of homelessness among the teen LGBTQ population. Even parents who do not go that far but who respond negatively at a less intense level, can cause higher levels of depression, suicide, and drug use in their children, who are six times more likely to be depressed, eight times more likely to attempt suicide, and three times more likely to use illegal drugs than their heterosexual peers.[20]

It also important to remember that homophobic bullying doesn't just take place in conservative areas of the country. Even in the Bay Area, which has long been known for its accepting attitude toward the LGBTQ community, both teens and adults, Sasha Fleischman, a white eighteen-year-old high school senior who identifies as gender neutral and sometimes wears a skirt, after falling asleep in the back of a local AC Transit bus on the way home after school, had their skirt set on fire. (Fleischman identifies as neither male nor female and prefers to use the plural pronoun "their" rather than gender-identifying pronouns.) Richard Thomas, sixteen, who is black, said he did it because he was homophobic, although he later refuted it. There was no doubt as to his guilt—multiple cameras on the bus recorded what happened from various points of view.

It is interesting to note that these two teens both lived in Oakland, a city full of contrasts, and would never have met had they both not ridden the 57 AC Transit bus regularly. Fleishman lived in the Oakland Hills, one of the wealthier parts of the city, while

Thomas lived in East Oakland in an impoverished neighborhood. Their backgrounds are reflected in the resolution to their story.[21]

Fortunately, this horrific story has a positive resolution for its victim, because Fleischman found concern and support not only from their parents and peers at their Berkeley high school, but also from the community at large. Thomas was charged as an adult with a variety of crimes, including two counts of hate crimes, and just a few days after the incident, students at Fleischman's high school all came to school in skirts, male and female, to support their classmate. After being released from the hospital, Fleischman expressed feeling a responsibility to inform people about the whole gender spectrum.[22] Fleischman has since graduated from high school and is attending MIT and doing well.[23]

In January 2015, the *New York Times Magazine* ran a story on the aftermath of the incident, when Thomas was charged as an adult, and in a plea bargain, sentenced to seven years in prison, in spite of the interventions of several groups who felt that he made a stupid, adolescent mistake and did not deserve an adult punishment. Fleischman and their parents were among them.[24] Thomas began serving his sentence at the Alameda County Juvenile Hall in February 2014, when he was seventeen. He will be transferred to prison when he turns eighteen.[25]


## CYBERBULLYING

Cyberbullying can take place any time and can involve both words and images, either stills or videos, which may be recorded without the target's knowledge or permission, especially when under the influence of alcohol or drugs. These can be shared instantly with large groups of teens, and some have gone viral online. Teens who are bullied in school are more likely to also be bullied online. Cyberbullying includes any kind of aggression (see previous section "Face-to-Face Bullying" for the content/format of that aggression) that occurs online in chat rooms, e-mail, text messages, websites, blogs, and instant messaging, using cell phones, tablets, laptops, and other electronic devices.[26] Two-thirds (or more, since this figure is from 2011) of teens between twelve and seventeen go online daily to do schoolwork, play games, chat with friends, or post on various social media platforms. And since anyone can be online 24/7, there's no downtime. Teens have created websites, videos, photo galleries, and profiles on social networking sites designed to mock and demean other individuals, and they share them with their entire peer group.[27]

Unlike in-person or face-to-face bullying, where some, if not all, of the bullies' identities are known to the victim, cyberbullying can be done anonymously. Messages and photos can be posted anonymously or under a false name. Texts can be sent from disposable or "burner" cell phones. According to CDC research, up to 46 percent of teens who have been bullied electronically don't know their tormentor's identity, and up to 22 percent of teens who do cyberbullying don't know their target's identity.[28] In the past, you had to know someone to some extent to bully them, but now that is no longer necessary. Bullying attacks can come out of thin air, without warning, and without any known source.

Cyberbullying has similarities to and differences from traditional bullying. Like traditional bullying, it is malicious, intending to be hurtful. It is repetitive, and goes on over time, sometimes becoming more intense and vicious, even encouraging the victim to commit suicide. As noted above, cyberbullies can be anonymous, hiding their identity from their victims. There are also no ways to regulate online communication, to enforce courtesy, or to prevent lies. While some parents do monitor their children's time online, many do not,[29] and when bullying is done via cell phone, the parent or caretaker may not be able to intervene, since the phone is always with the teen. Finally, it is much easier to be cruel to someone from a distance than it is face-to-face. When someone is bullied in person, the bully can see the effect of his or her actions on the victim. There is no such instant feedback in cyberspace, so it's far easier for the inappropriate behavior to continue.[30] And with a faceless victim, the bullying behavior can also intensify beyond what would happen in a face-to-face situation.

Technology also erases geographical boundaries. In the past, personal bullying might stay within one school in a community or within one interest group or clique in a large school, but today, cyberbullying can expand exponentially, to a town, a city, a region, and even all over the world. Teens don't always realize how fast and how far the information they post online can travel.[31]

Bullying can be done by one individual or by a group. The target may also be an individual or a group. It's logical that bullying increases during the school year—large groups of adolescents are forced together for the majority of the day, five days a week. After-school and social activities may also offer opportunities for bullying, which means that during the school year, there are few times when the bully's target can feel safe.

On Maslow's Hierarchy of Needs, the need for physical and psychological safety is one of the most basic, and lack of it can hinder the individual's growth, so it is no surprise that victims of bullying of any kind report a variety of physical or psychological problems, including sleep problems, depression, feelings of insecurity and anxiety, low self-esteem, isolation, and loneliness.[32] They may be afraid or reluctant to go to school, and are more likely to report family problems, academic problems, and behavior problems. As one teen in a recent study said, "It makes me hurt both physically and mentally. It scares me and takes away all my confidence. It makes me feel sick and worthless."[33] They also report suicidal or self-harming thoughts and activities at levels that are higher than those who are not bullied.[34] Feelings of self-worth and self-assurance are eroded with long-term bullying, and may not be regained, even in adulthood.

Eve Sturges, in an article in the online magazine *Rookie*, recalls being bullied in fourth grade, and how it impacted and changed her life for decades. The anger and the sense of being a helpless victim didn't fade over time; she had nightmares and imagined seeing her tormentors in crowded places, and panicked. But as an adult, when her bully found her on Facebook and sent her a friend request, Sturges found the courage to confront her about how difficult her life had been because of what she had to endure from this woman and her brothers. A huge part of her identity was wrapped up in her being a victim when she was in elementary school, and forgiving her bullies meant that piece of herself was gone. It was at once freeing and terrifying.[35]

One of the too-frequent results of bullying is suicide. Suicide is the third leading cause of death among adolescents in the United States, and a review of thirty-seven studies of the connections between adolescent bullying and suicide showed that 19 percent of high school students thought seriously about suicide, 15 percent made a specific plan to attempt suicide, almost 9 percent did attempt to kill themselves, and about 3 percent of these attempts were serious enough to require major medical attention. Both bullies and their victims were associated directly and indirectly with major depression, substance abuse, and antisocial behavior with self-harming tendencies.[36]

However, it is not only the victims who suffer in a bullying situation. Bullies also display higher levels of depression and antisocial activity than their peers, characteristics that follow them into adulthood,[37] although researchers disagree about how well adolescent bullying can predict adult violence. Some say that aggressive traits last a long time and that an aggressive teen is very likely to be an aggressive adult. Others suggest that there is a link between adolescent and adult violent behaviors, but the strength of that link is less certain. Adolescent bullies also tend to have less positive relations with their peers, and as a result, may be lonelier as well.[38] Observers or bystanders are also affected—they may not know what to do, what action to take, or fear retaliation if they take action. And in watching the victimization of someone else, they are also victimized,[39] which can result in lowered feelings of self-worth and increased levels of guilt for not taking action. It is important to remember that understanding and preventing bullying will help everyone involved, not just the victim.

Unfortunately, researchers have not been able to discover a way to determine who will become a bully and who will not—individual characteristics vary too much. The home life of bullies is definitely a factor, and so is their social life, both at school and away from it.

There are tendencies and possible signs that might point to future bullying behavior, but no direct links, no specific cause and effect.[40]

## FACTS AND STATISTICS

Perhaps a few facts and statistics will help demonstrate the impact of bullying, and show how widespread it is. In a 2013 study on bullying and suicide, almost 16 percent of the more than twenty thousand students surveyed reported cyberbullying and almost 26 percent reported school bullying. Most students were bullied both in school and online, and had a much higher level of distress than those experiencing either but not both, resulting in lower academic performance and higher social/mental stress. However, students subjected to any form of bullying reported higher levels of distress. Ninety-three percent of teens are active Internet users and 75 percent use a cell phone, so the technology for cyberbullying is widespread.[41] In addition, using social media can be done quickly, in the heat of the moment, without forethought or consideration, and an ill-considered Tweet or Facebook or Instagram post, picture, or video can spread across a school, a city, or a region with the speed of light.[42] Once online, it is virtually impossible to contain or remove the offending information, even if the person who posted it regrets his or her actions.

An FBI study found that in a study of student attacks done in 2004, examining the thirty-seven attacks that occurred between 1974 and 2000, that 71 percent of the attackers had been bullied and attacked themselves over a long period of time, and many were described as "the kid everyone teased." Seventy-five percent either thought about or attempted suicide, more than 65 percent had a history of depression, and 98 percent had a profound sense of failure or loss. Bullying is nothing new, but it is important that we recognize the damage it does to all who participate, regardless of their role.[43]

Instant messaging seems to be the most popular way to bully someone electronically, with 56 percent of bullies and 67 percent of victims reporting that it was how the bullying took place. E-mail and text messages are also used frequently, and 24 percent and 15 percent respectively of victims reported that bullies used these formats. Teens who are bullied by people they don't know in person are most likely to be bullied by e-mail and chat rooms, rather than IM. And no matter how it happens, teens who are bullied online are most likely to be bullied in person as well.[44]

## SOLUTIONS

There is little doubt that bullying behaviors are destructive and harm everyone involved, no matter their role.[45] A wide variety of theories have evolved about how to treat the bullies, from punishment to understanding, and there are an equally wide variety of opinions about how well they work. However, overall, several characteristics of successful programs have emerged.

Investment is the first requirement. Faculty, staff, and administrators must subscribe to the program being used, not just on a surface level, but on a committed, philosophical level. If the school leaders do not walk the walk and talk the talk, the students will see their duplicity, and the program will fail. The entire culture of the school must change, and all students must be just as empowered and involved as the adult leaders in order for this to happen.[46] Social skills and working positively with others must be taught, and positive, rather than negative, rewards must be supplied.[47] There must be a focus on the whole school, a systemic approach, rather than looking at individual bullies and targeting them. When students are taught that cruelty is harmful, and their efforts to prevent it are rewarded, they will be less likely to act in a harmful or bullying way, or let others do so in their presence.[48]

Teacher and poet Taylor Mali makes this point in his poem, "What Teachers Make," when he calls to let a student's parents know about how their son responded to bullying.

I make parents tremble in fear when I call home:

Hi. This is Mr. Mali. I hope I haven't called at a bad time,
I just wanted to talk to you about something your son said today.
To the biggest bully in the grade, he said,
"Leave the kid alone. I still cry sometimes, don't you?
It's no big deal."
And that was noblest act of courage I have ever seen.
I make parents see their children for who they are
and what they can be. [49]

We, as a society, have made great strides in reducing harmful
behaviors among adolescents because we have become more aware
of them and the dangers that they present. Today, teen pregnancies,
smoking, alcohol abuse, drug abuse (except marijuana), drunk driv-
ing fatalities, crimes, and suicide are all at lower levels than in the
1980s. There is less criminal violence among teens, and more finish
high school. [50] Now it is time to increase our awareness of bullying
and intolerance of differences, and make a firm resolve to reduce
them, changing the culture of our schools, and perhaps eventually,
changing the culture of our society as a whole.

# 14

## *SHATTERING GLASS*
## BY GAIL GILES

It took five years and several stops and starts to write, but it all started when Gail Giles was a substitute teacher, eavesdropping on a group of high school cheerleaders, high school royalty, who'd decided to do a makeover for the quiet, shy boy who shared a table with them in art class, a Bill Gates look-alike. They'd already persuaded him to stop belting his pants under his armpits, and were planning a trip to the mall for a new wardrobe and a haircut. But while he trusted the girls to help him, he also knew no makeover could elevate him to royalty status himself.[1] No matter what they did, he would still be a nerd, a geek, an outsider.

Giles watched, and listened, and wondered—and asked herself, "What if?" What if there were secrets on both sides, agendas that neither was willing to reveal? What if it wasn't cheerleaders and a nerd, but jocks and a nerd? How would changing the royalty to the king of the school and his posse change the dynamics of the situation? How much would the followers do for the leader?[2] How much would the geek do, and what if the geek was smart enough to know he was being played and decided to play the jocks while letting them play him?

Then Giles let the idea percolate for years, until she met a young man whose father had done something so unimaginable that it

ruined his son's life and changed him in some of the most fundamental ways possible. As she got to know him, she began to wonder
how this person might fit into her story, with his secrets that could
never be told and his flaws that could never be revealed.[3] And Rob
Haynes, charismatic yet twisted, stepped onto center stage.

*Lord of the Flies*, by William Golding, had been one of her
favorite novels since she was a teen, and she decided to take the idea
of absolute power corrupting absolutely as one of her themes,[4] nam-
ing her nerd Simon, in an homage. In Golding's novel, Simon was
beaten to death in a violent scene of group rage, and in her book, she
decided that Simon would die the same way.[5] Giles also admired
Golding's audacity at killing off major characters and not allowing
comfortable resolutions for everyone, and she followed his example
in *Shattering Glass*.[6] While Simon was the only one to die in her
book, two of the other main characters were changed so much in the
final denouement, they could be said to have died. Coop, the dumb
jock with a full-ride athletic scholarship to TCU, died when his face
and his knee were broken, and he was reborn as a college graduate
with a face that plastic surgery was not able to repair completely,
looking for a job as a fourth-grade teacher. Young, born with a
silver spoon in his mouth and a passion for writing, spent five years
in Huntsville Penitentiary because he refused to testify against any
of the other boys. Due to be released in the near future, he will be
living with Coop until he gets his feet on the ground, implying that
his wealthy family has turned their backs on him, although that's
not stated in the book. While his future has yet to be revealed, at
least he won't be forced to become a doctor like his father and
grandfather, but his life will surely be vastly different from the
privileged one he expected to live.

Another of Giles's favorite titles, *The Great Gatsby*, by F. Scott
Fitzgerald, helped her create her narrator, Thaddeus R. (Young)
Steward IV. Nick was the unreliable narrator of *Gatsby*; his involvement with the main character didn't allow Nick to see him clearly.
When Giles chose Young Steward as the narrator, she gave him that
same lack of dependability,[7] but made Ronna, Young's girlfriend,
the moral center of the book, the book's conscience.[8] Giles didn't

want Young to be that good—he had his dark side, just as much as Rob and Simon did, and in the final scene, Young realized just how dark that side was.

While she knew from the beginning that the book would be violent, she didn't want that violence to be the focus of the book, which is why Simon dies in the first paragraph. We all know the ending, we all know that Simon is going to die, killed by his friends, we just don't know why. So the whys behind the violence are the center of the book's focus. The little things, the details of everyday life that add up to the big things, can swiftly spin out of control.[9] Just as the sweep of a butterfly's wing can lead to a storm on the other side of the world, one misstep brought about a cataclysmic event that none of the players involved could have foreseen or prevented. The devil is definitely in these details.

Giles has always been drawn to the dark side of life, and she considers herself to be more cynical than most people. She knows people lie, and wants to know why. She also likes to poke at people and problems that hide in the dark places so she can see what happens and how they respond. Her books don't end with a neatly tied bow, because she doesn't really like happy endings, finding them unrealistic. Real life has very few happy resolutions. She understands that everyone contains inside them a part of the darkness in the world, and that it's the way each one of us handles that darkness that makes us a force for good or for evil—or perhaps a force for both at different times, with different motivations.[10]

She also feels that YA literature should show teens life as it is really lived, life that can't promise happy endings, that points out that there are no easy answers, and that sometimes mistakes can't be fixed. Sometimes an apology isn't enough to make it all better, no matter how regretful and heartfelt it is. And that dark path that looks so interesting, intriguing, and attractive? While it's frequently the one they want to travel, it's not always the one they should actually take, especially when there are no chances for U-turns. Books like these can show readers where the missteps are, and perhaps how to avoid them.[11]

Books with a focus on sweetness and light don't protect teens—they put them at even greater risk. Not knowing where the risks are, and what consequences they bring, can make it far more difficult to avoid those risks. Giles and other YA writers like her must have the courage of their convictions to produce titles that are unflinchingly real, that show how one small action can create echoes and reverberations throughout the rest of life. Lives don't always change in an instant, but they can, and teens need to know it. Unfinished or ambiguous endings require thinking and consideration—they help create a book that must be questioned, cussed, and discussed, not put away on a shelf with a "there, that's over" feeling, the result of a neatly resolved ending.[12] And books that require discussion and consideration are likely to also be ones that attract challenges, because they make the reader uncomfortable. And a fearful adult concerned about the safety of society's youth is not likely to remember that change and growth usually require discomfort of some kind.

As a result, these same authors also collect their share of criticism and censure for their determination to portray reality as they know it can be, making them some of the most respected and frequently defended authors of the YA canon. Giles's books, with their realistic characters, language, and situations, make her one of the most censored authors, but also one of the most important and valued ones, and one that teens turn to again and again.

In *Shattering Glass*, all the teens are a mixture of motives and intentions, actions and reactions, that spin suddenly out of control. If even one of those pieces had changed, the entire outcome of the book could have changed. What if Simon had been less arrogant about his newfound powers, and more humble? What if Rob's secret had never been revealed? What if Young had felt powerful enough to challenge Rob and not give Ronna away? What if Coop had not protected Simon when Rob began to beat up on him and thus avoided a beating that shattered his body and his life? The book provides a plethora of questions and perspectives that can make for almost endless discussion, leading teens to take a second look at their own lives, and the large impact that one small change can make.

Every author writes differently, and each has a different way to arrive at the point at which the novel and its characters come to life. Giles knows she has to get the opening scene perfect. It took her about fifty tries to do that when she started writing *Shattering Glass*. But once she had it complete, she knew that it would be about power, the power of fathers over their sons, of the insider over the outsider, of the group and its leader over the individual, and the consequences of going up against that power. It would be about secrets and the power that they hold when revealed at precisely the right, or wrong, moment. It would be about how a butterfly's flapping its wings can echo across time and create a hurricane of anger, of action, of damage, and eventually, of regret.

> Simon Glass was easy to hate. I never knew exactly why, there was too much to pick from, I guess, really, we each hated him for a different reason, but we didn't realize it until the day we killed him. [13]

This was Giles's first book, and its creation didn't proceed smoothly, even after she finally perfected the first paragraph and began writing. After almost a year of work on it, she hit a dead end. She was tired of the characters, sick of living in their heads, [14] and had written herself into a corner she couldn't get out of. [15] She scrawled "and then they all died" across the bottom of the last page, looked at it, then scratched it out and wrote, "After achieving great personal growth, they all died." Then she put the manuscript away for a year. [16]

Giles doesn't remember what happened, or what persuaded her to pick up the manuscript again, but she did, and realized that she had been focusing too much on plot, and not enough on characters. Or at least, she'd been too focused on the main characters, and ignored the minor ones. That's why she'd missed a key element of Lance's personality. Realizing what she'd done, she was able to go ahead and write herself out of that corner and finish the book, making the bullying and the role and influence of fathers its two main themes. [17]

While the flash-forward quotes at the beginning of each chapter give a different perspective to the action in the novel, they didn't become a part of it until later in the writing process, when Giles was doing revisions. Using Young as an unreliable narrator meant that she couldn't show sides of the other characters that Young couldn't see himself. Including the quotes from other people allowed them to speak for themselves.[18] They also offer some resolution to a book whose ending is abrupt and unresolved. This is how they all ended up—some were broken, some were healed, some escaped, some were punished, some relationships endured, and others ended forever. Some questions were answered, others remained. Many of these teens ended up taking the road less travelled, and Giles leaves it up to the reader to figure out what those futures did and did not include.

When Rob arrived on campus in the fall of his senior year, the school was ripe for a new leader. Everyone had gotten tired of Lance Ansely, who'd been the alpha male for years. Rob was confident, talented, charismatic, and able to unseat Lance easily. But Rob didn't just want to take Lance's place, he also wanted to make Lance into nothing, take away not just his leadership, but everything else he had as well. Lance was immediately outclassed, and shoved to the periphery of the in-group he had once led. But he was still a bully, and Simon Glass was still one of his favorite targets. The day it all began, everyone was hanging out in the commons before school, when Lance started in on Simon again, this time about his pocket protector full of pens and the ever-present waistband of his tighty whities peeking out of the top of his pants. Simon ended up on the floor scrambling around after his pens, as Lance yanked on the top of his shorts, before walking off cackling. Rob watched, and said, "He blew it . . . Lance." And with that quiet comment, life changed for all of the students of that small Texas high school. Rob wasn't just going to take Lance down, he was going to put Simon in his place, as one of the school royalty.

Rob was determined to make Simon into the most popular kid in school, but he was unaware that Simon had no intention of being made over. He might have looked like a geek, but he was rich and he was smart. He knew from the beginning what was going on and was just as ready to manipulate the system as Rob was. But Rob only manipulated people, Simon was able to manipulate computers as well. He used a computer to help Coop do his homework, in spite of the fact Coop was so far down on the IQ scale that sometimes he didn't get homework right even when he had someone else's to copy. He got Young back into Creative Writing after Young's dad forced him to drop it, by changing the computer records so it looked like Young was taking Biology when he was actually in Creative Writing. And he paid attention to details—like when he discovered that Rob's school records file didn't exactly fit with the stories Rob told about his past. He kept poking until he and Young both knew Rob's secret, the secret Rob would do anything to keep to himself.

Then things began to change for Simon. The guys taught him to drive, and his folks bought him a hot new car for Christmas. He looked better, and girls didn't laugh at him so much anymore. His confidence grew, and he even dared to needle Rob, something that was sure to have a bad ending. Once he knew how to hack the school computer, Simon could change anyone's record—and gave Lance so many absences that he spent all his time running from one teacher to another to explain that he had really been in class. Lance's father wasn't too happy about that, either. Then there was the day when Simon hacked into the school bells, so they wouldn't stop going off, and school was dismissed for the day. When Coop was sweating the ACT test he had to pass to get his athletic scholarship and get into college, the only way he could afford to go, Simon offered to go to a neighboring school and take it for him. He even paid for a good ID so he'd get in without a problem.

Rob's plan was working, but he needed one final coup—Simon had to win Mr. Popularity, Senior Class, and take Young's girlfriend, Ronna, to the dance where the class awards would be announced. Rob knew Simon had a crush on Ronna, and he twisted Young's arm until he agreed to pretend to break up with Ronna and go to the dance with someone else, so Simon would be free to ask Ronna. But Ronna knew what was going on and that Young was choosing to be loyal to Rob rather than to her, and she made the breakup official.

The night of the dance, when the winners are announced, Rob discovers that Simon used his computer skills to ruin Rob's plan, and is smugly pleased with what he's done—feeling every bit of the power he has accumulated over the past few months. When Rob attacks him for not sticking to the plan, as he'd promised to do, Simon retaliates by revealing what he knows about Rob's father, the secret Rob would do anything to protect. All the boys are caught up in the anger of the moment and begin to attack Simon, and when Coop tries to protect him, they attack him as well. Simon dies of his injuries, mainly inflicted by Rob, and Coop is seriously wounded. He will never play football or look the same again. In the end, Young is the only one who is punished, and goes to prison for five years.

The reader is left with only glimpses of the future, revealed in the quotes from those involved—friends, girlfriends, parents, teachers, counselors, the prison chaplain, and others, that begin each chapter. The final resolution is left up to speculation.

After the fact, it becomes easier to see the empty spaces in the lives of the teens under Rob's thrall, and how he manipulates each of them to achieve his goals. None of the teens are left unscathed, and while it might seem that Simon received the ultimate punishment, it can also be said that he is luckier than the survivors—he will not have to live the rest of his life knowing how his mistakes and arrogance affected and completely changed the lives of everyone around him. Each of them was a victim in one way or another. However, Giles notes that Rob is so shallow and so deep in denial that she doubts he will ever admit to his part in the escalation of events leading to the final crime, "if after five years after the killing, he can still say he had nothing to do with it." [19]

# 15

## *TEASE*
## BY AMANDA MACIEL

*Tease,* like many YA novels, is about bullying. But it's not from the perspective of the victim and how he or she suffered because of what was done to him or her. It's from the bully's point of view, and takes place after the bullying is over and the legal system has stepped in, and the bullies, or some of them, are on trial. Amanda Maciel wrote it to point out that bullying and its results are not black and white situations, but should be painted in shades of gray. When she noticed how vicious people could be to an accused bully, indulging in what they are castigating the bully for, making cruel comments about all aspects of his or her life, she wanted to show how we are just perpetuating the problem. It's as if the bystanders and critics didn't know what they were saying, and didn't see how they themselves had become bullies. She also wanted to show on a personal level the lives that are changed forever, the community that will never be the same, once criminal prosecution takes over to punish the bullies.[1]

This isn't say to that in framing her novel from the perspective of the bully Maciel is trying to create a sympathetic character. Nor is her victim sympathetic. The teens in this novel are realistic, multi-faceted, and show that the actions of a victim can be despicable, and those of a bully can be understandable. She feels that we are too quick to judge and find fault, which can be destructive to everyone involved, and even dangerous.[2]

We look at situations based on video clips, tweets, and sound bites and make a decision about them without thinking about the complexity that exists behind them, obscured by a surface of simplicity. In writing *Tease*, Maciel has tried to show that complexity, those gray areas where things are not necessarily what they seem. Written in 2014, it does include cyberbullying, but not to the extent that it is a factor today, when any story or video can suddenly go viral and collect thousands of responses from around the globe, condemning or praising the story's subject. These people know nothing but the headline and yet respond as if they know the whole story, and the combined impact of their messages, especially if they are negative, is sure to be emotionally and psychologically overwhelming to the teen (or adult) who is the focus.

Sara is a bully. There is no doubt about that. She and her best friend, Brielle, bullied Emma, the new girl at school, both face-to-face and online. But the book shows Sara from two different perspectives—when she was being a bully and now a year later, when she and several others are being prosecuted for the crime. A crime, Sara says, she didn't commit. Yes, Emma hanged herself because of the bullying, but Sara didn't tell her to do it; she didn't kill Emma herself, or even hand her the rope. She didn't even want Emma dead. She just wanted Emma to leave her boyfriend alone. She is a bully, not a murderer. She has to face some hard things about herself and figure out how and where she goes on from here, but is she entitled to go on? Should she be punished as any other murderer would be?

In interviews and in an Author's Note to her book, Maciel notes that her story is based on actual events from 2010, when a student at a high school Maciel had close connections with committed suicide after being bullied for a period of time. She began thinking about how so many lives had been destroyed or changed because of it and how the bullies involved surely could not have expected suicide—yet it was the result, and consequences had to be dealt with.[3] Setting the scenario in a fictional world was complex. She wanted to be true to life, but not rely too much on the incident that had inspired her.[4] She wanted to create a story in which everyone shared a portion of the blame, the perpetrators, the victim, the bystanders, and the community. This may be why few of the characters seem positive or sympathetic—she has given most of them a dark side. For Sara, the reader gets more than a glimpse inside that dark part, and one can see how the actions of the people surrounding her made it easier for her to be a bully, while still believing that she wasn't a criminal and shouldn't be treated as one.

While Maciel did get her inspiration from a specific incident, she had also been wondering about recent news stories showing that some teens were being prosecuted rigorously for doing things that adults would not be held so accountable for, noting the cyberbullying she had seen in the media. She says she "always pick[s] the wrong side of the argument," and likes to look at the point of view of the person not being interviewed on television.[5]

That being said, it's important to note that Maciel lets her characters make excuses for themselves, but doesn't excuse their behavior. Bullying is never okay—you never know what an unexpected result will be. But the bully isn't *only* a bully. He or she also plays other roles in life, because no one is a one-dimensional caricature. It is important to examine the whole person and the why behind the bullying.[6] In addition, it is also important to remember that the teen bully is not an adult, but an adolescent, with the brain of an adolescent, which is not capable yet of making adult decisions from adult understanding and perspective. Teens are impulsive, unwilling to consider the consequences of their actions, and slow to see situations from another's point of view—all because their brains have not yet matured to encompass these more complex processes. They react, rather than respond, to situations, and with the encouragement of their peers they take actions and chances that would make adults hesitate or turn away. Maciel's characters are teens, and they behave the way typical teens would. That makes them realistic and believable, but it also makes them somewhat unlikeable. Readers may find it difficult to decide whether they are sympathetic or not.

Maciel's decision to use flashbacks in her novel allows the reader to see Sara both before and during the bullying and months afterward, during the summer before her senior year, when she is preparing her legal defense. The before Sara is self-absorbed, desperate to be one of the popular kids, but a little shy and self-conscious, nervous about having sex with her boyfriend, Dylan, and resigned to doing it in order to keep him from straying. She looks up to her BFF, Brielle, who helps her feel more confident, even though Sara isn't always comfortable with the things Brielle persuades her to do. She's especially threatened by Emma, the pretty new girl at school, who seems obsessed by Dylan, and is determined to take him away from Sara. In Sara's eyes, she is a skanky boyfriend-stealing slut, who deserves to be bullied for what she's doing to and with every boy she can get her hands on.

Afterward Sara is completely changed. She feels threatened and has withdrawn from everyone, even her little brothers, whom she's been especially close to. She lashes out angrily at her parents and other adults, but deep inside is numb, unable to believe the situation she has gotten herself into, and unable to admit any part of her fault or blame. The only person able to break through the wall she's constructed is Carmichael, a fellow summer school student who seems to turn up wherever she is, and is willing to listen when she finally decides to talk.

These two perspectives allow the reader to see how Sara became involved in bullying Emma and why, and then shows how she struggles to find her part in Emma's suicide, learn how to accept what she did, and begin to move on beyond it. Sara has many issues to deal with at once: the bullying and its aftermath, plus the loss of several of the most important people in her life—Brielle, whom she has been forbidden to contact in any way; Dylan, who no longer has anything to do with her; and her parents, who are going through a difficult separation and divorce. Even her brothers have withdrawn from her and her angry explosions. She feels completely alone, defensive, betrayed, and seems completely unable to accept any of the blame for Emma's death, still determined to believe Emma brought it on herself by going after other girls' boyfriends.

The two perspectives also give clues about Emma's actions—hints about changing schools frequently, perhaps caused by her inappropriate behavior, and visits to several therapists over the years. Her parents seem to be rather clueless about exactly what is going on. Although well meaning, they don't take actions when past patterns begin to repeat themselves. It is also significant to note that Emma killed herself not just after the bullying she received, but after she learned that Dylan was breaking up with her to go back to Sara. This fact, something that Sara's detractors didn't focus on, puts her death in an entirely new light. Additionally, it's important to remember that Emma's actions were the original cause of the bullying—she was poaching other girls' boyfriends, something that is not tolerated in the world of teens. There is no definitive statement that she had done this at other schools, but if she had done so, it certainly would have led to trouble.

*Tease* is an important title in bullying literature, and Maciel is a courageous author who isn't afraid to ask the hard questions and to provide only enough of the answers to make her readers look within themselves for more complete responses. It is a book that will be read and reread, pondered and questioned by both the teens and adults who read it. It forces the reader to ask who the real human monster is, and why. It is all the more impressive because it is her debut novel.

# 16

## *SHINE*
## BY LAUREN MYRACLE

Lauren Myracle had just moved to Fort Collins, Colorado, when Matthew Shepard was flown into town after being beaten, tortured, and left for dead just outside Laramie, Wyoming.[1] He died six days later without ever regaining consciousness.[2] Myracle clearly remembers the candlelight vigils, the huge outpouring of support, and the pain of thinking that such a horrible thing had to happen, showing the very worst side of humanity.[3] But it was almost fifteen years before she decided to write about it.

By that time, she'd decided that she could share the part of her life that she had not revealed in any of her previous novels, a "slightly schizophrenic" childhood, because her divorced parents lived in Atlanta, Georgia, and in a tiny, rural mountain town in North Carolina. She identifies as both a Southern girl and a Christian, defying those that say the combination isn't possible. As a result, she could set *Shine* in the same area and know that her portrayal of the settings and the people would be authentic.[4] When researching the story, she not only looked at hate crimes, but also why they happen—what happens when people hate themselves and each other? Where does that hatred come from? Myracle believes that it frequently comes from fear, so that was also a part of her research, along with rural poverty, the KKK in the South, and the

culture of meth, and the people who make it and use it.[5] She also
wanted to examine the guts and bravery Patrick showed when he
decided to come out and live openly gay in this very small and
conservative town, and what Cat went through, deciding to support
and be friends with him, in spite of what everyone else thought
about him.

The book opens with a newspaper clipping about Patrick being
discovered battered and beaten outside the convenience store where
he worked. He's been tied up, and the nozzle of a gas pump hose has
been duct-taped in his mouth, and scrawled on his chest is a message, "Suck this faggot." Myracle's novel is based on that scene.
How did he get there? What happened to make someone do such a
despicable and horrible thing? What is the truth behind the horror?
In order to do this, she created the character of Cat, Patrick's best
friend, the two of them always knowing that they were different
from everyone else in town, but always able to be different together.
Cat's decision to find the missing pieces of the story allowed Myracle to explore not just questions of gender and sexuality but also
questions of identity, which has been one of her primary focuses
throughout many of her books. Who are you, and who is your tribe,
the people you belong with, the ones that really "get" you? What is
important, and meaningful, and worth fighting for? Where do you
belong in the world, and how do you create a life you can enjoy and
be proud of? It's a time of flux, of decisions made or remade, when
identity has not yet solidified, and everything is new, and intense,
and full of drama. She notes that teens' problems may be on a
smaller scale than those of presidents, or directors, or CEOs, but the
issues that they face are just as valid and important.[6]

Myracle also knew that while she wanted to create a story similar
to Shepard's, the pain his family and friends suffered when he died
was not fictional, but very, very real. She didn't want to exploit that
pain, she wrote the story about a boy who definitely wasn't Shepard.
They share some similarities, but *Shine* is Patrick's story. And it's
more than the story of a hate crime; it's a story about love and being
the best that you can be. It's about standing up against injustice and
finding out the truth behind the lies and evasions, about accepting

being different and not going along with everyone else.[7] Ultimately, Myracle's story is about hope, and overcoming, and demonstrating the quote from the Book of Matthew 5:14, at the beginning of the book, "You are the light of the world." *Shine* is about how we should all let our lights shine, no matter how difficult that seems to be. It is the best way to be true to ourselves, true to the best in each of us. It is about shining light into the dark places of our world and the people who live there, and seeing how we can confront what we find there, and learn and grow.

Myracle is well aware that her books are controversial (she topped the American Library Association's list of top ten banned books in both 2009 and 2011, and was included on it in 2007 and 2008),[8] partly because of her subject matter, partly because of her skill as a writer. Her editor once pointed out to her, "The fact that you're getting such extreme reactions shows that you've written something that matters." That sentiment was echoed in an anonymous e-mail she got shortly after *Shine* was published. It said, "I'm a gay teen in North Carolina. I want to thank you for *Shine*. Without it, I would not be alive today."[9] (Many YA authors have had similar experiences, as their readers respond to their books in e-mail, IMs, and tweets, and on their Facebook pages.) Responses like this one confirm that although Myracle may be controversial in some circles, her work is valued by her readers, and powerful enough to change their lives.

But she does realize that in order to reach a teen reader, she often must please an adult/parent/librarian/bookstore owner who is less comfortable with her subject matter than the teen the title is written for. It is a thin wire to walk without falling off, not caring about what those adults think, while caring very much about what makes her books relevant and relatable to teens, so the book will be available for them to care about. But while she walks that wire, she is also emphatically against censorship, believing with Chris Crutcher, that when you ban a book, you ban a person. She may occasionally doubt herself, but she comes down squarely on the side of the teens who need to know about the controversial content of her books.[10]

Cat and Patrick had always been friends, the two of them against everyone else. But all that changed the summer after they were in eighth grade. Cat suddenly withdrew from not only Patrick, but from everyone else as well. But as she listened to the gossip and the stories about the attack on Patrick that had left him in a coma, she knew she had to act. Something was missing—the stories didn't add up or make sense. People in town were denying that someone local could have done something that horrible. But why would a stranger stop at a convenience store in the middle of the night and beat up the teen working there until he was all but dead? How would a stranger know that Patrick was gay, and write "Suck this faggot" across his chest?

She is sure it had something to do with Tommy and his gang— Beef; Bailee-Ann; Christian; her own brother, Dupree; and Robert—and while she quickly uncovers some of their secrets, she can't put the pieces together. Bailee-Ann is cheating on Beef with Tommy; Beef is a meth addict, as are a lot of other folks in town; Robert spies on people and has a lot of his own secrets; and Patrick has a secret boyfriend. After she meets Jason, a college student who also knew Patrick, the pieces begin to fall into place, and Cat is convinced that Tommy attacked Patrick. But when she confronts Tommy, he denies it, and persuades her to believe him. If not Tommy, then who could it have been? Jason has proved it wasn't a bunch of frat boys, and the truth seems elusive until the two of them find out that Beef is really Patrick's secret boyfriend and while high on meth was responsible for the beating. But even when all the secrets come out, there are still questions that haven't been answered. Could it all have ended differently?

Myracle's consistent emphasis on light and letting the light that is in you shine so the very best part of you can be seen brings a depth and complexity to her characters that they otherwise would have lacked. This is most obvious in the final scenes of the book, when Christian, Cat, Jason, and Patrick agree to let the town's assumptions about Beef stand, and not reveal the true horror of what he did. Even though he deserved no mercy for what he'd done, they extended it to him, and to the town they all lived in. Is that as real as

Matt Shepard's death? Perhaps, or perhaps not. There's no way to know. Sometimes there are no final answers.

# 17

## *BY THE TIME YOU READ THIS, I'LL BE DEAD*
## BY JULIE ANNE PETERS

Daelyn is determined to get it right this time. She's tried suicide before, and failed every time. Killing yourself is harder than it looks. That's especially true when her parents have her on suicide watch 24/7. But this time Daelyn will have help. She's found a website for completers—suicide success stories—and she's sure that this time she'll succeed. The site, through-the-light.com, allows her to set the date of her death, called her Day of Determination, and then shows her how to spend the last twenty-three days of her life preparing for it. She and others on the site who are preparing to die, must spend those days blogging about their experiences and explaining how they got to this point in their lives.

Julie Anne Peters knew that for some teens, suicide is an impulsive act, born of intense emotion. But she wanted her character to really think about what she was doing, so the teens who read her story would also be forced to think about it, why she should do it, and why she should not. So Peters threw the book at Daelyn— loving and supportive parents, trained therapists, medical science, God, a new friend, a chance for romance, and a new start of a new life. Then she left it up to her character to decide what to do, including the unresolved ending.[1]

Peters doesn't necessarily outline her books, but she has an idea when she begins to write about where she wants to end up, and what the ending will be.[2] She always knew that the ending would be ambiguous and unfinished. She also knew that she didn't want to write a sequel to it and reveal what really happened after the last page of Daelyn's story. Readers will have to decide for themselves whether Daelyn and Santana live or die.[3] But *how* she wrote it is a different story.

On her website, she states that she wrote it in only two weeks, and still doesn't remember writing one word of it. It was like she was in a trance, writing as fast as she could, until she woke up one morning and the finished manuscript was sitting on her desk. It looked like her handwriting, and it was written on a yellow lined tablet like she always wrote on, but she couldn't swear she had actually written it. She just knew that it was a story that had to be told.[4]

Peters does know that this book came after the juxtaposition of two events: a panel on bullying that Peters was asked to participate in, as part of the 2006 ALAN Workshop, the theme of which was bullying. (ALAN, or the Assembly on Literature for Adolescents, is a division of NCTE, the National Council of Teachers of English.) About the same time she was preparing for the presentation and reading hundreds of letters from her readers about how they had been bullied after they came out as gay or lesbian, she saw a television documentary about children who had been so severely bullied at school from kindergarten on that they either dropped out of school entirely or chose to be homeschooled. Even though they had repeatedly asked for help, adults were unresponsive, saying that enduring teasing was simply part of growing up. (My mother's favorite platitude was that I was teased and mocked only because the boys liked me and didn't know how to express it—a statement that sounds as false today as it did when I was in elementary school and even high school. It also didn't explain why girls as well as boys did the bullying.) Near the end of the program, there were interviews with parents whose children had committed suicide after years of intense bullying because they saw no other way out, something now known as "bullycide."[5]

Peters was struck by the differences between children who could endure the bullying and survive it and those who were broken by it. There are children who are incapable of coping with the cruel feedback they get from peers and others about their worthlessness, their differentness, their aloneness, and their lack of support.[6] They may even be told they should kill themselves, because no one wants to have them around. These are the children and teens she is reaching out to in her books, trying to show them that they are not alone, that someone exists who has been there, someone who can help.

This is a book that makes the reader think about the thin line between life and death, and how frighteningly easy and how painfully difficult it is to cross. Peters wants this book to be an opportunity for teens and adults to open a dialogue about life and death.[7] While it is a difficult and uncomfortable topic of conversation, these very characteristics make it all the more important.

For many teens, bullying is a fact of life, as are adults who are oblivious even when confronted by someone who is being bullied and is asking for help. Ignoring the problem will not make it go away. Ignoring it will only make the problem worse and worse, as suicide becomes the only positive solution for desperate teens looking for a way out of their pain and torment.[8] While it is obvious to the outsider that it isn't the only option, and is certainly the most drastic and sometimes final one, for the teen whose pain and desperation can create tunnel vision, it may seem like the only way out.

If suicide seems to be the only option for some of those teens, as it does to Daelyn, Peters's story can help validate their feelings and let them know that they are not the only one suffering, that they are not alone. Perhaps that knowledge can persuade them to look for ways to cope that don't involve suicide. Sometimes, just knowing that they are not the only person being bullied, and that others have managed to find other solutions, can be enough to dissuade them from ending everything.

Unfortunately, for those who want to know more about how to kill themselves, the Internet is both a blessing and a curse. Peters found it remarkably easy to find different ways to kill yourself online, making her fictional website easy to create, and equally easy to defend. She has not included anything in this title that is not easily obtainable online, except the website itself. Curious teens who want to see the site for themselves will not find it, although they will find many others, just as Peters did.[9]

Peters doesn't censor or limit what she writes for teens, because of the wide exposure teens today have to all kinds of information, not all of it trustworthy. Reading about people and situations that teens can identify with and understand can help promote understanding and compassion, even when life experiences are very different.[10] People who don't talk about their feelings can tend to become isolated and separated from other people, which can lead first to depression and then suicide, not just for teens, but for people of all ages. Books who present situations that may be difficult to talk about with friends, family, or acquaintances, can connect isolated people with situations they are familiar with, and help them find new solutions by reading about how others have resolved similar situations. Reading about how someone handled bullying can help a bullied teen reach out for help in a way that could be more effective than the ones they might have used before.[11] Bullies can also benefit, since a book can show them how others see them, and see the consequences of their actions.

When she writes books, Peters wants them to be realistic, with settings and characters that teens can recognize and identify with easily. In the list of FAQs on her website, Peters notes that while she doesn't use the language of her characters in her own life, she carefully considers the language that comes out of their mouths, including words that her books have been criticized for. But she sides with her characters—and their language is part of her efforts to make them as real as possible. She doesn't even try to censor them when they begin to speak their minds, but let them say whatever they think and feel. She has little patience with authors who deliberately water down their books to make them more palatable to a wider audience. That, she believes would make them less real, and hence, less valuable. [12]

However, her perspective on her characters' right to free speech is even more interesting when contrasted with the fact that Daelyn is mute for most of the novel, as a result of her last suicide attempt. Daelyn's conversations exist only within her own head throughout most of the novel, until she very reluctantly begins to communicate with Santana. It's interesting to note that Peters herself didn't realize that her character was mute until one of her readers pointed it out to her. [13] She used Daelyn's neck brace and silence to show how cut off she was from the rest of the world, how isolated she was, even though she was surrounded by people all the time. Santana and his mother seem to be the only ones who can see beyond her appearance and her silence.

The novel opens as Daelyn notices that the boy who has been watching her as she waits after school for one of her parents to pick her up is still there, taking her place on the bench as she walks toward her mother's car. He is tall and skinny, with hair that's been bleached white and gelled into spikes. He wears clothes that seem too big for him and is determined to catch Daelyn's attention and make friends with her. He insists on talking to her, even though she doesn't want him to. He and his mother live in the house next door to the school, and even though Daelyn doesn't want to talk to him, she does think he's attractive, but only in a nerdy way.

Because she's tried to kill herself so many time, Daelyn is on 24/7 suicide watch. Her parents take her to and pick her up from school. They've networked into her computer, and watch where she goes on the web, and make sure she's doing her homework. Her bedroom no longer has a door, and her privacy is nonexistent. As a result of her last attempt, she can't talk, has to wear a neck brace to keep her from moving her head, and has to have all her food pulverized and blended into smoothies. A vegetable smoothie is bad enough, but a steak and gravy smoothie—gross. She can't eat anything she can't suck through a straw.

And while her parents love her and worry about her, they are completely clueless about what she thinks and feels, and what her life is like. Because they are both busy with their careers and have to go out of town frequently, they hand her off to each other rather like a football player handing the ball to a teammate.

Daelyn finds the website by accident, while searching for wills, which seem less likely to be upsetting than a suicide note. *Through the Light* is a website designed to help people who want to kill themselves—to help them become "completers"—to terminate their existence. Daelyn signs up and receives her DOD, Day of Determination, when she will become a completer, but it won't be for twenty-three days. And meanwhile she has to contribute to a discussion forum on the site, Final Forum, just as all the completers are required to do. This is familiar territory for her—she frequently contributes to online discussions of bullying or suicide, telling her story of how she has been bullied since she started school, and how adults either ignore it or join in. One of the topics is WTG—Ways to Go—how to kill yourself with the most efficiency and least pain. People discuss different methods, and rate them on how difficult or easy, painless or painful, and list reasons why each method might fail. Daelyn's already tried several of them.

As she continues to contribute to the various topics, she reveals the story of her life, and how one bully after another convinced her of her own worthlessness. She hasn't forgotten any of them, and holds tight to the pain she feels inside. She was ten years old when she first started planning her own death. The stories of how and why she was bullied are heart rending. She begged to be homeschooled, but her parents worked, and so she had to go to school. Their only solution to her pain was moving to a different school district, over and over and over. She was always the new kid, always the fat kid, and somehow the bullies always knew she was a victim, and the bullying got more and more intense with time. The boys were cruel, but the girls were mean, and she feared them. The hurt they administered was deeper and more crushing.

As the days count down to her DOD, Daelyn begins to cleanse herself, as the website recommends. She begins to let go of not only her stories, her memories, but also her possessions, carefully hiding their loss from her parents. She can feel herself getting lighter and lighter, beginning to fade away. But her purging is not always easy—bring back old memories is painful, as she has to endure the torture all over again as she writes it out. The most vivid memories, when Toomey and his gang assaulted her in middle school, and the fat camp her parents sent her to with sadistic and abusive counselors, are overwhelming, and as she remembers these and all the other bullying incidents, she realizes she never fought back, she never told anyone what Toomey and the other boys did to her. She just held her memories and her pain tightly inside her, where their intensity only increased—her only sin, not turning on her bullies. There was no one she could connect with, make friends with. She was too afraid and felt too alone. And now it's too late. She has only one choice, and she has made it.

She also has to answer questions *Through the Light* requires her to answer before she can enter the site. They force her to consider the specifics of her death—how will she do it? Will she be prepared? Who will find her afterward? What is waiting for her afterward? Some answers come easily. Others do not.

When she's nine days away from her DOD, Daelyn learns why Santana isn't in school—he has cancer, and was in remission, but he's just found a lump he's afraid to tell his mother about. His father died before he was born, and it's always been just the two of them, and he can't bear the thought of leaving her alone. He is fighting as hard for his life as Daelyn is fighting for her death. At first she doesn't believe him, but soon realizes he's telling the truth. He asks her to have dinner with him on his birthday—her DOD. He knows it might be his last, and wants it to be special.

Daelyn wants to reach out to him, but her ghosts are too strong. When Santana kisses her, she has a flashback to Toomey and what he did to her, she runs from him. But later that night when Santana won't stop IMing her, she finally tells him why she can't talk, and why she has to wear the neck brace. "i drank ammonia and bleach so i could die. r u happy now?"

When they meet after school the next day, he asks her again to be with him on his birthday. He hasn't given up on her, and won't, no matter how much she pushes him away. But Peters ends the story before we find out what happens to either of them. The next day, her DOD, Daelyn deletes her *Through the Light* account and takes one last bag of her possessions to the trash. Her room is cleared. Her head is cleared. Her father is ready to take her to school. She puts the laptop Santana loaned her in her book bag and leaves the house. The reader must decide if Daelyn chose life or death, and if she and Santana can actually help each other heal.

While this unresolved ending can be seen as frustrating, it is also a way for readers to have an active part in the story, whether they ponder the ending and its meaning by themselves, or discuss it with their friends, and perhaps parents and other adults. The book's brevity also makes it a good candidate for bibliotherapy, whether in a group or individual setting. It is illuminating about how bullying happens, why it continues, and how blind adults, even parents, can be to what is going on. It is a difficult book to read and to think about, which it is why it is so important. Had Peters been a less skillful writer, less able to create characters who live and breathe, it would have been far less impactful and controversial.

# Part III

# Monsters at School: Teachers, Coaches, Athletes, and Others

**M**any teens feel that school isn't safe because of the teen-on-teen bullying and name calling that goes on in halls, in classrooms, on playing fields, and online. But peers are not the only monsters on campus—adults can be monsters as well. Teachers and coaches intimidate and manipulate their students for a variety of reasons: a sports victory; sexual needs and urges; because they were bullied as a child and it is a familiar pattern; because they are afraid of their students; because they are tired, frustrated, overworked and lose their tempers; or to further their own goals. These adult monsters don't represent the majority of teachers, of course, who are hard-working and dedicated individuals, but they do exist, and they show up regularly in newspaper headlines. As a result, they also show up in today's literature for teens.

Teachers seduce their students in *Boy Toy*, *Teach Me*, *Friction*, *Nicholas Dane*, *Something Happened*, and *Gone*. Other teachers manipulate their students in a variety of ways, as we see in *The Chocolate War*. Coaches are verbally and emotionally abusive to their athletes in order to win more games and make themselves look better in *Leverage, Gym Candy, Crackback, Ironman, Whale Talk, Raiders Night,* and *Swagger.* Some settings where teens are abused by those in charge of them are not exactly schools, although there are some similarities, including a campus-like setting. Some of these titles include *The Buffalo Tree, The Bunker Diary, Boot Camp, Hoppergrass, Bunker 10,* and the classics, *House of Stairs* and *The Grounding of Group 6.*

But as noted previously, adults are not the only monsters on campus—those students who are in power, the elite, the athletes and the popular in-crowd, frequently abuse and manipulate those who are at the other end of the social/popularity spectrum. Abuse can be sexual, either gay or straight, physical, or emotional. Groups or teams can gang up on individuals, or the abuse and manipulation can be administered by just one or two people. Novels about teen monsters who operate independently and the adults who give active or tacit permission include *Geography Club* and other titles in that series, *The Body of Christopher Creed, Whale Talk, Breaking Rank, Shattering Glass, Breaking Point, Fair Game, Poor Little Dead Girls, Runt, The Knife That Killed Me, Plague Year,* and many others.

It's important to note that these titles could also have been included in the bullying chapter, but I decided to include them here because the school is more central to the setting. You may see them as more appropriate to the bullying chapter, and are welcome to include them there for your own use, and limit this chapter to adult monsters on campus.

Adult monsters on campus cast long, long shadows. I have never forgotten the most emotionally and socially abusive situation I faced, the high school band director who led the attack, or the students who followed suit, making my life a living hell for months, even though it was more than fifty years ago. The memory of how embarrassed, frightened, intimidated, and angry I was has never dimmed or lessened in intensity, even though time and adulthood have given me a less emotional response to the situation. I didn't drop out, simply because I refused to give him the satisfaction of having made me quit. Maybe that's why, for all these years, I've hung onto the letter jacket I earned by not quitting. Young adult literature is full of similar situations and stories.

Why do teachers bully? The teaching profession is a helping profession, filled with individuals who regularly go beyond what is asked of them to ensure that their students get the best possible education. But as in every profession, there are those who exemplify the darker side of teaching, and take advantage of and abuse their positions of power in their schools. There is even a Facebook page titled "No More Teacher/Bullies" citing one case after another. It has almost fifty thousand likes, and was created in 2012.[1]

Stuart Twemlow, a psychiatrist from the Menniger Clinic in Houston, conducted an anonymous survey of 116 teachers in seven elementary schools, and found that 45 percent admitted that they had bullied students.[2] About 45–50 percent of coaches have admitted to being bullies with their athletes, a scenario that is far more accepted than teacher bullying.[3] Teachers may bully because of personal problems they have to deal with outside the classroom, and bring the resulting emotional baggage into the classroom with them. Twemlow has identified two different kinds of teacher bullying behavior. Some teachers are sadistic, and get pleasure from humiliating students in various ways. They may also encourage other students to take part in the humiliation process, taking it from just the classroom or playing field, and including every other part of the campus. There is nowhere safe for the victim to hide or escape. (That was the worst part of my own experience—not knowing when the mockery, jeering, and name calling would begin. It happened not only during band practice but in hallways and classrooms as well. On band trips, it was relentless.) Other teachers are bullied by students and are afraid of them and bully back in an attempt not to appear weak or passive. Bully-victim teachers may also be passive-aggressive, let classes get out of control, and resort to anger and bullying behavior to regain control. In those cases, more training in classroom management can reduce the bullying behavior.[4]

Many bullying teachers have bullying in their backgrounds and may have been a victim in the past. This form of behavior feels familiar to them, and now that they are the ones in control, it's the pattern they follow.[5] Many coaches are former athletes and were bullied by their coaches, and they treat their athletes the same way they were treated, believing it is the most effective way to coach.[6] Several researchers note the fact that coaches are allowed far more leeway in the way they treat their students than classroom teachers, and are frequently verbally and emotionally abusive to student athletes, especially when they are trying to motivate them to play better and win more games. It is ironic that students actually perform better for supportive coaches than abusive ones.[7]

Formal and informal research have both shown that our culture is widely accepting of abusive coaches, including verbal, emotional, and physical abuse, even encouraging it as a way to produce winning teams. Players soon learn, as children and teens watching sports in person or on television, even before they begin to participate in sports, that this behavior is part of the sports culture and is supposed to help them improve their performance and win more games and more glory. It's called "tough love" or "discipline."[8]

And as teen athletes learn to deal with abusive coaches, they also learn to do whatever is necessary to win games, no matter what they have to do to achieve their goal. Athletes with abusive coaches are much more likely to cheat than those with supportive coaches. According to a recent survey of twenty thousand athletes at six hundred colleges, almost one-third of basketball players (these players were most willing to report on abusive coaches, although the study didn't give any information on causality) were willing to admit that they had been verbally abused by their coaches, and athletes playing all kinds of sports reported they had cheated in order to win a game and their coaches' approval.[9]

These athletes are also less tolerant of others who differ from themselves—racial or ethnic minorities, those who have differing perspectives on ethical or philosophical questions, those who are considered to be outsiders, "The Others" who are beneath those who are part of their teams.[10] Robert Lipsyte, one of the best-known and well-respected YA authors writing about sports, calls it "Jock Culture," and notes that it is endemic in youth sports. There are only two kinds of people in this culture, the Jocks and the Pukes, the entitled and adored athletes, plus their hangers-on, and everyone else in school—the goths, the geeks, the nerds, the band kids, the theatre/art kids. No one is exempt.[11] Lipsyte also notes that this attitude has spread to our society in general. Some of the most popular television shows now feature competitions of various sorts,[12] with individuals on competing teams who must cheat and scheme and play politics with team members to avoid being "voted off the island." The winner is frequently the person who has learned to be the most manipulative.

Verbally abusive behavior can include name calling, humiliation, and making the athlete feel worthless and inadequate. It is delivered not only by the words the coach uses, but also his or her tone of voice, which is likely to be scornful, derisive, and very loud, with accompanying facial expression, body language, and withdrawal of emotional support, reducing or removing the individual's status level in the eyes of the coach and other teammates as well. It is also important to note that students have different reactions to verbal abuse. Some may react extremely to it, while others may be able to shrug it off more easily. Those in the former group, who feel anxious or frightened because of what the coach is saying can also be undergoing emotional abuse as a result of the coach's actions.[13]

Research has shown that while not all coaches are abusive or negative, many are. In one study, 45 percent of the children included reported verbal abuse from their coaches, including name calling and insults during games and practices. Another study of 4,500 children who reported abuse named their coach as the source.[14] The effect of this abuse can be substantial, with athletes having anxiety and headaches even years after the abuse took place.[15] And even if physical problems do not persist, emotional and psychological problems can last throughout adulthood and impact the way an individual interacts with others when in a position of power—as when the bullied student later becomes the bullying coach. Athletic coaches wield tremendous power, and their toughness on their players has traditionally been upheld as a virtue.[16]

However, a 2007 study found that bullying results in physical changes in the victim. The levels of cortisol, the stress hormone, were higher in bullied students and those who anticipated being bullied. Heightened levels of cortisol have been shown to result in reduced learning ability, clear thinking, and remembering. Therefore, the athlete being verbally abused in front of his or her teammates is going to be less likely, rather than more likely, to remember or use the information the coach is trying to convey. In fact, 33 percent of verbally abused students have significant levels of symptoms of PTSD, which can make it extremely difficult for them to function effectively and result in a lowered self-image. Verbal abuse can have even more long-lasting effects than physical abuse, making a mockery of the old "sticks and stones" rhyme.[17]

Anyone who has watched or played a competitive sport recognizes the meme of the foul-mouthed and cruel coach who humiliates and demeans his or her players when they blow a play during practice and then in retaliation forces them to work out till they vomit.[18] And it's not just in real life—it's in the media as well. Television shows, movies, and of course, books, all show the myth of the angry, loudmouth coach with the highest expectations of his or her athletes, whose insults and screaming demands during practices and games result in victories.[19] The abusive behavior is seen as "character building."[20] With so many examples of bad behavior resulting in good results, our culture has become much less sensitive to the damage it can incur. While coaches' behavior is widely accepted, classroom teachers are allowed less and less leeway in the way they interact in negative ways with their students, in the classroom and out of it.[21] Parents accept levels of abuse from a coach trying to inspire the team to its ultimate effort that they would never accept from a math or English teacher. But until this is pointed out to them, they may remain blind to the damage being done to their child. And the aggressive and authoritative coaching style, with its violence and unpredictability, only leads to another generation of coaches who use and believe in it.[22]

Dr. Kody Moffet, a pediatrician who is on the Council of Sports Medicine and Fitness for the American Academy of Pediatrics and also an associate professor of pediatrics at Creighton University School of Medicine, notes that while most coaches treat their athletes with respect, bullying coaches are still problems that need to be addressed. Frequently, they lack training in classroom management and don't know how to deal with their students in a non-bullying way. They are therefore less effective in teaching the positive life lessons that can be learned from participation in various team and individual sports.[23]

Sometimes teens can learn just as much or more from losing than winning, and effective coaches who don't resort to name calling can ensure that those lessons are learned.[24] In 2013, a study done by members of the American Psychological Association showed that the most effective coaches used positive reinforcement, encouragement, and promoting autonomy to help their athletes create positive self-images that produced higher performance levels.[25] Unfortunately, many young athletes see the harsh methods employed by their coaches as just a part of the sport that they have to endure to be able to play. Boys in particular are at risk because of the macho expectations of both coaches and peers—objecting to the way they are treated can be seen as a sign of weakness, which will be quickly pounced on by their more powerful team members.[26]

The problem gets worse as the individual players increase their skill—a coach's recommendation can help ensure an athletic scholarship, which may be the only way college is affordable. Parents and athletes hesitate to rock the boat, and look the other way, hoping that denial that a problem exists will have a positive result. But that works for only a few—scholarships have always been limited. And what of the ones who endure, but don't get the payoff? What price will they pay? Perhaps some of them will find the books included in this chapter, and discover some of the ways creative athletes have fought back against their coaches. (I particularly enjoyed the last few chapters of *Leverage*, as this very scenario plays out.)

But there is yet another way that coaches and athletic directors abuse their athletes in order to win games—encouraging the use of anabolic steroids that allow young athletes to gain more bulk and strength, in spite of sometimes quite unpleasant side effects. Some coaches provide them to athletes, others tell their players where to get them and how much to take for the most added muscle. Recently, a powerlifting coach in Louisiana was terminated after it was found that he gave one of his students steroids, telling the student they were protein pills. He was caught when the parents noticed significant personality changes in their son.[27]

Teens also find out about these drugs on their own—from their peers, from muscle magazines or other media, from news stories about professional athletes who use them, and from researching their use online. All it takes is a quick Google search—there are many websites about their use and purchase. According to the CDC, 11 percent of high school athletes have tried steroids, and 6 percent have used them regularly. And even if they don't use them, students know how to find them, and consider them very easy to get. Four out of ten students said they were influenced by the belief that professional athletes were using them, and 57 percent of the teen users said that they were also influenced by men's or muscle magazines.[28]

It's also important to note that few high schools do drug tests on their athletes, and fewer still test for steroids. If teens decide to take them on their own, it's not likely they will be caught by tests.[29] However, the mood swings, the increased level of anger and aggression, the sudden increase in muscle mass, and the acne that accompany steroid use are fairly easy to spot, once someone knows what to look for. But some coaches are not alert to what is going on with their athletes and are unaware that athletes are using. Sometimes they do not want to know what is happening and turn a blind eye or convince themselves the evidence they observe is wrong.[30]

A 2013 study showed that use of human growth hormone (HGH) has more than doubled from four years previously, a statistic that can be attributed to the extensive marketing of growth-promoting substances and lack of drug testing in high schools. Teens always want the quick fix for their problems, and various forms of steroids are seen as the perfect way to get bigger and stronger quickly. However, given the high cost of these substances, it is likely that at least some of them are getting some kind of fake products that may have additional side effects.[31]

The National Institute on Drug Abuse reports on their website that more than half a million high school students are using steroids, and that the number of students that believe that they are not risky is increasing. These teens are taking these substances without knowing the long-term problems they create, since long-term usage of steroids in a teen population has not been studied.[32] Because the use of steroids is increasing among teen athletes, whether sanctioned by coaches or not, it is sure to continue to be a topic in teen literature.

Finally, after documenting the various monstrous and manipulative roles that teachers and coaches have played, it is essential to remember that, like other kinds of monsters we have already met, they are not the majority, but a small minority. Most teachers and coaches have chosen their careers because they enjoy working with teens and helping them grow into mentally, emotionally, and physically healthy adults who will contribute positively to the communities they live in. YA authors who create monsters on campus do so to let teen readers know what to do if they are faced with members of this small minority.

# 18

## *LEVERAGE*
## BY JOSHUA C. COHEN

Joshua C. Cohen was into athletics when he was growing up in Minnesota, especially gymnastics. But he was lanky and tall, a bad combination for a gymnast. And when he walked into the men's gymnastics program as a college freshman, he realized right away that there was no way that he could compete on a collegiate level, so there was no way he'd ever achieve his dream of being an Olympic gymnast.

After college, he studied ballet and modern dance to reach another dream—supporting himself by using his gymnastic and acrobatic skills. He spent years traveling the world with a variety of dance and musical theatre companies.[1] But he'd always been interested in writing, and would make up new endings for books and movies, making them funnier or sadder, or crazier.[2] He read a news story one day about a group of underclassmen who were attacked by their senior teammates and had to take abuse, but when they spoke up, the whole town ostracized them. Their actions had made the football team look bad causing the rest of the season to be canceled. So they were actually wronged twice—once by their teammates and then again by the town.[3] Cohen was interested in what effect such a series of events might have on all the people involved—the underdogs, the godlike jocks, the coaches, the parents, and the community around them. What is the effect of knowing that you are powerless against those who torment you, even if you ask adults for help?

This book is about sports, but it is also about power, and how that power can be ill-used. It's about what happens when sportsmanship goes out the window and a "winning-is-everything" mentality takes its place. It's almost flippant to refer to the well-known Lord Acton quote, "Power . . . corrupt[s], and absolute power corrupts absolutely,"[4] but Cohen has shown just how true it is. Football coaches use screaming, obscenities, and intimidation to inspire their players. They also encourage them to use steroids to get bigger, stronger, and meaner, making sure the players know where to get what they need. Predictably, juicing produces side effects that lead to horrific attacks on other athletes who are younger, smaller, and weaker.[5]

This attack is the linchpin around which the rest of the story revolves. It is a difficult scene to read, since Cohen doesn't pull his punches, revealing all the ugliness and horror of the encounter. This is what happens when locker room talk goes beyond talk and becomes action.[6] Scott, Mike, and Tom are seniors, the kings of the school, arrogant, entitled, scornful of anyone lesser than they, determined to win their last football season, and taking heavy doses of steroids to insure it. They already have it in for the gymnastics team, because the gymnastics coach tricked the football coach into letting his team use the weight room the football team considered theirs. Several weeks later, at the Homecoming pep rally, two of the gymnastics team members race onto the field on a motocross bike, and throw water balloons at the Homecoming Court, which includes Scott and Mike, soaking all of them. Then they zip off the field before anyone can rip off their masks and see who they are. The seniors are infuriated.

On Saturday, gymnastic practice is almost over when the three seniors break in and attack Bruce, the team captain, and Ronnie, who is the smallest, weakest member of the team. Danny is putting mats away in the equipment room, out of sight. The football players are convinced that Ronnie was one of the guys who ruined the pep rally, and they beat up on him, in spite of his protestations of innocence. When Bruce interferes, they tie him up and haul Ronnie into the equipment room, where they rape him over and over. Danny can see what's happening from his hiding place, but is too terrified to come out and help Ronnie. If they knew he was there, he'd get the same treatment.

Finally, Kurt, a football player who'd been practicing with Danny, returns to the gym, hears Ronnie's screams, and attacks the boys, flinging them off Ronnie. The scene brings back Kurt's memories of the group home where he and his best friend Lamar were raped over and over by the man in charge of the boys' side of the house. Lamar finally died from the abuse, and Kurt has never forgotten him or the guilt he felt for not being able to help his friend.

Now, in a fit of uncontrollable rage, he beats up two of the boys, while a third one sneaks off. He is knocked unconscious, and the other two football players leave. Danny emerges from his hiding place, and tries to help Kurt through the seizure he went into as soon as he regained consciousness. Kurt insists on leaving as soon as the seizure is over, and Danny finds Bruce, and releases him, and together they get Ronnie out and to the car and home. Bruce tells him to just take a hot shower and forget about what happened; tomorrow is another day. But Ronnie is so completely traumatized that it's not likely he will recover as easily as Bruce says he will.

A few days later, after trying to talk to Danny, Bruce, and Kurt, who all rebuff him and urge him to get over it, Ronnie commits suicide. The three football players have been out of school all week, as have Bruce, Danny, and Kurt. All three of them have their own reasons for not revealing the truth, and they all wonder whether if they had done something differently, Ronnie would have lived. Cohen makes it very clear that they didn't do the right thing, but also points out that telling the truth might not have changed things much at all. Both the football coaches and their team are so popular and so revered by the entire town, that it's unlikely the boys' stories about Ronnie's abuse would have been listened to, either before or after his suicide.

But secrets don't stay secret for long, and gradually everyone involved knows what happened, although nothing changes in the balance of power. The three kings still rule, as do their coaches. Oregrove High School has become a hunting ground, not a school, Danny decides. The jocks pick their targets and the teachers look the other way and say boys will be boys. When Scott is hurt in a football game and gets lots of sympathy and support from both students and teachers, both Kurt and Danny compare it to how Ronnie was treated, and their guilt becomes more intense. Finally, Kurt can't hold it back any longer and tells Scott that Danny saw everything that happened, and Scott finally realizes that he and his friends could be in danger.

Not long after that, Danny and Bruce are trapped in the gym with their nemeses. Danny is able to send Kurt their emergency signal for help before he's taken down. But before he can get there, Danny and Bruce are severely tortured. Kurt's interference allows them to get away, and Kurt faces off with the three players. He is able to goad them into talking about what they did to Ronnie and plan to do to Danny, but he doesn't reveal until he's fled the gym that he's been recording them from the time he broke into the gym.

Using that recording, they are able to set up the three kings and their coaches and reveal to everyone what has been going on and what happened to Ronnie. While probably not realistic, the final scenes are satisfying, showing that sometimes the good guys do win. This time the pure evil of the three kings is overcome by loyalty and friendship, helped out by a little technology.

# 19

# *BOOT CAMP*
# BY TODD STRASSER

Todd Strasser was on the Lower East Side in New York City, interviewing a group of homeless kids for one of his books (*Can't Get There from Here*), when one of the girls said she'd run away from home when her mother threatened to put her in a boot camp. A few days later, he read an article on "transporters," who are hired by parents to kidnap their children from their homes and take them to boot camp. On one hand, it made sense—it's difficult to force teens to get in a car or airplane, and then to get them to stay once they get to their destination. Teens can exhibit all kinds of out-of-control and disruptive behavior that can attract unwanted attention, and there can be questions about the level of force needed to make teens cooperate. Someone who can come into the home, restrain the teen, and take him/her away is a much less difficult and more efficient situation. Most parents who do this are completely convinced that there are no other options. Boot camp is the only way to keep their child from self-destructing in one way or another.[1]

Strasser was disturbed about the idea that teens have no rights at all until they are eighteen. The contracts parents sign with boot camps allow camp personnel to do anything necessary to change the teens' behavior. Such tactics sometimes produce rehabilitated teens who are able to return to their lives and function as capable and effective people in their communities. But many times, the opposite is true.[2]

There are many stories in the media about teens who die in boot camps. In November 2015, *Rolling Stone* published a lengthy article about one of those teens, that included research and statistics on the ways teens were mistreated and abused while in boot camps.[3] Teens are not allowed to contact their parents, and parents are warned to not believe their child's stories of mistreatment—beatings, starvation, excessive physical punishment, and solitary confinement.[4] Considering the personalities of those who are sent to boot camps, it's likely that more are broken than molded during their stays there.

One of the many problems with boot camps is that they are enterprises for profit. In order to make money, the entrepreneurs have to fill beds, so they are not likely to turn people away. Parents who send their kids to boot camps are desperate, convinced they have no other option. They are willing to send their kids away for unspecified amounts of time, even for years, and allow camp staff to discipline them in any way they choose. And until they are eighteen, teens have no legal rights to protect them from their parents' wishes.[5]

Strasser's novel has been called "disturbing," "vivid and realistic," with "horrifying violence and injustices experienced by teens."[6] Punishments at the boot camp have included brainwashing, temporary isolation during which the youth lies face down on a cold concrete floor, being shackled outside all night during freezing weather, and being beaten on the soles of the feet, as well as being beaten up by other teens and staff members. The fact that Strasser presents Garrett, his protagonist, as sympathetic, intelligent, and rational, makes his transformation at the end of the book, when he has finally yielded to the camp rules, even more heart-wrenching and horrifying. He is no longer the boy who was brought to camp months before, and the reader has to wonder what the rest of his life will be like.[7]

Garrett Durrell isn't really out of control, doesn't use drugs, or beat up on anyone else. But he's big—6'4" and 230 pounds—and he's smart. Too smart, his parents say, for his own good. When he discovered he could skip school and still pass all his tests, he quit going. When he fell in love with his former math teacher, who was eight years older than he was, they had an affair. He was rebellious, and stole, and basically did anything he wanted to do, and refused to do what his parents told him to do. So they sent him to Harmony Lake, a boot camp for teens whose parents are tired of putting up with them. There they are taught to be respectful, obedient, and polite enough to be released to their parents. Staff methods are harsh, abusive, and horrifying. Until a camper has risen to the higher levels by their good behavior (which includes tattling on the other kids when they do something wrong), they are subjected to unending physical and mental harassment and abuse. Garrett is sent to TI (temporary isolation) his first night there, and then continues to attract the negative attention of the staff, who are determined to undermine his self-confidence and break his will.

Eventually, he makes friends with two of the other campers, Sarah and Pauley, who have planned their escape, and they invite Garrett to join them. They succeed in getting away from camp and crossing the river into Canada. But when Garrett sees that two of the camp staff are about to drown in the river while following them because he'd sabotaged their boat, he turns back to help them. Predictably, they recapture him and take him back to camp, where his abuse reaches near fatal levels.

After being forced to spend the night outside, shackled to a stake, Garrett's mind and body finally break. He becomes a quiet, obedient camper, talking to no one, at last ignored by everyone. Weeks later, when his parents and their lawyer come to take him home, he no longer recognizes his mother until she hugs him. He refuses to say anything to his parents but "yes, ma'am" and "no, sir" because he knows he will be punished if he talks more. His mother begs him to tell the truth when the lawyer asks him if he was "hit, beaten, kicked, or injured by a staff member" while he was at the camp. But Garrett cannot. His fear is too deeply rooted; he has been changed in too many fundamental ways. His answer is only, "Yes sir, they did. But only because I deserved it." His abusers have won. He has been returned to his parents, respectful, obedient, and broken, perhaps irreparably. Strasser gives no hint of his future, forcing the reader to speculate.

# 20

## *BOY TOY*
## BY BARRY LYGA

**S**urprisingly for someone who decided he wanted to be a writer when he was in second grade, Barry Lyga doesn't like criticism or negative reviews. Even a relatively benign letter from his editor can mean a week of procrastination before he opens it.[1] (I think every writer could understand that reaction—I have had it myself!) Lyga does most of his rewriting while the book still exists only in his head—thinking about how characters will interact, how the setting will impact the story, how it will begin, how it will end—so when he sits down to begin the actual writing, most of the problems will have already been ironed out. However, sometimes a book can get away from him. This happened in *Boy Toy*, when he got about halfway through and realized that he had gotten off course, which made it impossible to get to his original ending. He had to decide whether he should start over or just let the story flow and see where he ended up. He ended up being very pleased with the result—his new ending was much better and more satisfying than the first one he had planned.[2]

While most critics see *Boy Toy* as being a sexual abuse story, Lyga disagrees. While the book does contain flashbacks to Josh's time with Eve, when he was twelve, the majority of the book takes place five years later, when she has just been released from prison, after having served only half of a ten-year term. During that time, Josh has withdrawn from all his friends, and focuses his attention on continuing to get straight As and raise his stats on the baseball diamond. He feels a tremendous amount of guilt about the four months he and Eve were involved and refuses to talk to anyone about it other than his psychiatrist, Dr. Kennedy.

In spite of years of therapy, Josh has yet to address the question of his guilt, and the part he played in making it happen. Lyga says that it's not a book about abuse, it's a book about recovering from abuse—a book about baggage. It addresses not the question of abuse itself, although that is part of the situation, but the lengthy and difficult process of recovering from abuse, about what we bring with us from the past, and how long we will feel the need to continue to hold onto it, taking it with us into the future. It's not about surviving abuse, but realizing you were abused, letting go of the guilt, and understanding that you were powerless to prevent it, because you were just a child.[3]

Toward the end of the book, Josh also has to deal with his parents' divorce, which brings back much of the anger and frustration he has pushed deep inside him for years, because his mother has been having an affair for years and has finally decided to leave Josh's father. Since Eve's husband has stood by her over the years, he doesn't understand why his father can't do the same.

Another source of tension is the reappearance of Rachel in his life. They were best friends since childhood, and during a session of spin the bottle on Rachel's birthday, Josh automatically begins to do some of the things Eve taught him to do to please her sexually, Rachel freaks, and the whole story splits wide open. Josh has not spoken to her since. Rachel finally decides to take things into her own hands and begins to pursue Josh romantically, even though he is still so traumatized he can't stand the most innocuous touch. He also refuses to listen to her, or to anyone else who tells him that it wasn't his fault, he did nothing wrong, and the blame is completely on Eve. Rachel's loyalty and persistence, her love and caring, finally persuade Josh to reconsider his stance.

But Rachel isn't the only one who is loyal to Josh—his best friend, Zik, has stood by him during all the years, and continues to challenge Josh to step outside his comfort zone. Josh, Rachel, and Zik were best friends all through childhood, and when Zik falls for Michelle, they become the Four Musketeers. All that ended the night of Rachel's birthday, and although Rachel and Michelle don't talk to Josh, Zik has always been there for him, in spite of the fact that Josh has never shared with Zik the details of what happened between him and Eve. Zik has also helped Josh stay focused on the two things that could help keep him stable—his record of getting all As (which Josh admits isn't all that difficult), and his ability to hit anything a baseball pitcher could throw at him. Josh is not only athletic, he is also a math genius, who's always wanted to go to Stanford. If they win this final season, he and Zik will both get what they want.

It's not until after Josh blows the last game of the season, and Zik confronts him about it, that Josh realizes that his mother had lied when she said kids couldn't fall in love, only adults could. Josh understands that what Zik and Michelle have, and what he and Rachel have, is real and true and pure. He also knows that he has to face his past, and he goes to see Eve to confront her about what she did. In one of the most gripping and intense scenes in the book, Eve tells him what he has never believed—*it wasn't his fault*—and he is finally able to hear her, forgive himself, and turn toward the future.

Difficult to read or even think about, Lyga has infused this book with genuine emotion, realistic characters, and a fast-moving plot that overcomes its length. The seduction scenes as Eve teaches Josh how to please a woman are as intense and sensual as they are repugnant and horrifying. While she has spent her time in prison teaching other prisoners to read and write, this doesn't overcome the pure evil of her scheme to draw Josh to her, plans that started with the first moment she saw him.

Lyga's novel is all about realizing that you are in a rut, caught in the past, and unable to see any way out of it or to see the friends that are waiting to give you a hand up and out. Perhaps reading it, teens stuck in similar situations can see how they can be resolved. It is not for the faint of heart, but for those who can weather its darkness, it can be a powerful example of overcoming and succeeding in spite of overwhelming odds.

# 21

## *RAIDERS NIGHT*
## BY ROBERT LIPSYTE

Robert Lipsyte has been writing his whole life, first as a journalist, and then as a YA author. His books center around sports, but they also describe the Jock Culture and what it does to both the Jocks and the Pukes, the insiders and the outsiders. His first book, *The Contender*, is one of the classics of the YA canon, along with *The Outsiders*, *The Chocolate War*, *Weetzie Bat*, *Forever*, and *The Pigman*. His books are hard-hitting and pull no punches, and the one that has had the most impact is *Raiders Night*. In it, Lipsyte takes an honest look at high school football today, the men who coach it, the boys who play it, and the community leaders that fund and support both groups. It has won critical acclaim, but has also stirred up angry and resentful responses from the adults who are involved in high school sports, particularly football and basketball.

Matt is a senior in high school and one of the captains on the football team. He has his posse, fellow backfield players he's known since grade school—Brody, Pete, and Tyrell. They are high school royalty and willing to do almost anything to keep winning games. Matt, Brody, and Pete are juicers, who take anabolic steroids to make sure they're big enough and strong enough to give their team an edge. Tyrell doesn't take anything, but he works out constantly to make sure he's as good as he can be. Matt suspects it's not so much that he objects to the juice as he can't afford it. Steroids aren't cheap. The prescription drugs he takes for pain, like Vicodin, are easier to get, and cost much less.

And they aren't the only ones who get shots—the linemen do too. The other captain, Ramp, is the leader of that group, and there is a rivalry between the two groups that sometimes seems friendly, other times, not so much. Ramp has a mean streak a mile wide, and enjoys showing off how much control he has over the rest of the team.

This year there's a new transfer student, a sophomore tight end named Chris. He's big like Tyrell, and graceful, but way too cocky about his place on the team, and way too much in Ramp's face about it. Other times, he seems vulnerable and lost, and Matt wonders if he's using being cocky to cover up how he really feels.

Football camp is just before school starts—a chance for the team to bond and for the seniors to prepare for their last high school season. There's lots of football, but there are also freshmen who have to go through hazing, which Ramp sets up, and Chris has to go along with them in spite of his protests. He's really pissing off the seniors, even Matt, who's uncomfortable around him, even if he can't pinpoint why. The coach tells Matt that, as one of the captains, he needs to get Chris to chill—he doesn't need Ramp and his friends to get on his case.

The last night of camp is Raiders Pride night, when the coaches leave the team alone to deal with the freshmen—a hazing tradition that this year, goes too far. It's a time for the freshmen to show that they are true Raiders, with Raider pride. They are stripped and their hands are cuffed behind them. The sophomores, except for Chris, and juniors leave, and the door is locked behind them. The freshmen are blindfolded, and the hazing begins. But Ramp is especially cruel to Chris and takes the game several steps too far, first urinating in his face and mouth, and then raping him with a baseball bat. Matt is frozen in fear and horror, but Tyrell, Pete, and Brody are not, and they attack Ramp, pulling him off Chris. But as soon as the three of them get Matt and Chris outside, Chris takes off, saying he wants to be alone, and they are unable to find him. He returns the next morning when the bus arrives to take them home. And by that time, everyone knows what happened. The coaches pretend ignorance, and say nothing.

Chris tries several times to talk to Matt, but Matt refuses. Matt's girlfriend, Mindy, is back from cheerleader camp, but while she was gone, Sarah, whom Matt likes a lot better, has decided to pursue Matt. Predictably, Mindy is livid, and Matt is caught in the middle. He hopes if he deals with the two girls and puts off Chris, Chris will stop trying to talk to him. And every time the pressure gets more intense, Matt pops more Vicodin—it's the only thing that can relieve his aching body and his constant headaches. He doesn't really realize that he's taking more than he ever has before.

Chris starts skipping practices because he refuses to change clothes in the locker room. Ramp's harassment has increased. He now calls Chris "Missy Chrissy." Coach puts pressure on Matt to get Chris back in line. Not having Chris as tight end is making winning much more difficult.

Matt and the coaches, and even some of the other players, are telling Chris to just suck it up and get on with it. Their platitudes are less than convincing. And somehow the news that something happened at camp has leaked out, and a local reporter is determined to get Matt to tell him the story.

The season staggers on, as tempers continue to rise. Matt's under pressure not only from his coach and teammates, but also from his dad, who wants Matt to get a full-ride scholarship to college. He wants Matt to live out his own dreams.

It all comes to a head just before Homecoming. Ramp is giving the team a pep talk in the locker room when Chris comes in with a gun and threatens to shoot Ramp. Ramp taunts him, and tells him to kill himself instead, and Chris puts the gun in his mouth and pulls the trigger. Matt tackles him in time to knock the gun out of his mouth, but it still fires, and Matt ends up with Chris's blood all over him. When the cops investigate, both Matt and Ramp hide what happened. But thinking back on what was happening just before Chris walked in, Matt realizes that the team is far less unified than it used to be. Even the Back Pack isn't standing together the way they always have before. Ramp is succeeding in setting team members against each other.

Because of the shooting, the Homecoming Dance is canceled, but the game is still on, thanks to Matt's dad, who wants his son to play out the season. If Matt can get into Division One, he can have a shot at the pros, something Matt isn't so sure he wants any longer. He is beginning to see how long his father has been pushing and manipulating him to bring his father's dream to life.

Matt finally realizes he has to stop Ramp—he can't let him get away with what he did to Chris, while the other seniors watched him. He decides to talk to Mr. Dorman, the school counselor, who's also one of the assistant coaches, and has always been straight with him. Unfortunately, Dorman isn't as surprised as he should have been—he already knew something had happened. He will discuss what to do with the other coaches, and get back to Matt later.

Matt goes to work out, and afterward, Ramp and his posse confront him in the steam room. But before he can do more than threaten Matt, the Back Pack shows up with three other players, ready to take Matt's side. Ramp and the linebackers back down and leave.

When Matt gets home, his dad confronts him and tries to persuade him to change his mind. It's a decision that will affect the whole team, college scholarships, property values, local businesses. But Matt has had enough—he's finally realized that he's his own person, and doesn't need to knuckle under to his dad any longer. He finds the card that the local reporter had given him. He'll start there. Once word gets out, no one will be able to stop it, not coaches, and not any of the other adults who want to bury the story. It will be a storm, but he's ready.

The storm wasn't only a part of the novel—it began blowing up around Lipsyte almost as soon as the book was published. *Raiders Night* tells the truth, and hundreds of high school players and former jocks confirmed it. They didn't object to the sex or the language, or the violence. They could handle that; after all, they saw it every day. What they wanted to talk to Lipsyte about was how they felt manipulated by their coaches, their fathers, and the businessmen in the community who wanted a championship team every year, and were willing to do anything to get one.

Lipsyte wasn't surprised that he heard that in Texas, or that he was invited by teachers and librarians to speak at their high schools about *Raiders Night,* and then quietly disinvited when the athletic department heard about it. Texans make a religion about high school football—but in other parts of the country, Lipsyte thought it would be different. It wasn't. High school sports is poised to be a huge money maker—just like college and pro teams. And videos of frightening tackles, reports of brain damage and concussions, and a rising awareness that maybe someone should do something have not stemmed the tide. Lipsyte is trying his best to make his readers and their families more aware of the dangers of steroids and other drugs, and the price that players have to pay to be champions. When coaches and other involved adults take their eyes off the game and begin to look at the money, rather than the needs and the futures of the teens on the playing field, something needs to change.

# Part IV

# Monsters You Live With:
# Nearest, but Not Dearest

Young adult literature is full of difficult home situations, in which violence is either threatened or played out—adults abusing children, children abusing adults, and siblings abusing each other. The abuse takes all forms—physical, emotional, sexual, and verbal. It can be intermittent or constant; it can be brief or last for years; it can seem to be superficial or can be debilitatingly intense. And it all reflects the realities that our children and teens live with every day. It is one of the more controversial topics in YA literature, and many titles containing family violence have been challenged, including those written by some of the genre's best known authors, including Chris Crutcher, Norma Fox Mazer, Todd Strasser, Walter Dean Myers, Sharon Draper, Neal Schusterman, Cynthia Voigt, Nancy Werlin, and Gail Giles.

Abusive families have been studied for years, highlighting the negative consequences on everyone involved—the perpetrator, the victim, and the observers. Researchers have looked at spousal abuse, parents abusing their children, children abusing their parents, but little examination has been done of sibling abuse and its long- and short-term effects on its victims.

While most people assume that familial violence isn't widespread, research shows that a majority of families experience some level of violence among their members at some point. If it becomes an ingrained pattern, those involved will be affected for years. What happens to people as children and teens can have a significant impact on who they are and how they live as adults.

Those with whom they are closest are frequently those with whom they live, whom they have been told are trustworthy, but have proven not to be. Who should have their backs, but don't. Who are supposed to protect them, but instead hurt them and allow others to do the same. Who prove that home is not a safe place where they are accepted and loved, but a dangerous place where it's impossible to relax. There is no one there to protect them, to prevent them from being attacked by other family members. And if there is someone on their side, that person may be too afraid to speak up. Having friends helps, but many teens hide what is happening at home from their friends, feeling embarrassed or that they themselves are to blame.

Many researchers have studied the problems of family violence, but from different perspectives, using different definitions. As a result, statistics show conflicting numbers, but overall, do show that family violence is widespread. In addition, a number of these studies include only information reported to governmental agencies, and much violence is never reported. Studies that feature self-reporting from both perpetrators and victims may also have skewed results, depending on how violence is defined and whether the individual feels that it's safe to tell the truth. The American Humane Association notes that results are most likely under-reported, and that the actual instances of abuse against children from other family members is probably much higher.[1]

Reports of family violence come from a wide variety of sources, over half of whom are considered to be "mandated reporters" or professionals who are required by law to report suspected abuse. They include teachers, social workers, police personnel, legal and criminal justice personnel, and mental/medical health practitioners.[2]

(Librarians are generally not mandated reporters, other than teacher librarians, who are considered faculty members. Local, regional, and state laws can change this, however. If you see something that concerns you, ask your supervisor what is required in your library system.)

Boys and girls are equally likely to be victims, and abuse happens across ethnicities and social classes.[3] A CDC study reported that 44 percent of the victims were Caucasian, 21 percent were African American, and almost 22 percent were Hispanic.[4] Only 1 percent were Native Americans, and less than 1 percent were Asian.[5] Substance abuse is reported to be an underlying factor in 70 percent of reported incidents and is the primary reason why children are put into foster care. Parents are most frequently the abusers (almost 89 percent), but 7 percent were other family members. In addition, unmarried partners of parents accounted for almost 4 percent of the cases. But this is only the tip of the iceberg, since about three times as many incidents go unreported as are reported.[6]

The Domestic Violence Roundtable also reports figures on children witnessing violence in the home, and reports that between three and four million children and teens are at risk of witnessing domestic violence, most likely committed by the male partner/spouse of their mothers or stepmothers. Witnessing is defined as seeing, hearing, observing the aftermath, or being aware of tension and fear between the adult couple. Children in this situation feel anxious and on guard, since they may not know why the violence happens or how to predict it. And when the violence is consistent over time, the repercussions can continue throughout adulthood. A study of abused teens found they were 25 percent more likely to have a pregnancy and 80 percent more likely to have at least one psychiatric disorder by age twenty-one.[7] In a study of homeless youth done by the U.S. Department of Health and Human Services, 46 percent had left a home where they suffered physical abuse, and 17 percent had left home due to sexual abuse. Finally, abused and neglected children and teens are 59 percent more likely to be arrested as a juvenile, 28 percent more likely to be arrested as an adult, and 30 percent more likely to commit violent crimes as adults.[8] And while not every abused child grows up to abuse his or her own children, statistics say that about a third of them do, creating a self-sustaining cycle of violence.[9]

However, a major study published in the March 2015 issue of *Science* looked into whether parental violence was passed down from parents to children. It was shown not to support past research that seemed to show that being abused as a child is an important factor in whether or not an individual will be abusive as a parent themselves. Lead researcher Cathy Spatz Widom, a professor of psychology at John Jay College of Criminal Justice in New York City, found that previous studies of this topic had been flawed because they worked backward, asking abusive parents if they had been abused as children. However, those studies did not involve non-abusive parents who had been physically abused as children. Using three different predictors, (contact with Child Protective Services, interviews with parents, and interviews with children of those parents once they had reached adulthood), Widom and her team found that differences between children from physically abusive and non-abusive homes who went on to become abusers themselves were not statistically significant. Almost 7 percent of children born to abused parents were abused, but just over 5 percent of children born to parents who had not been abused were abused. But this has to do only with physical abuse. The risk of sexual abuse or neglect was significantly higher in children born to abusive parents. Widom had no explanation for the difference, but intends to do more research into the question.[10]

It is important to note that this study shows that children of abusive parents are not doomed to replicate those mistakes. The vast majority of children who are abused grow up to be non-abusive parents.[11] One reason for this can be the individual's determination to treat his or her children differently, and the increasing availability of information, including books, videos, classes, online forums, and other formats, that offer a variety of perspectives for training for new parents. Today, more is known about parenting than in the past. Seeking out formal or informal ways to improve one's parenting skills is no longer something to be ashamed of. It is seen to be an indication of parents' devotion to their children and their determination to be the best parents possible. In addition, divorcing parents (still about 50 percent of marriages end in divorce) seem to be more aware of the impact their actions can have on their children, and also have a variety of resources aimed specifically at them, to help them and their children through the trauma involved when families break apart.

While abuse between children and parents has been researched extensively, sibling violence has not. Many times, it is downplayed as a part of growing up—that is, "kids will be kids."[12] But in reality, the effect of sustained sibling violence or abuse can be just as pervasive and long lasting as violence or abuse by peers unrelated to the victim.[13] In a recent study, Dr. Murray Straus, author of *Behind Closed Doors: Violence in the American Family*, said that 74 percent of siblings push and shove each other; 42 percent kick, punch, and bite; and an amazing 85 percent engage in regular verbal abuse.[14] It seems from these figures that very few households are exempt.

There are multiple causes for sibling violence, including absent or uninvolved parents, parents who don't set boundaries, parents who assume that children will engage in rough play or tease their siblings, or parents who unintentionally escalate the violence by playing favorites, automatically assigning blame to the older children and ignoring the part the younger children play in provoking the older ones. And many parents and other adults simply turn a blind eye, refusing to recognize that sibling violence exists, deeming it simply part of growing up, and not just as dangerous as violence from other peers, and even more impactful than the violence parents perpetrate on their children.[15]

In another study from New Hampshire, over two thousand children were asked about the levels of violence in their families. Thirty-five percent said they had been hit or attacked by a sibling. Forty percent of those were attacked repeatedly, 13 percent were injured, and 6 percent were attacked with a weapon. In addition, the study found that the violence crossed ethnic and socioeconomic boundaries, and boys were only slightly more likely to be violent than girls.[16] A 1994 study found that children are the most violent members of families, and sibling abuse is more common than spousal or parental abuse.[17] The *New York Times, Social Work Today,* and *Psychology Today* have all published recent articles on the alarmingly high levels of sibling abuse in our society today. It is also important to note that sibling abuse does not have to involve physical violence. Emotional abuse, including teasing, name-calling, and isolation can also cause long-term effects.[18]

However, sibling abuse does not typically occur in families who have functional family systems. Families with parents who make little or no attempt to attend to the physical, emotional, and social needs of their children, or who have not formed a supportive, functional parental dyad, are likely to be susceptible to sibling violence. Parental absence or unavailability, whether emotional, physical, or both, is one of the most common markers of family systems that are likely to exhibit sibling abuse. To a great extent, the responsibility for sibling abuse falls on the parents, but it is also important to note that even functional families who are experiencing an extreme stressor from outside the family may also exhibit various dysfunctional characteristics, such as sibling abuse. In many cases, the abused sibling may be so heavily impacted that he or she may struggle with establishing or maintaining intimate relations with a variety of other people during adolescence and adulthood. These relationships include spousal relationships, relationships with their children, family of origin relationships, or peer relationships, and can likely be attributed to the consistent minimization of the abuse by both involved and uninvolved adults.[19]

But children do not have to be victims to be affected by violence at home. Even witnessing violence between family members can have a seriously dilatory effect, and children witness family violence (hear, see, and experience the results) much more frequently than parents realize. For instance, a study of battered women showed that children witnessed the violence that their parents thought they were unaware of, and were able to provide detailed descriptions of it. Data collected by police officers responding to domestic violence 911 calls showed that children were present in about 50 percent of these calls, and 81 percent of those children either saw or heard the violence take place. College students reported that about half of them had witnessed violence in their homes during their childhoods. [20]

Children want to know what is going on in their families, what secrets are being kept from them, even if those secrets are unpleasant. They will listen at doors, hide and peer through cracks, sneak down staircases or into rooms, and pretend to be asleep when they are not, in order to find out what is really going on. Even infants are affected by the noise of parents fighting. They may exhibit disturbed sleep and feeding patterns, show increased screaming patterns, and experience developmental delays of various kinds. [21]

Preschool children may become excessively clingy and anxious about being separated from the parent who is a victim, and exhibit fear of the abuser. They may also show disturbed sleep patterns and may regress to coping behaviors such as thumb sucking and bed wetting because they are being forced to cope with trauma at an age when they have not yet learned how to deal with it. [22] And many children feel that they are somehow responsible for the violent behavior, since they have not yet learned to attribute causality correctly. Teens, who are beginning to move into the stage of development that includes creating a self-identity and beginning romantic relationships, will frequently show inappropriate behavior as they act out the violent relationships and situations they see at home.

But the further children and adolescents get from domestic violence, the less likely they are to be affected by it. There is a plasticity in the brains of youth that allows them to learn new patterns and behaviors and set aside the old ones, once they have been given consistent positive role models.

This is one of the reasons why books containing family violence are important to teens: they can see the situation from an outside perspective rather than the more limited one they had as a participant, allowing them to be more objective about it. They can make decisions about whether or not to follow that example or to look for another one. They can realize that they are not the only person experiencing a violent situation, and find strength to get out of it.

Even if they are not in an abusive situation, but know someone who is, they are able to see it differently and may be more likely to empathize and provide support to that person. Fictional titles that show victims overcoming difficult circumstances can help provide new patterns for real-life teens to follow that can lead to a more positive outcome.

No parent wants to admit that violence exists in their home, whether or not it was in the past or the future. Remembering difficult times can be painful, uncomfortable, threatening, and even dangerous, and seeing such situations in books their child is reading can cause the same effects. Banning such books and other materials may seem easier than allowing their children to read them so the problems can be discussed and questions answered. As a profession, we are lucky that information is leaky and infective, and even when teens are forbidden to read a book or see a movie, they figure out ways to do so. Sometimes it is just as important to stock and promote and display controversial materials on family violence and the monsters that live at home as it is to check them out. If these materials are available and teens are aware of them, they will find a way to get access to them, even if they cannot read them in their own homes.

# 22

## *THE RULES OF SURVIVAL*
## BY NANCY WERLIN

After I read *The Rules of Survival* for the first time, shortly before it was published, when Nancy Werlin asked me to write a teacher's guide for it, I asked her how she could stand to have such an evil person as Nikki walk around in her head while she wrote. She said it was really hard—she had to keep taking breaks from writing just to keep her sanity.[1]

She also says that it is the darkest book she has ever written, even though it ends on a hopeful note. After meeting a woman like Nikki Walsh, the mother (and the monster) in this book, Werlin found herself thinking about what it might be like to grow up as one of her children, in a world that isn't ever safe, because it is never predictable, never a place you could trust.[2] The result was "Safe," a brief (just over a thousand words) short story she wrote in 2001,[3] that featured a scary incident she retold as the opening of the novel. It is as powerful today as it was fifteen years ago, especially since it is about the edge of violence, the potential of violence, violence just barely averted. And had Werlin written it today, and set it in Texas, with its new open-carry law, it might have had a very different ending. The characters in 2001 don't carry guns. Today, they might, and the resolution could be much more final and deadly.

After she'd written the story, Werlin began to realize that there was more going on with the characters and their situation than could be included in a short story, and that she needed to explore it, going into the dark places she didn't particularly enjoy visiting in order to tell it.[4] So she began the research for this novel.

This is a story that is almost too horrible to tell, made even worse by Werlin's skill in creating characters who are all too real, even though we wish they weren't. It is written in the form of a letter that Matt, Nikki's oldest child, writes to his youngest sister, to tell her about their mother, the things she did that Emmy was too young to know about, or that her older siblings shielded her from.

Werlin chose to make her job as a writer more difficult by giving away the ending on the first page—all three children have survived, and are doing well. She would have to do something to keep her readers turning the pages even though they knew the ending. What could she do to bring the reader into the story on a visceral level, to make him or her feel the fear that the children had to live with every day? By writing the story in first person with Matt as the narrator, and having him write to Emmy, he could address his story to both Emmy and the reader using "you." The reader would be forced into the story, not only as an observer, but also as a participant, one of Nikki's children, living with fear. The happy ending would become less important because of the tension and the hell that those children had to live through to get there.[5]

Fear has been a part of Werlin's psyche ever since she can remember, and she uses that fear when she writes, channeling it into a pull/push force for her characters to deal with. She knows what fear is like; she lives with it, owns it, and maps it into her characters and makes it real for her readers.[6] Her knowledge of what her own fear feels like enables her to inspire that same fear in her readers. We are all afraid, some more than others, and we all look for a way to escape or outwit that fear with as little risk of danger to ourselves as possible. Werlin's skill as a writer makes her characters' fear real, tangible, and yet safe, between the pages of a book, where, like the author, we can close the cover and pause the story when it becomes more grim than we can handle.

This is why her books are so valuable to teens living in difficult situations: they offer solutions to ponder that have been previously unknown; they offer recognition and reduce the reader's isolation— "I'm not the only one who feels this way, lives with this problem, is treated like that." They offer hope of a better future, and they increase teens' knowledge, emotional strength, and vicarious experience, all from a place of safety.

It is interesting to note that since Werlin created Nikki Walsh and spent three years living with her, she has not published another realistic novel, focusing instead on a fantasy trilogy with supernatural elements. Perhaps she needed a longer break from the monstrous characters she creates so deftly. But her suspense fans have something to look forward to—there is an announcement on her website about her next book, coming in 2017, *And Then There Were Four*, about five teens who discover that their parents want to kill them. The tag line is reminiscent of Julian Thompson's classic *The Grounding of Group 6*, and plenty of chances for more monstrous families.

*The Rules of Survival* begins with a letter Matt is writing to his youngest sister, Emmy, who is nine. He is about to leave her and the middle sister, Callie, for the first time, to go to Austin, Texas, to attend the University of Texas. He doesn't know if he will ever give the letter to Emmy—it might be better if she never knows the totality of what happened to them. He'd like her to live happily ever after, but he knows that there is no guarantee of that. So while his memories are sharp and clear, he wants to write down everything that happened because of their mother, a woman who never should have been a mother. It's a "just in case" letter, a letter to let Emmy know what he learned from living with Nikki—not ever to trust anyone, to expect danger around every corner, to understand that there are people out there that choose to harm you, that want to harm you, and sometimes they are also the people who say they love you.

For Matt, it all began when he and Callie saw Murdoch for the first time. He was thirteen, Callie was eleven, and Emmy was only five. It was a sweltering summer night in Boston in the middle of a heat wave, but it was also Saturday, date night for Nikki, their mother, so they were locked in a third-floor apartment as hot as an oven. As soon as Emmy was asleep, Matt and Callie snuck out and walked over to a convenience store to get popsicles. Matt worried about Emmy waking up, but they were only going to be gone a few minutes, and she almost never woke up once she was asleep.

They were picking out popsicles when the yelling started. A big barrel-chested man had grabbed his kid by the shoulders and was shaking him and screaming at him. Then suddenly, this other man snatched the boy away from his father and shoved him behind him, away from the big man. He said to the father, "You want to hurt someone, hurt me. I promise I won't fight back. You can hit me till all the anger's gone. I'll let you." And suddenly it was over. The big man mumbled something and turned back to the counter to pay for his stuff. Murdoch just ignored him, and knelt down in front of the little boy, and said, "It's wrong for anyone to hurt you. Can you remember that? You don't have to do anything, just remember what I'm telling you." The big man hustled the little kid out of the store, Murdoch paid for his iced coffee and the Reese's Pieces that the little boy had had in his hand, tossed them to Callie and Matt, and he and his date walked out as well.

Murdoch wasn't a big man. He was medium in every way— height, weight, overall appearance—but he was outstanding in one way: he wasn't afraid, or if he was, he acted anyway. For Matt, who'd lived with fear his whole life, it was a revelation. "Living with fear every day, like we did," Matt wrote to Emmy, "changes you, gets into your blood, becomes your master. I know that I'm not who I was supposed to be, who I could have been, because I was afraid for too long. It made me think about things I never should have had to think about. I learned to live with it, we all did. And it changed us in ways that we can never fix."

Then Matt goes back to his childhood, before Emmy was born, when he was only four years old, and the night he fully realized the depth of his mother's insanity and evil, and accepted that his first job was to keep his sister and himself alive, any way he could. At that time, all he could do was hide, muffle Callie's screams of terror, and hope Nikki didn't remember about them. When Emmy was born, Callie helped him protect her from their mother, but nothing could take away the threat of danger they confronted on a daily basis, and the fear that they lived with, knowing that they could depend on no one but themselves.

There were few adults in their lives other than the men Nikki brought home and took to her bedroom, and there was a steady stream of them. None of them really paid any attention to the children—the kind of men she chose weren't the fatherly type. Nikki was smart enough and beautiful enough to attract men who were ready only for a good time, since that was all she wanted. Most didn't even know the children's names. But the men did keep Nikki amused and out of the house a lot of the time, which made everything easier and safer for the kids.

When Matt got older, he realized that the chances of any of them surviving long term with Nikki getting more and more insane and destructive were slim indeed, and he went to the adults in their lives and asked for help. No one was willing to confront Nikki. They all sympathized—Ben, who was Matt and Callie's father; Bobbie, Nikki's sister; Murdoch, the best of Nikki's boyfriends—but no one was willing to take a chance on Nikki's temper and her finely developed talent for revenge. And while Child Protective Services might have gotten them out of their home, it would most likely have split them up, and then returned them to Nikki when she got her act together long enough to act like a sane and loving mother—which she could, when she needed to.

Murdoch was with them for only one summer, the miracle summer, Matt called it, but that was far longer than anyone else had been with Nikki, and longer than she had managed to stay stable (at least in front of Murdoch) for years. But by Labor Day weekend, when Nikki dumped the kids on Murdoch without any warning and left them there for almost a week, Matt knew it was over. But that wasn't all he'd learned—he'd realized just how insane their lives really were. Being with Murdoch had given them a glimpse of reality, a taste of what normality was like, and the contrast with their own lives was stark and bleak.

Finally, after Matt comes to him yet again for help, Murdoch begins to work quietly behind the scenes with Ben and Bobbie to cobble together a way to get the three children away from Nikki. And after Nikki's final meltdown, when she kidnaps Emmy and nearly kills her, their makeshift family finally succeeds in ending Nikki's custody of her children. But in this realistic and straightforward novel, this is not the ending, but a new beginning, with new problems and setbacks and frustrations and even regular meltdowns. It takes years for Nikki's malevolent influence to wane and allow them all some peace and safety, something the children have never known.

Yes, this book ends on a hopeful note, but not an unrealistic one. The insightful reader knows that all three of the children have years of struggle ahead of them, learning how to leave their years of living in fear behind them, and learning how to survive without the rules they had lived under for so long. What were those rules? Here they are, from the back of the hardback dust jacket.

*Matthew's Rules of Survival*

1. Sometimes, even the people who mean you harm are the same ones who say they love you.
2. Fear is your friend. When you feel it, act.
3. Protect the little ones.
4. If you coped before, you can cope now.
5. Always remember: In the end, the survivor gets to tell the story.

Werlin never lets go of the tension, and doesn't reveal or even hint at the problems that Matt, Callie, and Emmy face because of their years of following the rules, or how those years will impact their lives as adults and the rules and relationships they live with for the rest of their lives. But the discerning reader is forced to consider this and wonder if they will be able to un-limit their lives, after living under such rigid and limited circumstances for so long.

There is certainly much to consider, discuss, and educate in this finely crafted and difficult-to-read novel.

# 23

## *HOPE IN PATIENCE*
## BY BETH FEHLBAUM

**B**eth Fehlbaum doesn't write fiction, but she doesn't write nonfiction, either. She blends the two. In her Patience trilogy, she creates fictional characters in a setting and a situation that comes from her own deeply disturbing past. In doing so, she shows not only the horror of sexual abuse at the hands of a stepfather, but also the destructiveness of a mother who chooses over and over, not to believe her daughter and also to stand up for and support her husband. The protagonist, finally able to escape the abuse, is left to find her own way back to emotional health and normalcy, assisted by adults who are able to demonstrate to her what those are. The books have been praised for their "courageous and accurate portrayal of the many small steps that lead toward psychological healing,"[1] "testament to the strength and resilience of the human spirit",[2] "intimate portrayal of the impact of [sexual] abuse and PTSD . . . [in which] emotions . . . ring true [and the] . . . intense, graphic scenarios . . . including Ashley's descriptions of her physical abuse and her occasional self-mutilations,"[3] and "true testament to the strength and resilience of the human spirit. Written with elegance and fearless honesty, . . . [it is] quite simply a must-read for anyone who suffered abuse."[4]

Fehlbaum began writing her first novel at the suggestion of her therapist, as a way of confronting and putting behind her what she had experienced as a child. It took a while to get started because she kept getting stuck in her own memories and anger at the people who victimized her. It took seeing her protagonist as someone else other than herself to begin to put the pieces of Ashley's story together. She wrote for herself, and didn't consider having it published until she had actually finished it and realized that she did not have a story of abuse, but one of *surviving abuse,* a story of hope, rather than one of despair.[5] She wanted to show that while recovering from childhood sexual abuse is one of the most difficult things an individual can do, it is possible. It is also possible to not just recover and survive, but also to succeed at life itself, and to become stronger than ever.[6] Fehlbaum's life today is an excellent example of that philosophy, as she is successful as a teacher, an advocate, and an individual, with a strong marriage and happy family life.[7]

Fehlbaum's day job is a middle school teacher, and she has excellent advice on how teachers can learn to be aware of signs of abuse, and learn how to respond to them in ways that are most helpful to and supportive of the student.[8] She knows the statistics— 25 percent of children in any school classroom either have experienced abuse of some kind or will experience it at some point of their lives. She also realizes the reality of Abraham Maslow's Hierarchy of Needs, and that physiological and safety needs (food, water, air, sleep, safety of body, home, health, and family) must be met before children (or adults) are able to deal with any of the higher needs, among them social skills, academic progression, and success. It's difficult to focus on the lesson of the day when you've spent the previous night hiding in the closet to escape the abuser waiting down the hall, or to focus on becoming friends with peers you can't invite to your home because of the dysfunctional family system that exists there.[9]

Given that Fehlbaum has a therapeutic, supportive approach to first approaching and then working with students she suspects are being abused, it is no surprise that one of her favorite authors is Chris Crutcher,[10] a family therapist who also includes therapeutic aspects in his books, including characters who are therapists for teens in difficult or desperate family situations. *Ironman* and *Whale Talk* are excellent examples of this, and both have been widely challenged, as have other of his books, because of the unrelenting reality of his depiction of abusive characters.

Fehlbaum didn't depend only on her own memories when writing *Hope in Patience*; she also researched the book carefully, so as to maximize the accuracy and realism of the individuals, settings, and situations in the book. She consulted legal, law enforcement, and therapeutic adult experts, and talked with a variety of teens about what their experiences with abuse had been, and what it is like growing up different in a small town. Even the classroom lessons taught in the high school Ashley goes to were vetted for accuracy with professionals in the same areas.[11]

Ashley's story opens as she wakes up from a frequent nightmare—Charlie, her stepfather, is standing over her, about to molest her. As she sits up in bed, shaking and finally awake, she realizes she's safe in her own bedroom in her father's house. The hell she lived through for six years is finally over. She no longer has be afraid. She survived. However, she does have to figure out how to go on with her life, and begin looking ahead at her future, not back at her past.

Her life changed that weekend afternoon last May, while her mother was getting them a pizza for supper and made Ashley stay home with Charlie, who'd been squirting them with a water gun. Ashley remembered only flashes of what happened next. She knew she'd been running away from Charlie, and he was chasing her, and then he tackled her and she fell down flat on her face. Then she blacked out, and when she woke up, she was covered with blood from her waist down. When her mother wanted to know what had happened, she said that Charlie had been molesting her for years, but her mother just blew her off.

The next day in school, Ashley was really spacy, and her best friend made her tell a teacher what had happened. The teacher called Child Protective Services, and a couple of hours later, a doctor's exam proved what she'd already known—Charlie had raped her, "back and front." The hospital called the police, and Charlie was arrested, and CPS called Ashley's father. She couldn't go back to her home—her mother said she was a slut who liked it rough. Her mother's parents loved Charlie and wanted nothing to do with their granddaughter. There were only two choices, David, her father, or the emergency shelter.

That's how Ashley ended up in Patience, Texas, a small rural town in the Big Thicket area of East Texas, where she found a family, friends, a support system, and a psychologist who helped her see herself and her past more accurately than she could alone, so she was able to begin to move toward a future that was full of love and hope. She was no longer stuck in her past, looking over her shoulder, but facing the future knowing that it would be as bright as she could make it.

What lies ahead for Ashley? *Truth in Patience* begins where *Hope in Patience* ended, as Ashley begins to see more clearly that recovering from sexual abuse is a journey made up of many steps, only a few of which she has taken. As Dr. Matt, her psychologist puts it, it's like walking barefoot from Texas to Alaska and back. It's the hardest thing you've ever done, and it takes a long time to accomplish it. Ashley's journey has just begun.

Fehlbaum has recently moved to a new publisher and is rewriting the Patience trilogy; she expects to publish it beginning in 2017, including in Ashley's stories the growth and insights she has gained since 2008, when the first book was published. She looks forward to sharing Ashley's story with a new generation of teens.

# 24

## *WHAT HAPPENED TO CASS MCBRIDE?*
## BY GAIL GILES

Gail Giles wrote *What Happened to Cass McBride?* during her last winter in Alaska. It was a tough time for her in several ways. First of all, it was a snowy winter—a record breaking snowy winter, with short days and long, dark nights. (Alaska usually gets about three to five hours of daylight a day during the winter, depending on how far north you are. In the Arctic, there is a period of about two months when the sun doesn't ever rise above the horizon.) There was a snow pack of eighteen feet, and they lived in a single-story house. When Giles looked out her windows all she saw was snow piled against the glass, snow way over her head. She felt buried alive, claustrophobic, and unable to do anything about it. If she wanted to go somewhere, she had to use snow tunnels dug by the snowplows. It felt surreal to her. [1]

At the same time, she was also stuck about what she was writing, letting things said to her matter more than they usually did. That led her to start thinking about the power of words—the kind of offhand remark that had her stymied, almost paralyzed every time she sat down at the computer. The things we say, the things we don't say, and how words and the amount of attention we pay them change and control our lives. How words can be used, misused, not used, and the harm that they can do, whether intentionally or not. All of this led up to Cass McBride's birth and burial.[2]

Giles believes strongly in the power of words to change lives, and it's one reason she writes the psychological thrillers that she writes. She feels that too many books are "too soft," with happy endings, neatly tied in bows, giving readers the impression that they somehow reflect real life, when many times they do not. While teaching remedial reading at a Texas high school, she discovered that one reason her students didn't like to read was that their lives were not reflected in the books available to them. They had nothing to identify and connect with. So Giles decided to write books those students would want to read—books that said there weren't always happy endings, that said saying "I'm sorry" isn't always enough, and sometimes doesn't make any difference at all. Real life is not always pleasant, and while dark paths may look exciting and intriguing, they are also dangerous, and don't allow room for changing your mind once you have started down them. Frequently, they end with harsh lessons painfully learned, what Giles calls "the abyss" into which the unwary can fall, only to discover there's no way out.[3] Giles's titles warn her readers of those dangers, and perhaps also persuade some of them to stay away from those darkest paths. She also writes from the perspective of someone who didn't grow up in a "warm and fuzzy" home, and didn't really feel safe there. She grew up (as I did) in a time when it was acceptable and expected for parents to discipline their children by hitting or whipping them, or by using cruel and crushing words. Life for many children and teens was both physically and emotionally risky. Her way out was books, and she wants her books to give today's teens the same opportunity to escape and to learn how to find solutions that will improve their lives and their ability to respond appropriately to danger. She wants them to let kids know there are ways out that don't involve those dark pathways.[4]

Giles is also curious about why people do what they do, why they make the wrong decisions, why they continue to walk down paths that will lead to destruction. If we know the why of what we are doing, is it easier to stop doing it? What keeps us on paths we know aren't the best ones for us? Are people born with a genetic bent to go wrong, or does something happen in their lives that turns them in that direction?[5] She believes that many times it is our insecurities that make us take actions we otherwise might not.[6] This is one of the central themes in *What Happened to Cass McBride?* Why did Kyle do what he did to Cass? Yes, he had been severely emotionally abused by one of the most despicable mothers I have ever met in YA fiction, and was traumatized by his brother's death, but his home life alone wasn't enough to take him over the edge.[7] He made a cold and deliberate choice, and took deliberate measures to carry out his plans. He was methodical, not impulsive. While he had been victimized, he was not a victim himself.[8] He chose his path, rather than having it thrust upon him. He lived with a monster, but he didn't have to become one himself. Cass wasn't given a choice, however. Kyle made that choice for her. Her only choice was to outwit Kyle and survive or to give in and go insane.

And if Kyle isn't a sympathetic character, neither is Cass. She lives with her father after totally rejecting her mother, and has totally bought into his salesman philosophy. She is driven, self-centered, and well aware of her position as one of the popular crowd at school. When dorky David asks her out, she turns him down politely, then makes a snarky comment about it in a note that is meant for her best friend but is intercepted by David. Shortly afterward, he hangs himself in his front yard with a suicide note pinned to his chest that says, "Words are teeth. And they eat me alive. Feed on my corpse instead." His older brother, Kyle, immediately decides that Cass's note was the reason his brother killed himself, and sets out to get his revenge.

He decides to bury her alive and jerry-rigs a coffin with an air supply and tapes a walkie-talkie to her hand so they can talk. He kidnaps her, drugs her, and buries her. She wakes up in a box just barely big enough for her, and with no way out. From then on, it is first Cass against herself and then against Kyle, as she decides to talk her way out of the box by making him see that David's death is not her fault.

There are three narrators to the story, Kyle and Cass, of course, and also Ben, the police detective in charge of the case, who is determined to find Cass before she dies. But first he has to figure out why she disappeared, who took her, and where she is. Finding the answers is no easy process. Giles writes in short, pithy chapters that keep the reader engaged. Each narrator has his or her own typeface, making it easy to see who is speaking, as the plot is gradually unraveled.

The ending is pure, unadulterated Giles, as it gives no real answers or glimpses of the future. Cass's voice is the last voice we hear, still talking in the night, no longer buried alive, but now shut up in a box of her own making, from which she may never emerge. It is a stark and haunting scene that is impossible to forget. The world is waiting for Cass, and all she has to do is reach out and grab it—we can see it so easily, and Cass is so blind to it. She has come so close, and yet has so far to go.

It is the book that Giles found most difficult to write, and that readers find equally difficult to read. It is a brief book, and the action spans only a few days, yet it is impossible to forget. The power of words to help and to harm, to imprison or to set free. Kyle set out to imprison Cass, yet as the book ends he is the one imprisoned and restricted from going his own way and making his own choices. Cass is free to live her life and make her choices, yet she is just as imprisoned as Kyle.

# 25

# *THE CHOSEN ONE*
# BY CAROL LYNCH WILLIAMS

**W**hen Carol Lynch Williams heard the story of a young girl living in an isolated religious community, who ran away because she was being forced to marry a much older man who was actually related to her, who was found, dragged home, and beaten, yet ran away again as soon as she could, she knew that one day she would write a book about it.[1] But it took years for her to begin. It was a difficult book to write, she says, and it took time to percolate.[2] She also wanted to show the difference between polygamous groups and the Mormon Church, or the Church of the Latter Day Saints, of which she is a member.[3] But before she could begin to write, she had to do a huge amount of research on polygamous groups, their beliefs, and their characteristics. While some of the situations and characters in the book are based on real life—the beatings, the forced marriages, the disciplining of children including infants in various ways—others, such as Patrick's story, are purely fiction. While the majority of her research was online, she also watched and read news stories and positive and negative accounts of polygamous communities.[4]

Williams felt very connected to the topic and to her research, but freely admits that it was a depressing subject to immerse herself in.[5] Her research resulted in a problem frequently encountered by writers: what to include and what to leave out. She had to create a whole religion and a strict and rigid community that believed in it. She had to explain the tenets of that religion and the rules of the community. She had a character—but that was all. How was she going to include the necessary backstory while keeping her readers interested in her character?[6]

Williams decided to make her community a group of "severe" polygamists—ones who believed in older men marrying younger girls, some while they were still teens, making for a more dramatic story. There are many types of polygamous groups and beliefs around the world, but Williams wanted her readers to have something in the book and its central character that teens would be able to identify with, so she set it in the southwest desert of the United States. The Chosen Ones represent the more extreme type of polygamous communities, with leaders who are rigid, cruel, and convinced of their own righteousness. They enforce the rules of the community without any mercy or flexibility. Children, even infants, are punished as severely as adults. Disobedience results in physical abuse and torture. They rule with threats of violence and fear. There is little doubt that these men are fearsome and dangerous people to those both within and without the community. The possibility of death at their hands is very real, which makes the risks Kyra takes that much more dangerous.

In addition, the community is fenced and guarded, both to keep outsiders and their sinful ideas and appearance outside, and to keep the community members inside and isolated. There is no radio or television, and members leave the community only under close supervision. The only members permitted to speak to outsiders when they are outside the community's fenced property line are the most senior of the men or their wives. And there are always members who will not hesitate to report even minor infractions, whether they happen on the outside or the inside.

But Williams wanted a way for Kyra to escape the community, to find out about the larger world outside the tall chain link fences that surround it. So she gives her a way into the world of books, books that are forbidden, because any reading material other than what is approved of by the community leaders is forbidden and members are severely punished if they are caught reading it. Kyra meets Patrick, who drives the local bookmobile on a route that goes close to the fence enclosing the community. That first meeting changes the course of Kyra's life completely and irrevocably.

Getting a library card means that she can sneak away from the community and read about the outside world she's seen little of. She learns of the ideas, the opportunities, and the freedoms she has missed out on, and when she's told she will have to marry her sixty-year-old uncle, she rebels, and tries to escape. When that fails, and she is returned to the discipline of the community leaders, she's told that leaving again may result in death—others who defied the decisions of the elders have been killed for their sins. Those who rule the community will brook no disobedience, and harsh punishment of those who defy and disobey the elders' pronouncements will help the others in the community remember not to follow their examples. Once a decision is made, it becomes law, and laws are not to be broken without swift and harsh punishments.

Not every novel catches the reader's attention with the very first sentence, but *The Chosen One* does: "'If I was going to kill the Prophet,' I say, not even keeping my voice low, 'I'd do it in Africa.'" She is speaking to her youngest sister, Mariah, who's only eight months old. Kyra doesn't know it, but in just a few hours her life will change forever. The Prophet, the leader of their community, has had a vision, and decided that Kyra is to be married, married to her father's cruel older brother, Hyrum, who is sixty years old, already has seven wives, and is well known for punishing them harshly for any infraction of his rules.

Predictably, Kyra rebels, and flees to Joshua, the boy she is in love with and wants to marry. The boy she has kissed, the boy she has held hands with, the boy who doesn't want three wives to ensure he gets into heaven. The boy who wants only her, only one wife.

Love matches had been permitted with the previous Prophet, but not under Prophet Childs, who decides who will marry whom. The girls are saved for the old men who are closest to the Prophet. Kyra can't remember the last time a young girl married a young boy. The Prophet decides when the girls are ready to begin to have babies and then selects the person they will marry. Women and girls are kept pregnant as much of the time as possible, and some have babies annually, even the ones whose children are stillborn or die in infancy, or the older women for whom pregnancy is physically dangerous, like Kyra's mother.

Joshua decides to appeal to the Prophet for permission to marry, but it results in even more punishment. He is severely beaten and cast out of the community with several other boys who have sinned in other ways. The Prophet says they will die in the desert long before they can reach the nearest town, just as all the other boys who have been cast out over the years have died.

And Hyrum himself beats Kyra to show her that she must obey him in all things, while the Prophet and his "God Squad" of sycophants looks on. She is left bloody and battered, her face wrecked, her arms, legs, and back covered with deep bruises. That night, Kyra's mother goes into labor, even though she is only seven months pregnant, because of her stress and worry about her daughter. The tiny girl dies after taking only a few breaths, and Kyra's mother may be near death as well.

The next day, the Prophet comes to threaten Kyra's father and warn him to keep his girls in line or they will be taken away from him and given to other men, where their punishment will be harsh and long lived. After he leaves, Kyra confesses to her relationship with Joshua, devastating her family. But she doesn't tell them about her other sin—the bookmobile and the books she has been reading, and the friend she has made in Patrick, who drives the bookmobile and tells her about his wife and little boy, and the books they like to read.

Kyra has always taken walks, ever since she was a small child, first with her parents or one of her twenty siblings, later all alone. People have gotten used to seeing her walking, beyond the fences, beyond the property line, out near the highway that leads to places she can only dream of. The community is isolated, and few cars come along the highway, but one day a week the bookmobile drives by. Kyra frequently goes to see it, and one day it stops, and Patrick, the driver, offers her a library card. That's the beginning of Kyra's discovery of the world outside her community, from *Bridge to Tera-bithia* to *Harry Potter and the Sorcerer's Stone* to the books she remembered reading with her little sisters, like Dr. Seuss and other picture books. But that was before Prophet Childs said that books from outside the community were from Satan and ordered that all of them had to be burned. Kyra had created a hideaway in one of the Russian olive trees near her mother's trailer, and she was able to hide the books there, sneaking away when she could to read. She told no one about the books except Joshua and dreamed of the day when they could read them together.

But after her beating, when she went to the bookmobile, Patrick is appalled that she's been beaten, and Kyra confesses everything—having to marry her sixty-year-old uncle, Joshua, the baby sister who died so quickly, the beatings, and how anyone who speaks out against the Prophet or tries to leave the community is beaten and sometimes killed. Patrick immediately decides to take Kyra out of the county, only a few miles down the road, so she can call the police. She can live with him and his wife for as long as she wants to. Unfortunately, the bookmobile is old and not built for speed, and the "God Squad" catches up with them. They run the bookmobile off the road, and capture Patrick. Just before he's taken away, he manages to tell Kyra where his cell phone and a spare key to the bookmobile are. She never sees him again. The next day, the book-mobile is parked where it was every week, and when Kyra peeks in the window, and sees the interior covered with blood, she knows that Patrick is dead.

This is her final breaking point. Joshua is gone; her face and body are battered, with the promise of more punishment to come; her youngest sister is dead; and her mother may die too. She knows she cannot marry Hyrum, and even if she does, it's no guarantee that her sacrifice will save her family. She gets up in the middle of the night, cuts her wedding dress into tiny strips, scatters them over Hyrum's front porch and bushes, goes to the bookmobile, finds the key, turns on the cell phone, and drives away. Patrick said she'd get cell service when she got to the county line, and then she could call 911 and ask for help.

And she manages to do just that, in spite of the "God Squad" chasing her and shooting at her. She tells the detectives at the police station about everything—Patrick's death, Joshua and the other boys, the dead children, the forced marriages, the beatings, the punishments, the young girls being saved for the old men, the book burnings, and the rules of the Prophet and how everything changed when Prophet Childs became the community leader. She is safe, but she has given up everything in her whole life, with no promise that she will be able to survive in the new world she will now live in, and only uncertainty about ever seeing Joshua and her family again. She has escaped, but at what cost?

Like many YA novels, this is another one that just stops, rather than coming to a predictable ending. Williams leaves plenty of room for discussion and speculation about what might happen in Kyra's future. Like *Hope in Patience*, it is a hopeful ending, but not a happy one.

# Part V

# Manipulators: Rapists, Kidnappers, and Other Predators

Of all of the human monsters I have written about, these are the ones who are the most difficult to understand. They are people who may hide their evil beneath a beautiful or handsome face, people who may have tried and failed to hold their urges and obsessions in check, people who torture and kill simply for the pleasure of it. Of all the minds I have peered into, these are the most evil, the darkest. But this is why this final section is so important—because they have the ability to hide in plain sight and appear normal, until the victim is captured, the door is shut, and they are free to do as they please.

The headlines are full of stories of children who are abducted, raped, or abused in other ways. Parents wonder how to bring up their children in a culture of fear, and how to educate their children about the risks in society without teaching them to hate and fear those who aren't like them. Statistics are alarming. Thinking it will never happen to me or my town works only until it does happen.

According to the National Center for Missing and Exploited Children, there is no way to know how many children are missing, because many such cases are not reported. According to the FBI, in

2014 there were over four hundred fifty thousand children reported missing, slightly more than were reported in 2013. But each time a file is updated, it adds to the total. That means that one case, updated five times, would look like five separate cases.[1] Other statistics offer different numbers.

According to *Parents* magazine, every forty seconds a child is abducted or reported missing—about two thousand a day. About half of those cases are family kidnappings, where the perpetrator is a parent or other relative, about a quarter are acquaintance kidnappings, where the victim knows the kidnapper, and the remaining quarter are stranger kidnappings, where the victim doesn't know the kidnapper.[2] This latter group includes both those children who are stalked by their kidnapper, or those kidnappings that are planned, as well as those that are spontaneous or spur of the moment.

Family kidnappings are most often committed by parents, and occur most frequently with children who are younger than six. Acquaintance kidnapping has the highest percentage of injured victims, occurs at homes or residences, and has the largest percentage of teenage victims. Stranger kidnappings usually happen at outdoor locations, and the victims are more frequently girls. It is generally, but not always, associated with sexual assaults on the girls and robberies of the boys. It is the kind of kidnapping that is most closely associated with the use of a firearm. About 75 percent of nonfamily (acquaintance or stranger) abductions are girls.[3] Thankfully, only about one in ten thousand missing children reported to local police are not found alive, although about 20 percent of the children reported to the National Center for Missing and Exploited Children (more than ten thousand in 2014) are not found alive, and one in six were likely to be involved in child sexual trafficking.[4] In recent years, Amber Alerts and calls to the Cybertips line at NCMEC have helped in recovering hundreds of missing children, but more needs to be done. Eighty percent of stranger abductions take place within a quarter mile of the child's home when the child is lured to a stranger's car or is snatched off the street. Fast action is essential—almost three-quarters of abducted children who are killed die within three hours of being taken.[5]

In 2013, the *Washington Post* published five myths about abducted or missing children, which are worth examination. The first of these is reflected in the statistics above: *Most abductions are done by strangers.* In fact, stranger abductions account for only about .01 percent of all missing children, according to the last comprehensive study, using information from 1999. The second myth says that *more and more children are missing every year.* In truth, the number of missing people, both children and adults, is declining. FBI figures show a 31 percent drop between 1997 and 2011. There is little doubt that this figure is partly due to increased cell phone use—parents are able to track their children more easily, and those who are in accidents of various kinds are able to call for help. Third myth: *the Internet had made kidnapping easier.* There are many reasons why the opposite is true: online activity leaves tracks, and online predators can be traced. Parents and other responsible adults are educating their children about online dangers and becoming more proactive in controlling Internet access. Fourth, *preventing abductions means teaching children to fear strangers.* To begin with, everyone is a stranger at first, and children are much more likely to be kidnapped by someone they know, or who is at least familiar to them, than by strangers. Rather than teaching them to fear, it's important to teach them the signs of dangerous behaviors— inappropriate touching, trying to get them alone, asking too-personal questions, trying to control them, or using weapons. Children need to know what to do when the situation becomes uncomfortable for them, how to say no, how to get away, and how to get help. Finally, *the goal is to bring the children back to their families.* For many children, that's an appropriate goal, but for others who ran away because of family conflicts or abuse from parents or siblings, putting them back into that dangerous and frightening environment can make the situation worse. Now the child will not only have to deal with all the stressors with which he or she was coping before, but with additional stress or condemnation as a result of running away.[6]

There have also been headlines about priests manipulating the younger members of their congregations, about Internet predators taking advantage of naive teens, and about human traffickers who buy and sell human beings. Manipulators exist everywhere, and teens need to be taught how to recognize them and their tactics. They tend to have psychopathic and narcissistic qualities, putting their own needs and preferences above anyone else's. But they also have the ability to concentrate completely on the task at hand, whether it is or isn't socially acceptable. Obsessing about something comes easily to them. They are also able to appear interesting, attractive, and exciting, and draw people to them. But there is little substance below the attractive surface, and no matter what they say and do, ultimately their actions will benefit themselves before anyone else. A master manipulator is able to create a façade of emotion in order to draw in his or her victim, gaining their empathy and sympathy. But when the victim least expects it, the manipulator pounces, and the victim is caught.[7]

Psychological manipulation involves changing someone's perceptions and even behavior. Manipulators work to benefit themselves, using methods that are exploitive, underhanded, and devious. They work to learn the vulnerabilities of their intended victims to gain power over them. While they can be extremely aggressive, they have learned to hide it. In addition, they are ruthless in their attack, uncaring about any psychological or physical damage the victims may suffer. They are detached from the conventional tenets of morality and see themselves as being above moral issues or questions.[8]

Manipulators can show up in positions of power, where they can be even more dangerous. Police officers have been trained to take control of situations and persuade suspects and perpetrators to say what the officers want to hear. Appearance is a part of this, including an authoritative voice and body language. Tone of voice is also a way to intimidate someone they want to influence. A variety of techniques can be used, ranging from a "good old boy" approach, to "good cop/bad cop" scenarios, to outright threats and physical punishments.[9]

Manipulators also can use denial and protests of innocence to convince the people around them that they are doing nothing wrong.

The most talented of them are skillful enough at this to make the victim or the observer question their own memory and perceptions. They are also able to justify their behavior, to make it appear normal or average, and to do this with a clear purpose of furthering their own goals.[10]

It is essential that teens (and adults too, for that matter) learn to recognize the signs of the manipulator and understand how to resist their attraction. Manipulators don't validate the feelings or actions of others unless it helps them toward their own goals. They take advantage of others' insecurities, playing passive-aggressive games with them. Belittling others in public when it will be the most embarrassing is another way of making other persons feel diminished, while the manipulators add to their own superiority. Not taking responsibility for their behavior, always finding someone else to blame, is another of their characteristics. The blame can go anyplace else, but it never rests on the manipulators' shoulders.[11]

In order to be able to persuade and twist people into doing what they want, manipulators have to have knowledge about them. Knowledge is power and the more they know about the other players in their sphere, the better. They can use this knowledge to divide and conquer, setting one person or faction against another. A situation with conflict between two or more groups is perfect for them if they are able to play puppet master and maneuver others so that they lose and the manipulators win.[12]

There is no doubt that these people exist in every level of society in a wide variety of situations and professions. I have seen them in almost all, if not every, book I have examined for this text. They are chameleons, able to take on any necessary coloration to hide their motives and actions. They are in families, in schools, online, at work, at play, and far too often in our heads, where they can do inestimable and long-lasting damage. Books that feature these evil souls are an essential part of young adult literature. While it may be unpleasant for parents and caring adults who work with teens, it is necessary to introduce young people to these hidden villains. They must be able to recognize the manipulators in their lives, no matter what faces they wear, so they will be able to outwit them, ignore them, report them, and render them powerless.

# 26

## *THIS GORGEOUS GAME*
## BY DONNA FREITAS

**D**onna Freitas writes because she loves to do it and can't imagine doing anything else that is as much fun. Her books begin when a character shows up in her head and won't stop talking to her. She even laughs with friends about the voices in her head, but she enjoys them and the stories they tell.[1]

Years before she began writing *This Gorgeous Game*, Freitas was stalked by someone she trusted, someone with so much position and power that it never occurred to her that he might fall for her, especially since there was no way that she would ever return his feelings. (She was courageous enough to include his name and titles in her acknowledgments at the end of the book.) She was able to escape, recover, and go on with her life, and when she became a writer, she thought that perhaps she'd write about the episode. But she soon realized that her memories were so repulsive and terrifying that she didn't want to immerse herself in her them to re-create the story. *This Gorgeous Game* might never have been written had Olivia not shown up in her mind, talking about her experiences and her fear. By the time Olivia had given her the first lines of her story, Freitas knew she had found the spokesperson who would help her tell her own experience. She wanted to let girls who are being stalked or who might someday be stalked to know that they are not powerless. No matter how revered or powerful or charismatic their stalker is, what they are being subjected to is wrong, and even if some people brush off their concerns, it is important to continue to tell those in authority what is happening and request, even demand, help.[2]

Writing this novel was an intense experience, made even more so when Freitas's editor told her she needed to go back to the beginning of Olivia's relationship with Father Mark, when she idolized him, and show the insidious process he used to try to tie her to him more and more closely. It was not what Freitas wanted to do—having escaped from that trap once, she didn't want to go back and relive it. She didn't want to be with Olivia during the time when she was eager to begin working with Father Mark, when she saw him as a figure of light, not one of darkness and evil. But she also realized that her editor was right—the whole progression of the relationship, from beginning to end, was a necessary part of the book—a necessary evil. Once the book was finished, Freitas was glad she had decided to tell the whole story. It allowed her to confront and conquer her own monsters, and in so doing, craft a tale that would allow her readers to recognize similar situations and similar monsters, and know that reaching out for help is a way out, even if that help doesn't come quickly.[3]

Freitas didn't mean for this to be an easy book to read, and it isn't. The tension builds constantly, almost forcing the reader to keep going, watching Olivia change from being engaged with life, excited, and eagerly looking to the future, to being threatened, doubting, unsure, and withdrawn. Finally she becomes hopeless, avoiding Father Mark and anyone else in her life who is close to her, afraid that telling what is happening to her will bring condemnation.[4]

The story is told completely from within Olivia's head, which makes it easy for the reader to identify with her and become caught up in her world. The reader is the only witness to her growing discomfort about Father Mark's actions, her questioning about how she might somehow be to blame for them, and whether or not anyone else would believe her. The fast-moving pace of the book makes the reader hold her breath, anxious to see what happens next, yet fearing it at the same time. It is a relief to the reader as much as it is to Olivia when someone finally believes her story and steps in to change things.

The contrast between Father Mark's reputation and the reality of what Olivia is experiencing from him becomes more and more intense. It is significant that what finally convinces her to ask for help is far more reprehensible than anything he has done before. In putting his feelings and intentions down on paper in a short story he gives to Olivia about how he sees the two of them, he finally condemns himself. Anyone reading it will know the wrongness of the relationship and pay close attention to Olivia's story of what she has been living through.

While this is a story that is deeply involved with faith, it is important to note that Freitas is not writing a diatribe against the Catholic Church or about priests who are pedophiles. She even comments at one point on the inappropriateness of what is happening in the Catholic priesthood, and that it must be stopped.[5] This is a story of one man, a man who is a priest, and his obsession with a girl in his community and in his power. Olivia's faith makes her situation even more difficult, because of Father Mark's position, but it was not destroyed by what happened to her. In fact, when she finally goes outside her family to ask for help, she goes to a nun who is less impressed with Father Mark than everyone else.[6] Ultimately, the people in Olivia's life who are able to save and support her are people of faith, who help her regain her own faith.[7] As a result, Olivia is able to separate Father Mark's role as a priest and his role as an obsessed stalker.

Freitas could conceivably have written the story using a man who wasn't a priest, omitting the question of faith. The emphasis is not just on the priest as a man of God, but on the wrongness of his actions, actions that would be equally wrong for *any* man. This is what makes the story universal, the idea that no matter what, stalking and obsession are wrong, and not the fault of the person being stalked.[8] It shows the power of the Catholic priesthood, and how that power can be, and is being, corrupted.

It is also important to note that Freitas is not describing pedophile priests about whom headlines are written. The relationship between Father Mark and Olivia never becomes physical, nor does it involve physical or verbal threats, which somehow makes it even more chilling.[9] It is never depicted as being romantic or sensual.[10] This makes it hard for Olivia to convince those around her that something is wrong, as Father Mark's attention moves from flattering to smothering and others are completely taken in by his charisma. The lack of sexual intimacy explains the victim's inability to describe exactly what the stalker has done wrong, because his actions seem to be innocuous and easily explained to someone not experiencing them personally. The teen being stalked may feel that confessing will be more likely to bring derision or disbelief than understanding, and because of that, she may refrain from speaking up.

It is important to note that the book is carefully and deliberately crafted, including its use of the initial Thomas Merton quote and later references to the Trappist monk, and how he fell in love with and pursued a young nurse who was caring for him while he recuperated from surgery. Freitas was also deliberate about the chapter titles. She patterned them after the way priests title their sermons or homilies, indicating the subject in the title: "On Love," "On Repentance," and so on, with Olivia as the priest, and her chapters the sermons she is sharing about what is happening to her. It felt important to Freitas to give Olivia that power and position, especially since she is being taken advantage of and terrified by a priest. She hopes readers will ponder the titles' layers of meaning, and their relationship to what is happening in their respective chapters.

The reader knows from the opening page of the prologue, which is set in the present, that something is wrong in Olivia's life, and that it centers around "him," who wants to mentor her, telling her she has such a wonderful, God-given talent that it would be a sin for her to waste it. It would be a sin for him not to help her nurture it. It would be a sin for her not to accept his help. And the pages he has given her to read for him, and discuss with him seem to glare at her from her bedroom table. Her phone rings, but she doesn't answer it.

She knows who's calling and why. She still has not read what he's written for her. Then her phone signals that she has a text—no, three of them. Confused, unwilling to see him or talk to him, she glares back at the stack of manuscript pages, and leaves the room, closing the door behind her.

Then the story travels back to the day that Olivia found out she had won the emerging writers contest, with its $10,000 scholarship, and would be mentored by her idol, Father Mark, and given a place in his college summer writing seminar. She can't believe it at first, especially how much Father Mark loves her writing. He wants to spend time with her, and showers her with phone calls, e-mails, texts, and invitations to coffee to discuss her writing. Her best friends, Jada and Ash, think it's a little creepy, but don't say anything for six weeks. By that time, Olivia is spending all her free time with Father Mark and has put off multiple invitations from her friends. Her world has become very narrow without her even realizing it. But when Jada and Ash bring it to her attention, Olivia sees how much she is giving up.

She and Jamie (a friend of her older sister's boyfriend, whom she was instantly attracted to) are also getting closer, and she wants to spend time with him as well. When he interrupts a session she is having with Father Mark in his campus office, the priest first ignores him and then is rude to him, Olivia recognizes that Father Mark is jealous of Jamie, and perhaps of anyone else in her life. When she leaves the session, he says he will see her in class in two weeks, and she is relieved that she will be free to make plans with her girlfriends, with Jamie, and with her older sister, Greenie, who is getting married, and wants Olivia to be her maid of honor. But his messages don't stop. Olivia decides to ignore them, and fills her days to the brim with what she wants to do—being a high school girl involved in doing things with her friends and family, and paying attention to her first important romance.

But Father Mark gets even more intense in his attempts to see and talk to Olivia—he follows her when she is with other people, and his messages of all kinds increase until she's afraid to answer her phone without checking to see who is calling. When class starts, it becomes obvious from the very first meeting that Olivia is his pet, something she's not only uncomfortable with, but tries desperately to avoid. It isn't until he invites himself to dinner at her house that she again realizes how charismatic he is, and how everyone around her admires and kowtows to him. Would anyone believe her if she told them how he is trying to take over her life?

The final straw comes when he forces her to accept a story that he has written, telling her she *must* read it, and then discuss it with him afterward. She refuses to give him the promise he wants, but she takes the story. She reads no more than the title before setting it aside, vowing she won't read it, no matter what Father Mark says. Olivia decides she will just ignore him, and hopes he will go away. Unfortunately, it doesn't work, and his attempts to contact her continue to increase, becoming more and more frantic and demanding.

Jamie and Olivia discuss what the priest is doing, and Jamie tells her that he thinks that there's something wrong with Father Mark. He isn't acting normal, the way he follows her around, calls her constantly even though Olivia never answers his calls, and leaves all kinds of little gifts for her at her home. Afraid to confess what is going on, Olivia makes excuses Jamie doesn't seem to accept.

The only time she sees Father Mark now is in class, and Jamie is always with her there, and they leave just as soon as class is over, so the priest doesn't have a chance to get her alone to talk to her. Finally, one afternoon she can't force herself to go to class, and calls Jamie to let him know she won't be there. Unfortunately, the phone rings just after they hang up and Olivia forgets to check who is calling before she answers, and it is Father Mark. He has to talk to her in person, he says, frustrated because not only will Olivia not answer his calls or respond to his messages, but her mother hasn't told her about all the times he has left requests for Olivia to call him back. He makes her promise to meet him after class, and she agrees, knowing she won't be there.

The next day, she goes to Starbuck's on her way to meet Jamie, and Father Mark catches her there. He forces her to talk to him, frantic to have her read his story and talk to him about it, becoming frighteningly intense when she doesn't respond as he wants her to.

When she finally leaves, he follows her, so she doesn't go to the meeting place where Jamie is waiting for her, but to her high school campus instead, where she heads for the chapel. Father Mark lets her go, but before he does, he steps close to her and kisses her. It's on her cheek, but it is so far beyond what is appropriate for their relationship that Olivia is frozen, unable to respond. She goes into the chapel to think and meets Sister June, her high school principal, who has come to pray. Olivia wants to tell her what is going on but is afraid she won't be believed, and leaves without confessing. Father Mark is waiting for her and follows her for several blocks, calling her name over and over. When she begins to run to get away from him, he stops, and she is able to get home.

When she gets there, she finally realizes she's going to have to read the story. She is horrified to discover that it is the story of a love affair, *their love affair*, based on the writings of the Trappist monk, Father Thomas Merton, whom Father Mark greatly admires. Merton fell in love with his young student nurse who was caring for him when he was in the hospital after surgery. She returned his love, and they had an affair. Just as Father Mark wants to have an affair with *her*. Olivia is horrified, repulsed, and terribly afraid. He has not just given her a story, he has given her a proposition, a proposition to have an affair with him, like Merton and his nurse. The first thing she does is run to the bathroom and throw up.

She is alone. There is no one she can turn to for help. There is no evidence to prove what he has done to her. There is nothing she can do. Until she realizes that she can use her talent to fight back. She is a writer, and she can write her story, her version of Father Mark's story. She sits for hours, tapping away at her laptop, ignoring all the people who want to talk to her. When she finishes, she feels lighter and more like herself than she has in months. Now it is *her* story, not his. Now she is ready to tell that story.

When she does, she discovers that she is not alone, and has never really been alone. There is evidence—mountains of text messages, voice mails, e-mails, and finally, the story. It's all there, and the picture it paints is damning. And Olivia doesn't even have to tell her own story—others are more than glad to tell it for her, first Jamie, then her family and friends, and as she listens, the story changes. It's the story of a smart, beautiful, popular girl who is stalked by a priest, taken advantage of by a priest. And *it's not her fault.* The blame belongs to Father Mark, who found ways to control and take advantage of her, who would not quit until finally she broke down and began to talk.

We don't find out what happens to Father Mark, only that he has left the university and his office is being packed and sent after him. But that's appropriate—this is Olivia's story, and what she cares about is that he is out of her life, not so much that he was punished for what he did. Freedom from him is what she wanted and needed, and finally, it's what she has.

# 27

# *CUT ME FREE*
# BY J. R. JOHANSSON

"**F**ear and pain can only imprison hope for so long,"[1] is how J. R. Johansson describes her recent book *Cut Me Free*, a thriller that involves horrific physical and emotional abuse, human trafficking, and the lengths to which courageous victims will go to escape and rebuild their lives. It began as a blend of two of Johansson's interests. The first was a writers' group that challenged her to write a story that involved a puppet in an attic. The second was the research that she'd done on child abuse and child trafficking and her desire to create a character that accurately depicted the effects, physical and psychological, of living through years of intense abuse, affecting the victim's physical health and status, emotional state, and psychological responses to the world after the abuse ended.[2] The resulting book is intense, painful to read, and hard to put down. Reviewers' opinions have been mixed, but all confirm that it is a chilling, brutal read.[3]

It took Johansson two months to plan the book, doing extensive research that must have been difficult for her to immerse herself in. She investigated the most sadistic, most brutal forms of torture, including men with "torture closets," where they keep a wide variety of weapons, tools, belts, whips, and other instruments used to inflict pain on the women and children in their control. When look-

ing at human trafficking, she must have encountered toxic people
willing to sell human beings for money. Much of what she knew
about the psychological effects of long-term abuse came from what
she learned because she minored in psychology in college, but she
admits to having to do more research on these topics because she
needed a "refresher" course.[4]

She also did extensive research on Philadelphia, when she fell in
love with the city while visiting her sister, who lived there. The
research made the city become a real character in the book, and
allowed the reader to walk the streets of the city just as her characters did.[5] Those familiar with the city will no doubt be able to locate
places in the book where they themselves have been.

After the planning and research process, Johansson was able to
write the first draft of the book in only two months. She noted that
once the main character, Piper/Charlotte, had come to life in her
mind, she felt compelled to keep writing until she had found an
ending. Then she spent six months rewriting and honing the novel
before she was satisfied with it.[6]

Johansson hopes readers will come away from the book with
more awareness, and the ability to notice things that they might
have overlooked previously.[7] Piper/Charlotte has a very educated
eye, after years of harsh and frightening abuse, and is able to read
the signs as easily as others recognize stereotypes in the people they
see on the street. She immediately knows as soon as she sees Sanda
in Rittenhouse Park, that she is being abused. She is being all but
dragged along by a man who emanates evil. Her hair and clothes are
dirty and shabby, and while she walks hand in hand with the man,
her hand is limp within his grasp. Her fear of him is all too easy for
Piper/Charlotte to see. It reminds her of her little brother Sam, who
didn't live long enough to escape—Sam, whom she failed, and who
lives as a voice in her mind, forcing her to take action.

People are complex, so Johansson makes her characters complex
as well, portraying them in shades of gray, rather than in black and
white.[8] She looks at the conflict within her characters, as well as
those between them and around them. Piper/Charlotte is an excellent example of this, as she argues with herself about the rightness

or wrongness of killing her parents, no matter how much they deserved it. She spent six years with her mother, who drank and abused her physically, with bruises, burns, and other "punishments." Then her mother decided she was tired of being abused by her husband, and offered up Piper in her stead. Piper spent ten years in the attic after that, let out only occasionally, and mostly for visits to the torture closet. She never went to school, and gained her knowledge of the outside world by watching the television through cracks in the attic floor. Their home was isolated, and the only people she saw were her parents and Sam, after he was born, and finally, for just a few weeks, her grandmother, who came to live with her son when she was dying of cancer. She hadn't known of the children's existence, and tried to rescue them when she found them. But her son and his wife were able to create a believable story for the cops, and so they did nothing.

When the chance for escape was presented, Piper didn't hesitate to use a shovel on her mother and a knife on her father. It was justified, there was no doubt about it, but Piper could not completely convince herself of it. This seems to be a reasonable response from a child who has spent virtually all her life being told that she was worthless and undeserving of anything good. She knows that what she did was wrong, and it is difficult for her to see the rightness of doing whatever it took to get herself out of the reach of her abusive, brutal, inhuman parents.

Piper/Charlotte also knows that rescuing Sanda is the right thing to do, and doesn't regret the actions that allowed her to do that. But her self-condemnation about killing three people prevents her from making connections with those around her, especially Cam. It is easier for her to connect with women than men—which also makes sense, since her torture at the hands of a man was so much longer and more intense than what she endured at her mother's hand.

The novel is made more intimate and more intense because the only perspective we see is Piper/Charlotte's. Her paranoia, her memories, her instinctive responses to anyone who tries to get near her or touch her, all combine to draw the reader into her world, where everyone is a threat, and no one is to be trusted.[9] The reader feels every flinch, every jump backward, every suspicion, as she twists everything to fit her distorted and twisted view of the world. Even Cam, whom she trusts to provide her with a new ID, who helps her find an apartment and a job, is held at an arm's length. She alternately pushes him away and then pulls him close again, showing the power of the demons that have just begun to loosen their grip on her. The reader can only watch and hope that she is able to stop going to extremes with him and figure out how to begin a more normal and accepting relationship.

Moving from an extremely brutal and obsessive situation, from a world with only four other people in it, to a world with many people, she has to decide to trust or not trust. Her fears and memories seem to jerk her from one extreme to another. Yet, when courage is necessary, Piper/Charlotte comes through. Terrified, wanting nothing more than to turn and run, she still fights back. And she takes the reader with her on her journey, seldom able to explain her actions rationally, unable to move beyond her memories, unwilling to take chances, even when they promise something good. Yet her determination to succeed never seems to waver, even when she has to learn to be welcoming and cordial as a restaurant hostess, learning to do what she herself has never experienced. She might not agree, but she has much to teach teens about strength, and courage, and survival.

Johansson also hopes that readers will find a sense of hope in the book, a sense that abuse can be overcome with courage, effort, and the support of others. While the ending doesn't resolve all the problems the characters have, there is hope that at least some of them will be able to survive. They have gone through all different kinds of violence and have fought back. It will influence what they do and how they do it, but it doesn't define who they are or who they will become.[10] They have learned how to survive by taking action to create change in their worlds.[11] Their survival skills have been hardlearned, costly, and painful, but the lessons they take into the future will serve them well. Not everyone in similar situations will be able to survive, but it is important to remember not only that some will, but *how* they will. Johansson's goal is to write books that deal with the dark side of life, but that also show at least glimpses of the lighter side, and allow discussion of both sides in a safe environment.[12]

It's taken her a year, but Piper is exhilarated by downtown Philadelphia, the skyscrapers surrounding her in the middle of Rittenhouse Square, the people around her living their own lives, free do to whatever they please. Somehow they all make her feel safe—something that has not happened very often in her life. She is waiting for the man whom she hopes will give her a new life, a new identity, a chance to start all over again.

But then her attention is caught by a couple walking past her—a girl holding hands with a man. Suddenly a cold feeling spreads through her, because she sees what others don't notice—the bruises on the girl's arm before she pulls her sleeve down, the way the man clutches her hand, but the girl does not hold on to his hand. Hers lies quietly in his as he tugs her along, a prisoner. His prisoner. The same aura of evil, of blackness, that he carries within him, just like her father did. The girl's dirty dark hair falls around her face. She flinches when the man raises his arm to scratch his shoulder. She is hiding, hiding in plain sight, and Piper is the only one who sees. The voice in her head, Sam's voice, whispers to her—*You have to help her. No one else will.* But as they disappear in the distance, Piper knows that there's little she can do.

Then her attention is drawn to the boy who has walked up behind her. It's Cam, the person she was waiting for, the one everyone she has talked to says is the best in the city at making fake IDs. Getting a new identity isn't cheap, $7,000, but his work is supposed to be as good as the real thing. Piper is sure that no one is after her—she doesn't think her parents survived her attack—but just in case, a new identity will make her harder to find. The next morning, after her hair is cut and dyed, Piper becomes Charlotte, Charlotte Thompson, who is eighteen and has a GED. Soon, with Cam's help, she has an apartment and a job. But she hasn't forgotten the little girl in the pink coat she saw in the park.

She waits until she sees the girl and the man again, and follows them to their apartment, where she discovers that the girl lives in a cubbyhole underneath the stairs, locked in, unable to escape. With Sam's constant whispering in her mind, she knows she has to get the girl away from him. And she does, leaving the man unconscious as a fire lit by his cigarette begins to burn his clothes. The entire apartment house is destroyed, and both Piper/Charlotte and Sanda are safe, and Piper/Charlotte can give Sanda the world she deserves, the world that Piper/Charlotte never had.

Or are they? In only a few days, Piper/Charlotte is sure someone is watching her—her finely honed sense of survival says so. But she's unable to see or hear anyone. Then she comes home one day to find a black box outside her apartment door, addressed to Piper. But no one knows her name! No one but Cam and his assistant Lily. Who has found her, and how?

The tension winds up more and more tightly—there are more boxes, a man is watching the apartment, and finally it's broken into. Everyone is in danger—Piper/Charlotte, Sanda, Janice, her landlady who lives downstairs with her granddaughter Rachel, Cam, Lily—and Piper/Charlotte knows she has to do something to find out who is stalking her and how to make him stop.

The ending is dramatic, even sensational, as Piper/Charlotte struggles to save herself and her friends. But Johansson's lesson of hope comes through in the end. The only people who die are the ones that need to, and while we don't know what will happen in the future, for now everyone is safe and at peace.

# 28

# *RUTHLESS*
# BY CAROLYN LEE ADAMS

Carolyn Lee Adams was born to write horror. She was born on Halloween. Her mother read to her when she was a young child, but unlike most mothers, she chose Edgar Allen Poe and dark, haunting poems like "Richard Cory" by Edwin Arlington Robinson. Plus, Adams grew up near King County, Washington, the dumping grounds of the most prolific serial killer in the United States, Gary Ridgeway, the Green River Killer.[1] Everyone she knew was changed by the experience of knowing that so many dead bodies had been found so close to home.[2] Ridgeway was convicted of forty-nine deaths, but confessed to nearly twice that many.[3] By the time she was in sixth grade, she was reading Stephen King, and her future was set in stone.[4]

*Ruthless* started as a dream. Adams dreamed the first three chapters, woke up and wrote them down.[5] Ruth was right there, a fully formed character.[6] She was revising a previously written but unpublished book, and intended to start on Ruth's story after she finished it,[7] but Ruth's voice was so insistent, refusing to be silenced, that she just had to stop and tell her story.[8] It took about a year from the first to the last page, but she had to quit writing for several months when she was about halfway through, because her marriage was ending, and she needed time to grieve.[9] She worked her way through her grief, and when she picked up the novel again, she was writing about Ruth's escape into the woods, coming face to face with her own mortality, just as Adams was coming face to face with the death of her marriage. When she was able to go back to her book later, she realized that when Ruth has made her peace with death, Adams had made peace with her divorce. She had overcome her demons as she wrote.[10]

She showed the first draft to a friend who was an editor, who told her what Adams already knew but didn't want to admit. It's a two-person book, essentially, and while Ruth was a fully formed character, Wolfman was just a cardboard cutout, not inspiring any fear or dread at all. She had to go back and write his backstory. Why did he kidnap Ruth? What happened to him that made him want revenge so ferociously?

It was not an easy revision, showing how a human being can become a cold and vicious predator, capable of unspeakable violence, and even addicted to killing, his vice of choice, no less alluring and seductive than drugs or alcohol. Adams ultimately decided to reveal his history in flashbacks, as he remembers turning points in his life that set him on a collision course with Ruth. This may be because Adams found him so difficult to write. His story arc is only about five thousand words, but they were the most difficult words Adams had ever had to write. Every day for a month, she'd sit down at her desk and write a couple of paragraphs, and then, sick to her stomach, get up and pace around her living room for a while, then go back and try to get down another few paragraphs. She was nauseated every day for the month it took her to write his story, yet it is the part of *Ruthless* that she is most proud of.[11]

The scene she found the most difficult to write is part of this backstory, when Jerry, who became the Wolfman, meets his first victim. Because Adams had been bullied by girls not unlike the ones who bully him, it was difficult to write. She had never truly dealt with those experiences and was able to use writing that flashback to help her confront her own past and let it go—one of the best things, she says, she got out of writing the book.[12]

When Adams is working on a book, her writing day generally starts with a few quotes from Conor McGregor, an Irish mixed martial arts fighter with the Ultimate Fighting Championship. Adams is a huge fan. Unlike some YA authors, she doesn't listen to music while she writes, finding it distracting. And when she gets stuck, she needs to have a window. It doesn't really matter what the view is, as long as there is something to look at while she tries to figure out how to get unstuck. When she's seriously stuck, and the view doesn't help, she takes a "thinking shower," and lets the white noise of the water act like an idea faucet, pouring solutions right into her brain. She notes that when she is her most productive, she is also *very* clean![13]

*Ruthless* was always Ruth's story, but she has a lot of Adams's characteristics in her, which made her sometimes difficult to write. Adams doesn't cut herself much slack for her shortcomings, and she was not inclined to give Ruth much either. In addition, Ruth is not a particularly likable character. She has a deep sense of entitlement, because she belongs to the Carver clan, and looks down her nose at anyone she considers lesser than they. Unfortunately, her best friend, Caleb, is a bona fide redneck, who lives in a trailer on the Carver ranch with his mother, complete with Wrangler jeans, cowboy boots, country sayings, and bad grammar. She knows he is in love with her, and she loves him as well, although she's never told him so. But Caleb is still her best friend and understands and accepts her more than anyone else does. She doesn't want to need him, but she does.[14] She calls him the other half of her soul. Many of the most difficult lessons Ruth has to learn during her time in the wilderness have to do with trust, loyalty, and romance.[15]

Five years before the story opens, Ruth won her first major riding competition, a twelve-year-old girl on a three-year-old horse, besting the top pros in the Worlds competition. It was a necessary win, an essential win, because it meant that her mother's horse farm would be put on the map, and she could get the kind of top clients that she needed to stay in business. And after she won, she knew she had to do it again, and again, and again. She had to stay on the top so her mother could stay on the top, too. She knew the responsibility for their success was on her shoulders. And maybe the success of her parents' marriage as well—there was less conflict when there was more money. Ruth didn't realize how the pressure had changed her, how well she had begun to fit her nickname, Ruthless. While Ruth does reveal some of her past in the main narrative, the story of the Worlds competition is told in flashbacks that highlight her relationships with her horse, her mother, and Caleb.

But for Ruth to change, she needs to see herself as others see her, something that the Wolfman is able to provide, since he has been following her for years. She needs to realize that she does indeed deserve her nickname, and that in taking on the burden of responsibility for the horse farm and its success, she has pushed away everyone who is close to her. It is an interesting twist that Wolfman, who wants to torture and kill her, is the person who gives her the clues she needs to change into the new Ruth, leaving the broken Ruth behind.

She has an epiphany the night she spends on the river, which is Adams's favorite scene in the whole book. Looking at the stars that fill the brilliant sky above her, drifting down the river in her little inflatable boat, Ruth releases her past and embraces her present in a way she has never done before. It is the heart of the novel, a time of reclamation and redemption, that empowers her as she moves into the last parts of her journey and her battle with the Wolfman. [16]

One of the things that makes this novel so gripping and engrossing is the seesawing changes in power between Ruth and the Wolfman. In the beginning, he has the power, then she snatches it from him, only to see him get it back. When she tries to get away in the woods, and he tracks her to the very tree she is hiding in, Ruth finally decides to shoot him. She does, only to discover that he isn't dead, just unconscious because he fell on a rock, hitting his head when she shot him. The bullet Ruth had hoped would kill him falls into her hand when she begins to search the body. This tension doesn't let up, as both characters grab the advantage as many times as they can. It is not until the very end that Ruth is finally able to make her voice heard and keep her own power for good.

Another thread that Adams explores is that of the attitude of a bystander to a plea for help. Several people in the novel refuse to help Ruth, no matter how she begs them. She seems to be in so much danger that it could rub off on them. The Logans are the first people who literally shut their doors to her, more concerned about their own safety than about the obviously wounded, mud-covered, naked girl who is begging them for help. They even refuse to call the police until long after Ruth has left the area. It is tempting to wonder how they reacted when the whole story was in the head- lines. Closer to the end of the book, Ruth tries to flag down several cars on the highway that refuse to stop, until she realizes too late that the one that did stop was driven by the Wolfman. And the gas station attendant who hears her cries for help turns his back on her, afraid to enter the darkness of the woods, although he does call 911 and alert the police, bringing the chase to an end.

Adams hopes that in addition to showing her readers the tenacity and persistence that it takes to survive on your own, they also take away from the book a willingness to fight. We all go through dark and difficult times, and when we are surrounded by darkness, it takes time and perseverance to get back to the light. We each have our own demons, as dangerous and painful as Ruth's were, and we all have to learn what is necessary to defeat them.

But Adams also would like for her readers to see the flip side of that willingness to fight our way out of the dark, and know that just as we are fighting, so are others around us. Life is full of torturous circumstances or situations, with accompanying trauma and pain, and no one remains unscathed. Darkness touches us all. No matter how perfect anyone acts on the outside, there is little doubt that they suffered through their own brand of darkness, and bear inner scars that are not visible on the face that they present to the world. She would have her readers remember that those they are fighting are fighting their own battles at the same time. We are shaped and molded by the battles we have fought and the outcomes we have reached.[17] Even Wolfman was once a tortured and unhappy child, unable to control his circumstances or his life.

Ruth woke up with a blinding headache, unable to see and unable to move. Gradually, she figures out that she is lying in a pile of manure in the bed of a moving pickup truck. She has been kidnapped. The truck stops, and she is pulled out of the dirt and shoved into the cab. Her hands and feet are tied. When she tries to question the man who has taken her, he knocks her out again, and when she wakes up, she is sitting in a wooden chair, still bound. No one answers when she calls out, and panicking at the thought of being alone in a strange place, she struggles with her bonds until she is free. She peels off the blindfold, and discovers that she is in an old cabin that smells of mildew, dust, and mold. Every surface is covered with garbage, and the cabin is surrounded by woods. She knocks out one of the windows and gets out, only to be immediately caught by the man who kidnapped her. He reminds her of a wolf, and so she decides to call him the Wolfman.

Ruth doesn't know who he is or why he's kidnapped her, but she is determined to get away. She's pretty sure someone will be looking for her, but no one will think to look in the middle of the woods. She is determined to escape, but she had no idea where she is or which direction she needs to go to find help and get home.

Her first conversation with the Wolfman gives her bits and pieces of information: he used to work for her father but was fired because he made her nervous, following her around. She's not the first girl he's kidnapped—there have been six others before her, all redheads, all dead and buried under the cabin. A phone call means that the man has to go to work, even though he is supposed to be on vacation so he can deal with her. He drugs her, wraps her up in rope like a mummy, and leaves.

When she wakes up, she notices a pile of panties on a table. Panties worn by little girls, not by teens like her. But she's very petite—maybe he thinks she's a little girl. She isn't, and she is determined to get free. There's a pile of magazines close enough for her to see the address labels. She memorizes his name and address.

When Wolfman comes back, he forces her to strip so he can wash her off with the outside hose. When he's distracted and aroused by her nakedness, she dashes into the forest, soaking wet and naked. The good news is that she's escaped. The bad news is that he's stopped chasing her and gone back to get his gun.

The chase starts there, as Ruth tries to figure out how to get away from a dangerous man who knows the woods far better than she does, and has the clothes, boots, and weapons that she lacks. When it gets dark, Ruth realizes her white body is too easy to see, so she rolls in mud until she looks more like the forest floor. She decides to double back and steal the Wolfman's truck and get back to civilization. But there are no real roads in the woods, only trails that lead to switchbacks and dead ends. Finally she sees a house, and hopes that it won't be deserted. It isn't, but the couple inside, the Logans, won't let her in and even refuse to call 911 for her. She gets some food out of their trash can and heads back into the woods. She finds another house, and also a hunting jacket and lots of rifles. But both her shoulders have been wounded, and the rifles are too heavy for her to pick up. There is a handgun, but only three bullets for it. When the Wolfman gets into the house, Ruth holds him at gunpoint with the empty gun, and ties him up. She cleans and bandages all the injuries she can reach, and then discovers that the Wolfman has escaped.

She heads back into the woods and finds a place in a tree where she thinks he won't find her, so she can sleep. But he tracks her right to the tree, and using her last bullet, she shoots him in the back. He falls, hitting his head on a rock with a loud crack. When Ruth searches the body, she discovers he has on a Kevlar vest and is unconscious only because of the rock he fell on. She takes what she can use from him, ties him up, and continues her escape. But she's bruised and battered, with a gash in her head, and terrible wounds on her feet from running through the forest. Both shoulders are damaged, and she is hungry and exhausted, as near death as she has been so far. She has collapsed, almost passing out, when she sees the ghosts of the six murdered girls, who lead her through the woods, leaving her when she hears the sound of rushing water. It is a huge river, and she finds a little inflatable boat beside it. She blows it up and patches it with the duct tape she took away from the Wolfman, and launches it into the river. That night she has a revelation, letting go of her past, and being profoundly grateful that she is here, in this present moment, able to experience it to the fullest.

The next morning, her boat has gone aground, and when she begins to explore, she finds mussels clinging to the rocks at the edge of the river, and eats them raw. She realizes something happened the previous night, something healing, something that has given her back her sanity and strength. She also realizes that she needs to communicate with her friends and family, knowing that although they must be searching for her, they may never find her. She prays for each of them, then she pushes her boat back into the river and continues on. But the river isn't as placid as it was the night before, and she has to steer her boat through one set of whitewater rapids after another. By the time she is through the last of them, it's dusk. During the afternoon, she heard the baying of hunting dogs and got a glimpse of a search and rescue helicopter, so she knows they are searching for her—but in the wrong place.

By the time she hears the sound of a car on a highway, it's foggy and she almost misses the bridge. But she is able to steer her little boat to shore and scramble out. When she gets to the highway, she tries to flag down two cars, but neither of them stop. Realizing that she must look a little scary, with the huge hunting jacket, a gun strapped over the T-shirt she has on underneath the jacket, and layers of athletic socks on her feet, she decides to lie down and play dead, thinking she'll look less scary if she isn't moving. A car does stop, but it's the Wolfman, and she is back in his power again. He hauls her into the cab of the pickup and starts to drive, but he has to use one arm to control Ruth, who is determined to get away. She bites him, hard, and when she sees a police car coming, manages to throw herself out of the truck.

When she wakes up she realizes that she is in worse shape than ever, and has broken several ribs when she fell. The policeman is dead. She sees Wolfman dragging him away. But she is close to civilization now, and knows that if she just keeps going, she will get help. She gets within sight of a gas station, and calls for help as loudly as she can. The attendant comes out to the edge of the woods to see who called for help, but the Wolfman has caught up with her and chokes her, preventing her from speaking. Hearing nothing, the man goes away.

Ruth decides to pretend to be dead, so the Wolfman will stop trying to kill her. It works, and he buries her in a shallow grave. Suddenly, she hears a siren coming closer and closer. She struggles to sit up, and someone pulls her out of the pit—she's been found.

Ruth doesn't really understand what is going on, and she fights her rescuers until one of them convinces her that she's safe. But as she is put on a gurney and headed to an ambulance, she sees the Wolfman in the crowd of people around her. Frantic, she tells her rescuers that her captor is there watching what's going on. She describes him, tells them his name and address, repeating herself over and over until they tell her he's been caught, and is in one of the police cars. Finally she is safe.

# 29

# *THE RAG AND BONE SHOP*
# BY ROBERT CORMIER

Robert Cormier's *Rag and Bone Shop* was his last book, and it was controversial at the time it came out. The book was unfinished at the time of his death, but what did "unfinished" mean? Reviewers speculated, coming to a variety of conclusions, but it was Connie Cormier, his widow, who had the final say. In a preface to the advance reading copy, she explained that Cormier loved to tinker with his books long after they were completed, trying to make them more right, more perfect. He had reached that point with *Rag and Bone Shop* when he died. So in one sense, it was incomplete. In another, it was complete, because he was doing his final tinkering, not making significant changes in the plot, characters, or the text.

Like most of Cormier's books, this final one is about the conflict between good and evil. Trent, a depressed and unhappy but manipulative police interrogator with a reputation for always getting a confession, no matter what, faces off with Jason, an innocent twelve-year-old boy, accused of the beating death of Alicia, the seven-year-old sister of one of his friends. The boy has no chance against Trent, who is more interested in getting a confession than finding the truth. Every word, every movement and gesture, every expression, is calculated. How can he make the boy confess?

But if Jason is set up by Trent, Trent is just as callously set up by the head of the local police force, who has become fixated on Jason because he was the last person to see Alicia alive. When Trent is called in, he's told that a local senator who knew Alicia would be willing to move him up the ladder professionally if he is successful at getting a confession. Burned out and tired of his profession, Trent is energized at the thought of getting special treatment from the influential senator. It is at this point that Trent becomes what he does rather than who he is and stops looking for the truth of what happened and focuses on getting a confession, no matter what that requires. His conviction about the boy's innocence, which grows as the interrogation progresses, doesn't hinder his determination to get a confession.

The bulk of the slim novel takes place in the small, crowded, hot interrogation room, where Trent and Jason sit opposite each other, knee to knee. Trent's dance of interrogation is chilling, frightening, and reminiscent of a cat playing with a captive bird or mouse. Jason wants to please Trent, to say what he wants him to say, while at the same time restating his innocence, over and over. The reader is caught in that small, uncomfortable room with them, and it is a relief when Trent finally leaves the room to get Jason something to drink. That such a break is needed and so welcomed by the reader is proof of Cormier's skill as a writer, and the level of tension he has created.

Of course, the ending is almost predictable. We all know from the moment Trent steps on stage that he will wrest a confession from Jason, one way or another. And he does. But he emerges from the interrogation room with Jason's confession, only to be told that the real killer, Alicia's brother, has admitted to the crime. Trent did what he was told to do—get a confession. But the cost is far more dear than he had expected. Cormier's coda takes the aftermath of the interrogation and gives it a twist, a final chance to show how thoroughly broken Jason is. It is one of the finest of Cormier's final twists, for which he is deservedly famous.

While Cormier's books focus on the battle between good and evil and the corruption of innocents' innocence, this one does so more succinctly and pointedly than any of his other titles. In the tiny interrogation room, we have two contrasted characters of the purest light and dark. Jason is young, naïve, by his own admission not that bright or sophisticated, enjoying the company of children younger than he because they look up to him and don't laugh at him. His peers make his life miserable, but mostly by ignoring him. They perceive him as too insignificant for them to bully or harass. He knows what they think but is at a loss about how to change their minds. He just hopes eighth grade will be better than seventh. He is a child who has not yet become acquainted with the darker side of life. He is willing to be interviewed to help find Alicia's killer, because she was his friend, and he enjoyed her "little old lady" ways and her ability to solve jigsaw puzzles.

In fact, when Trent begins to imply that Alicia might have been putting Jason down when she tried to teach him how to do a puzzle more quickly, Jason is confused. Why would he resent her for trying to help him? Trent has to lead him, step by step, cajoling him to change his perception of Alicia, until Jason has to admit that maybe that could have happened. But he doesn't really believe it.

Jason struggles not only with wanting to say what Trent wants to hear, but also with what he remembers about Alicia's last day alive. It was an ordinary day—the first day of summer vacation. Jason was free to do as he pleased—go swimming, ride his bike, finish his Stephen King book, go visit Alicia—the world was full of choices. But on such a day, when he had no plans, no deadlines, it's hard to remember the details of what he did and whom he saw. Trent pushes for those details until Jason toys with the idea of making up a suspicious stranger for him. But Jason is a truth teller and discards the idea almost as soon as it occurs to him.

Trent, in contrast, is one of Cormier's most evil characters, brought back from one of his earliest books to make one final appearance. Cormier didn't like to talk about his works in progress, but when he was writing *Rag and Bone Shop*, he had a chance to talk with Patty Campbell, his friend and biographer, and gave her a hint about his newest work, tentatively titled "The Interrogator." When she heard the title, she asked if the character was like Brint,

Adam's interrogator in *I Am the Cheese*. Cormier's response was that it *was* Brint, leaving her to puzzle over what he'd meant. Trent's deliberate, cunning manipulation is also reminiscent of another of Cormier's earliest characters, Brother Leon, from *The Chocolate War*. Both of them are focused on their own agendas to the exclusion of anything else, and they are willing to destroy anyone who gets in their way. However, when Trent's story ends, he seems to have some understanding of what he has done, and some regret about it. Brother Leon came to no such realization.

When considering Trent as an evil character it is important to remember that not only does he have doubts about Jason's guilt at the beginning of the interview, based on his body language, tone of voice, and general demeanor, he also has a "blazing moment" in the middle of the interview, when he realizes that Jason cannot possibly be guilty. His innocence is no longer in doubt, but a fact. Yet he shakes off that insight, shoves his humanity away, and gets back to the job at hand. Getting a confession, maintaining his perfect record of convictions, is more important than revealing the truth. The mind game he plays with Jason to convince the boy of his own guilt, twisting his words, anticipating his thoughts, and smoothly, persuasively reshaping them into something much more sinister, are all he concentrates on. He has no idea what is going on outside the interrogation room, nor how the case is progressing. And he doesn't care. All he cares about is the confession, no matter what he has to do to get it. The vision of this "blazing moment" will come back to haunt him, first when he learns the truth, and later when he looks at how his life will be different because of what he did in that small, hot room with a shy, scared, and intimidated young boy.

Cormier's last scene resembles other ambiguous endings in YA literature, notably among them the ending to Lois Lowry's *The Giver*, which gives no clue about what happens to Jonas. Trent has been vanquished and is likely to live his life in obscurity, a manipulative loser who forced an innocent to admit to a crime he did not commit. But he doesn't know what is going on in Jason's mind and life, as he thinks about what he did. He confessed to murder when he was innocent. Does that mean he could actually do it? If someone really deserved it?

The reader is left hanging, just as he has been at the end of so many of Cormier's other books. True to his readers, as always, Cormier once again dares to disturb not only his universe, but also those of his readers. There are many things to question: will Jason decide to become a murderer? Was he, perhaps, a murderer all along, and Trent merely helped him realize it? Was Brad's confession real, or the result of another case of a manipulative interviewer? And is Trent's life over, as "stuck in amber" as it seemed to him to be? Is there any redemption for him?

When his readers demanded to know what happened after the end of *The Chocolate War*, Cormier resisted writing a sequel, only to give in ten years later, writing *Beyond the Chocolate War*. This time, those readers will have to look inside themselves for answers to those questions—which is where Cormier preferred they go, anyway. His reply is simply, *"What do* you *think?"*

When the book opens, Trent is finishing up yet another successful interrogation, during which he has used all his skills to get Carl Seton to confess. It is a particularly vicious and brutal murder, a random and motiveless one that resulted in three unnecessary deaths. Once he has persuaded the murderer to share his story, Trent has to listen to the grim recounting of what Carl did, moment by moment, how he felt about what he did, and why he did it. Trent needs to make sure that the criminal says enough to ensure his conviction. It is a terrible thing to have to listen to, but afterward it usually leads to a surge of triumph at another case resolved. But that's missing now. Trent is lost in the grief of his wife's death, his lonely and solitary life, and his preoccupation with her judgmental words—"you are what you do."

Jason had awakened at his usual time on the first day of summer vacation, lying in bed luxuriating in the wealth of options he had for the day. He was scheduled to go to the Y with his mother that morning, but the afternoon was completely free. He decided to go over to Brad's and visit Alicia, Brad's seven-year-old sister, who was a jigsaw puzzle whiz and one of Jason's favorite people. When he got there, Alicia was trying to do a puzzle on the patio, and Brad was being a pain in the ass, jumping in and out of the pool and horsing around with his two buddies. He kept trying to get the puzzle wet, knowing that it would make his little sister mad. At one point, she turned to him and said, "Haven't you done enough damage today already?" When she spoke, she didn't sound like a seven-year-old kid sister at all. Brad grew quiet, and he and his friends left. Jason helped Alicia pick up the puzzle pieces and take them inside. She offered him some lemonade, but Jason could tell she was still mad, so he decided to go home instead.

Alicia's body was discovered that evening, just before dark. The medical examiner said she'd been killed instantaneously by a blow to the head with a blunt object. Her body and clothes had been arranged neatly—her hair framed her face, and her hands were crossed on her chest. She was covered with a light layer of leaves and brush. She'd left her home between about 4:00 PM, after Jason left, and 4:10, when her mother got home. The ME set the time of death at about 5:00 PM.

Lieutenant Detective George Braxton was in charge of the case. He was an insomniac who couldn't make himself relax, whether at work or at home. He loved his job when a case was clear cut and he could put the bad guy in jail. He hated his job when it was a case like this one—no physical evidence, no clues, no suspects, and no quick resolutions. To make it worse, Senator Gibbons, who was an influential man in the community, was sniffing around wanting to know how the investigation was going and asking about suspects. Braxton tried to brush him off, annoyed at his interference.

He spent the night at his office, going over the case, and when the next day dawned, he still didn't have much, but he did have a possible suspect, Jason Dorrant, who'd been at Alicia's home the afternoon before, and was the last person to see her alive. Braxton decided to interview him.

Jason was confused and intimidated by Braxton's questions and by how impatient he acted. He wanted to provide the detective with the quick answers he seemed to want. He didn't lie, but he had never been interviewed by the police before, and didn't know what he was supposed to say or what was important to the detective. But he did the best he could.

Meanwhile, as soon as Braxton got back to the station, he was caught in a storm of inquiries—the senator was getting increasingly demanding, the news media wanted updates on the case, and friends and neighbors in the neighborhood where Jason and Alicia both lived were scared, angry, and had their own set of demands. Braxton had not slept at all the night before, and was feeling stressed out. His gut, that had often been right before, was telling him that Jason was a viable suspect, but he had no hard evidence linking him to the crime. He needed a confession. And he thought he knew how to get it. He talked to Alvin Dark, the district attorney, who was anxious for a conviction, and mentioned Trent, a skilled interrogator with a perfect record of getting confessions from the most recalcitrant suspects. The DA approved of bringing him in, and Braxton made the call.

Trent got that call only minutes after finishing the interrogation of Adolph Califer, who had finally admitted he had killed his next door neighbor, with whom he'd been having an affair. It hadn't been an easy interview, Califer evaded some of Trent's questions, but answered others confidently and eagerly, certain his story would stand up to scrutiny. But Trent had an ace in the hole, and he was waiting for the right time to play it. He knew if he played it at the wrong time, Califer might be his first failure, and he knew the other officers he worked with would be gleeful to see it. He had never fit in, never become one of the guys, and his interrogation record was his only claim to fame. Trent watched Califer carefully for a crack in his façade, and when he saw one, he pounced. Ten minutes later Califer confessed, and five minutes after that, Trent got Braxton's call.

Trent thought about turning down the job, but Braxton brought up Senator Gibbons, implying that the senator had been part of the decision to hire him. Gibbons was solidly anticrime, and could wield power and influence. He was a good man to have on your side. Trent accepted the job. It was the third interrogation he'd done that week, and he was tired after Califer and Seton, but the lure of

Senator Gibbons's ability to help him up the ladder and reinforce his reputation was too strong for him to turn it down.

The senator sent a limo to take Trent to Monument, and Braxton sent a member of Dark's DA staff to bring him up to date on the ride. When Trent stepped into the room where the interrogation would take place, he was prepared. He knew that Jason was the only real suspect, although three other boys were also brought in for questioning to hide the fact that they were concentrating on Jason. He had about three hours to get the confession. Jason's mother had an appointment she didn't want to break; and the officer who picked up Jason was warm and reassuring, promising her that several boys were being brought in to discuss what they remembered about the day of the murder, and that none of them were suspects. He promised he would have Jason back home in no more than three hours. As a result, Jason was on his own, with no adults to look out for him.

The room was small, and hot and crowded, forcing Trent and Jason to sit close together. Trent warmed him up by asking easy questions to put the boy at ease, but very shortly began asking more pointed and personal questions, and observing Jason's responses to them—facial expression, emotions, body language, anything that could give Trent clues about how Jason was reacting to his questions. He carefully led Jason through his story about what happened that afternoon, then decided to give him a short break, and to let him think about what he'd said.

Jason was surprised, but then he appreciated the time to get his thoughts together. As he did, he remembered that he was a volunteer, not a suspect. He didn't have to answer questions if he didn't want to. He got up and walked out. But he only got as far as the parking lot before Trent saw him and persuaded him to come back inside. If he left, Trent told him, it would look suspicious.

The questions continued, and Jason revealed more and more about what had happened that afternoon, finally mentioning that Alicia and Brad seemed to have been quarreling. Trent wondered briefly about the brother's validity as a suspect, because the conflict could have been a motive. But then he refocused on Jason, telling himself that *he* was Trent's suspect, not the brother. Trent kept on probing, suggesting, twisting, questioning, until Jason was confused and uncertain of what to say, knowing only he wanted to please Trent and do the right thing. But the flow of the interview changed when Trent asked if Jason had ever thought about or touched Alicia in a sexual way, and at that point Jason asked to leave. It was his last rebellion, and Trent skillfully reeled him back in, even while agreeing that he was free to go.

And then Trent sums up what he's heard from Jason, carefully twisted to exhibit the boy's guilt: Alicia was younger but smarter than he was and made him feel inferior when she beat him at games. Jason enjoyed books and movies that were violent and daydreamed about violent things. Sometimes he couldn't tell the difference between fantasy and real life. He had been in the woods where Alicia was found, and he knew that a rock had killed her, something even the police didn't know. He had both motive and opportunity. But as he watched Jason's reaction to Trent's accusations, Trent suddenly knew that without any doubt whatsoever, Jason was innocent. He'd seen too many criminals try to wiggle out of confessing, and Jason wasn't doing that. He couldn't reveal how Alicia had been killed because he didn't know.

Trent has to make a decision—let the boy go and look for the real killer, or stay the course. He ignores his gut and the inner voice that whispers the truth, and continues the interview. Eventually, Jason is broken, and confesses. Trent leaves the room with the cassette in his hand, only to discover that the real killer, Alicia's brother, has confessed. He has forced an innocent boy to confess to murder.

Days later, Trent looks at the wreckage of his life—his career is over, his reputation gone, his future bleak and lonely. While he recognizes the mistakes he made during the interview, he still envies Jason, who at least is now free to live his life. Sadly, he doesn't realize that his twisting of Jason's words have had a sinister and perhaps long-lasting effect. If Trent had been able to make him say he would do something he never would have done, does that mean he is actually capable of it? Jason considers carefully the people he could kill, and one name becomes clear and bright in his mind. Where? When? He considers, plans, and reaches into the kitchen drawer to take out the butcher knife.

# AFTERWORD

Once again, the end is in sight, and we have come to another fork in the road. Bookshelves once stuffed with books on monsters of all kinds have been cleared out, waiting for the next project. The love-seat can now seat two, rather than one plus piles of books and legal pads for note taking. The cats have reluctantly gotten used to not sitting in my lap while I write, although their pitiful begging for attention has been hard to deal with. They get their lap time when they can, and if I am not at the desk, my lap is seldom empty. And I am taking a deep breath and planning on doing some light reading not involving monsters.

This has been by far the most difficult book I have ever written and I have a newfound respect for YA authors who create and bring to life these challenging, difficult, and emotional titles with their evil characters that are far less fun to read about and analyze than vampires, shape-shifters, and zombies. But I have also met people who have overcome their demons and gone on to succeed. I have also watched characters break under that pressure and wondered if they were able to survive after the last page was turned. And over and over, I have been aware that these titles, no matter how dark and difficult they are, teach lessons and provide insight that today's teens very badly need.

Did I include every kind of monster? No, of course not. I had to do a lot of cutting, like any other author, to make this book fit the length and the format required, and my cutting room floor is littered with corpses. There are titles on a wide variety of predators, rapists, manipulators, abusers, and other criminals, that I was not able to capture in these pages. With one exception (*My Friend Dahmer*), all the titles I presented are fiction, in spite of the fact that nonfiction titles exist. Parameters must be adhered to, and no title such as this one can be truly comprehensive. However, I hope the ones I was able to present will help you see how books with other kinds of monsters should be defended and protected and made available to teens.

Human monsters wear human masks, and can masquerade as friends, peers, family, teachers, neighbors, or the person next to you on the bus, or at the movies, or in line at Starbuck's. Most of us will never meet monsters as dangerous as the ones I've gotten to know, or the others in the books I didn't have time to include. But that doesn't mean we can't learn something from their stories. It's always best to be prepared, and no one really knows what is going to be waiting around life's next fork in the road.

That's why I decided to take a moment to introduce you to two additional and brand new titles that didn't make it into the previous chapters, but demanded to be talked about. Michael Cart's newest anthology, *Taking Aim: Power and Pain, Teens and Guns,* brings together stories from some of the best YA authors around, looks at guns in history, in culture, and on the streets of our society. We live in a culture of guns, Cart says in his introduction to the title. A third of American children grow up in homes with guns, and 43 percent have unlocked firearms readily available. There are guns on TV, in movies, and in the hands of friends, family, and strangers. The debate on gun control has divided the country for decades. Many people use them for hunting, to put food on the family table, and many others use them for recreation. But there is no way to deny that they are also used for less honorable purposes, and in a variety of violent scenarios.

Cart asked sixteen well-known YA authors to contribute to this collection, sharing their thoughts about guns and gun control by sharing their stories. Chris Crutcher, Marc Aronson, and Will Weaver collaborated on an essay about their views on guns and America's gun culture, and other authors share their stories designed to make readers stop and think, consider, and perhaps change their own ideas and beliefs.

With so many deaths occurring all over the world, and the frightening number of weapons available on the streets and from legal sources, including automatic and semiautomatic weapons that were designed only to kill other people, this is certainly a title that is both timely and necessary. Cart's anthologies have always been popular, but I would argue that this one is a title that *must* be popular, and is deserving of promotion that will put it in the hands of as many teens as possible.

*Violent Ends: A Novel in Seventeen Points of View*, by Shaun David Hutchinson, would have fit into the "School Shooters" section, had it arrived on my desk in time to be included. However, it also would not have fit, because it is not a novel with just one author, but a novel with seventeen. Hutchinson had been toying with the idea of writing a book about a boy named Kirby, a sixteen-year-old who came to school one day and began to shoot students and teachers at a before-school pep rally. Some he aimed at trying to kill. Two students were saved because he made sure they wouldn't be at the rally. He killed five students and a teacher before he killed himself. There was no one to explain what happened, why it happened, and why no one had foreseen it.

Hutchinson realized he wanted to tell the story of the shooter and how the people who surrounded him saw him, instead of the story of the shooting itself. So he asked YA authors whom he knew and admired if they would be interested in working with him to write a joint novel. All of them would contribute to the plot and the characters, but each would write one story from one person's perspective, giving their unique view of Kirby. This project would be completely different from the way school shooters are portrayed in the media, from a rather one-dimensional point of view. He wanted a multidimensional view of his character, one that could be provided only by having the people in Kirby's life talk about who he was to them. It would require a group of authors, rather than just one, working as a team, to make a fictional person and event as real as they possibly could be.

The stories are not all equally powerful or evocative, but that unevenness makes Kirby even closer to reality, since no one sees the same person the same way. And while they answer some questions about who he was and why he decided to do what he did, they do not provide all the answers, any more than those who knew the real shooters from the headlines could provide all the answers. In including himself among the victims, Kirby ensured that those who knew him would continue to have questions.

And now, even though we still may have questions for the human monsters who might now not seem that purely monstrous, it is time to end. Close the book, remember the lessons, and take them with us into the future, so they can help us when the fork in the road reveals something or someone more dangerous and threatening than we'd expected.

As for what's in my future, I'm planning a little vacation from the dark and dangerous, from the monsters of all kinds, from the challenging and difficult books that keep me up at night, and the ones I throw across the room when I read the final page because there are no answers or neatly tied endings. I'm going to spend some time looking at short fiction for teens and tweens of the twenty-first century who have a book report due *tomorrow*! *World Class Thin Books 3* will be coming your way soon!

# NOTES

## INTRODUCTION

1. Stephen A. Diamond, *Anger, Madness, and the Daimonic: The Psychological Genesis of Violence, Evil, and Creativity* (Albany: State University of New York Press, 1996), 3.

2. Craig A. Thompson, "Commentary: Youth Violence—the Elephant in the Room," *Daily Record*, March 1, 2012.

3. Diamond, *Anger, Madness, and the Daimonic*, 6.

4. "Assault Rifle," *Wikipedia*, http://en.wikipedia.org/wiki/Assault_ rifle (accessed November 26, 2013).

5. Google search on "how to get an automatic weapon illegally," accessed November 26, 2013, https://www.google.com/search?num=100& safe=off&espv=210&es_sm=91&q=how+to+get+an+automatic+weapon+ illegally&oq=how+to+get+an+automatic+weapon+illegally&gs_l=serp.3.. .4177.5650.0.6155.2.2.0.0.0.0.458.847.3-1j1.2.0.crnk_timepromotiona...0. ..1.1.32.serp..2.0.0.A0SEfMGrn_M.

6. Diamond, *Anger, Madness, and the Daimonic*, 5.

7. Joni Richards Bodart, *They Suck, They Bite, They Eat, They Kill: The Psychological Meaning of Supernatural Monsters in Young Adult Fiction* (Lanham, MD: Scarecrow Press, 2012), xxii–xxiii.

8. Diamond, *Anger, Madness, and the Daimonic*, 7.

9. Ibid.

10. Ibid., 8.

11. Heather Vogel Frederick, "What's Known Can't Be Unknown," *Publisher's Weekly*, February 20, 1995.

12. Ibid.

13. Rummanah Aasi, "Author Interview: Alex Flinn on Writing *Breathing Underwater* and Censorship," *Books in the Spotlight*, accessed November 26, 2013, http://booksinthespotlight.blogspot.com/2012/05/author-interview-alex-flinn-on-writiing.html.

14. Ibid.

15. Ibid.

16. Gail Giles, "How I Wrote '*Dark Song*,'" *GailGiles.com*, accessed November 26, 2013, http://www.gailgiles.com/How_I_wrote_Dark_Song.html.

17. Gail Giles, "How I Wrote '*Right Behind You*,'" *GailGiles.com*, accessed November 26, 2013, http://www.gailgiles.com/How_I_Wrote_Right_Behind_You.html.

18. "Interview with Gail Gailes," *YARN: Young Adult Review Network*, accessed November 26, 2013, http://yareview.net/2011/10/interview-with-gail-gailes/.

19. Gail Giles, "Why Teens Need Edgy Fiction," *GailGiles.com*, accessed November 26, 2013, http://www.gailgiles.com/Why_Teen_Need_Edgy_Fiction.html.

20. Gail Giles, "Wrath," *GailGiles.com*, accessed November 26, 2013, http://www.gailgiles.com/Wrath.html.

21. Ibid.

22. Arialdi M. Miniño, *Mortality among Teenagers Aged 12–19 Years United States, 1999–2006* (Hyattsville, MD: U.S. Dept. of Health and Human Services, Centers for Disease Control and Prevention, National Center for Health Statistics, 2010), http://purl.fdlp.gov/GPO/gpo6936.

23. "National Child Abuse Statistics," Childhelp, accessed November 24, 2013, http://www.childhelp.org/pages/statistics.

24. "Abuse in America," The National Domestic Violence Hotline, (accessed August 21, 2013), http://web.archive.org/web/20130821205212/http://www.thehotline.org/get-educated/abuse-in-america/.

25. Ibid.

26. "Dating Abuse Statistics," *Love Is Respect*, accessed November 24, 2013, http://www.loveisrespect.org/is-this-abuse/dating-violence-statistics.

27. "Youth Violence: Facts at a Glance," Centers for Disease Control, 2012, accessed October 31, 2013, http://www.cdc.gov/violenceprevention/pdf/yv_datasheet_2012-a.pdf.

28. Ibid.

29. "Connection between Bullying and Sexual Violence Perpetration," Centers for Disease Control and Prevention, accessed October 31, 2013, http://www.cdc.gov/violenceprevention/youthviolence/bullying_sv.html.

30. "Facts on Children's Mental Health in America," NAMI: National Alliance on Mental Illness, accessed November 24, 2013, http://www.nami.org/Template.cfm?Section=federal_and_state_policy_legislation&template=/ContentManagement/ContentDisplay.cfm&ContentID=43804.

31. Karen Peart, "Bullying-Suicide Link Explored in New Study by Researchers at Yale," *Yale News*, accessed November 23, 2013, http://news.yale.edu/2008/07/16/bullying-suicide-link-explored-new-study-researchers-yale.

32. L. Alvarez, "Felony Counts for 2 in Suicide of Bullied 12-Year-Old," *New York Times*, October 16, 2013.

33. Carol Kuruvilla, "Rebecca Sedwick Case: Both Suicide Victim and Bully Grew Up in 'Disturbing' Family Environments, Cop Says," *New York Daily News*, October 25, 2013, accessed November 25, 2013, http://www.nydailynews.com/news/national/rebecca-sedwick-case-suicide-victim-bully-grew-disturbing-family-homes-article-1.1496991.

34. Joseph Gregory Kosciw, *The 2009 National School Climate Survey: The Experiences of Lesbian, Gay, Bisexual and Transgender Youth in Our Nation's Schools* (New York: GLSEN, 2010).

35. M. Birkett, D. L. Espelage, and B. Koenig, "LGB and Questioning Students in Schools: The Moderating Effects of Homophobic Bullying and School Climate on Negative Outcomes," *Journal of Youth and Adolescence* 38, no. 7 (2009): 989–1000.

36. T. R. Coker, S. B. Austin, and M. A. Schuster, "The Health and Health Care of Lesbian, Gay, and Bisexual Adolescents," *Annual Review of Public Health* 31 (2010): 457–77.

37. C. Ryan, D. Huebner, R. M. Diaz, and J. Sanchez, "Family Rejection as a Predictor of Negative Health Outcomes in White And Latino Lesbian, Gay, and Bisexual Young Adults," *Pediatrics* 123, no. 1 (2009): 346–52.

38. "Youth Risk Behavior Surveillance System: 2011 National Overview," Centers for Disease Control, accessed October 31, 2013, http://www.cdc.gov/healthyyouth/yrbs/pdf/us_overview_yrbs.pdf.

39. Alex Kingsbury, "Gangs in the U.S.," *CQ Researcher* 20, no. 25 (July 16, 2010): 581–604.http://library.cqpress.com/cqresearcher/cqresrre2010071600.

40. D. D. McDaniel, "Risk and Protective Factors Associated with Gang Affiliation among High-Risk Youth: A Public Health Approach," *Injury Prevention: Journal of the International Society for Child and Adolescent Injury Prevention* 18, no. 4 (2012): 253–58.

41. J. R. Bodart, "Young Adult Authors as Trusted Adults for Disconnected Teens," *ALAN Review* 38, no. 1 (2010): 16–22.

42. Miniño, *Mortality among Teenagers Aged 12–19 Years*.

43. Ibid.

44. James Dawes, "Understanding Evil," *Chronicle of Higher Education*, July 1, 2013, accessed June 5, 2014, http://chronicle.com/article/Understanding-Evil/140025/.

45. Arthur G. Miller, *The Social Psychology of Good and Evil* (New York: Guilford Press, 2004), 5.

46. Ibid., 4.

47. "Kitty Genovese," *Wikipedia*, accessed June 4, 2014, http://en.wikipedia.org/wiki/Kitty_Genovese.

48. "Diffusion of Responsibility," *Wikipedia*, accessed June 4, 2014, http://en.wikipedia.org/wiki/Diffusion_of_responsibility.

49. Miller, *The Social Psychology of Good and Evil*, 85.

50. Ibid., 87.

51. Ibid., 89.

52. Roy F. Baumeister, *Evil: Inside Human Cruelty and Violence* (New York: W.H. Freeman, 2001), 1–2.

53. Ibid., 5.

54. Ibid., 6.

55. Ibid., 7.

56. Ibid., 10.

57. Ibid., 14.

58. Ibid., 14.

59. Miller, *The Social Psychology of Good and Evil*, 91.

60. Ibid., 93.

61. Ibid., 96.

62. Thomas Blass, *The Man Who Shocked the World: The Life and Legacy of Stanley Milgram* (New York: Basic Books), x.

63. Jerry M. Burger, "Replicating Milgram: Would People Still Obey Today?" *American Psychologist* 64, no. 1 (2009): 1–11; Thomas Blass, "Understanding Behavior in the Milgram Obedience Experiment: The Role of Personality, Situations, and Their Interactions," *Journal of Personality and Social Psychology* 60, no. 3 (1991): 398–413.

64. Blass, *The Man Who Shocked the World*, xvii.

65. Ibid., xxii.

66. "Milgram Experiment," *Wikipedia*, accessed June 4, 2014, http://en.wikipedia.org/wiki/Milgram_experiment.

67. Ibid.

68. Kendra Cherry, "The Milgram Obedience Experiment," About.com, accessed October 27, 2013, http://psychology.about.com/od/historyofpsychology/a/milgram.html.

69. Miller, *The Social Psychology of Good and Evil*, 28.

70. Cherry, "The Milgram Obedience Experiment."

71. Burger, "Replicating Milgram."

72. "Philip Zimbardo," *Wikipedia*, accessed June 4, 2014, http://en.wikipedia.org/wiki/Zimbardo.

73. Philip Zimbardo, *The Lucifer Effect: Understanding How Good People Turn Evil* (New York: Random House, 2008), 23.

74. Ibid., 171; "Stanford Prison Study," *Wikipedia*, accessed June 4, 2014, http://en.wikipedia.org/wiki/Stanford_prison_study.

75. Zimbardo, *The Lucifer Effect*, 31.

76. Ibid., 197.

77. Ibid., 54–55.

78. Ibid., 54–55, 74, 106, 115, 129

79. Ibid., 48–50, 76.

80. Zimbardo, *The Lucifer Effect*, 169–71.

81. Ibid., vii.

82. Ibid., x.

83. Ibid., 3.

84. Ibid., 5.

85. Ibid., 6.

86. Ibid., 7.

87. Romesh Ratnesar, "The Menace Within," *Stanford Alumni*, July–August 2011 accessed June 5, 2014, http://www.stanfordalumni.org/news/magazine/2011/julaug/features/spe.html.

88. "BBC Prison Study," *Wikipedia*, accessed June 4, 2014, http://en.wikipedia.org/wiki/Bbc_prison_study.

89. Ron Jones, "The Third Wave," Thewavehome.com, accessed June 6, 2014, http://www.thewavehome.com/1976_The-Wave_story.htm.

## MASS MURDERERS: SERIAL KILLERS AND SCHOOL SHOOTINGS

1. Brian Truitt, "'*My Friend Dahmer*' Depicts the Boy before the Monster," *USA Today*, March 22, 2012, accessed December 28, 2013, http://usatoday30.usatoday.com/life/comics/story/2012-03-22/Derf-Jeffrey-Dahmer-graphic-novel/53708368/1.

2. Betsy Fraser, "Shooting Monarchs," *School Library Journal* 49, no. 6 (2003): 143.

3. Kathleen T. Isaacs, "Reality Check," *School Library Journal* 49, no. 10 (2003): 50–51.

4. Chris Crutcher, "The Outsiders," *School Library Journal* 47, no. 8 (2001): 54.

5. James Alan Fox and Monica J. Delateur, "Mass Shootings in America: Moving Beyond Newtown," *Homicide Studies* 18, no. 1 (2014): 126–27.

6. Ibid., 128.

7. Ibid., 129.

8. Mark Follman, Gavin Aronsen, and Deanna Pan, "A Guide to Mass Shootings in America," *Mother Jones*, February 27, 2013, accessed January 12, 2014, http://www.motherjones.com/politics/2012/07/mass-shootings-map.

9. J. Pete Blair, M. Hunter Martaindale, and Terry Nichols, "Active Shooter Events from 2000 to 2012," *FBI Law Enforcement Bulletin*, accessed January 19, 2014, http://leb.fbi.gov/2014/january/active-shooter-events-from-2000-to-2012.

10. James Allen Fox, "Mass Shootings Not Trending," *Boston.com*, accessed January 12, 2014, http://www.boston.com/community/blogs/crime_punishment/2013/01/mass_shootings_not_trending.html.

11. Ibid.

12. Fox and Delateur, "Mass Shootings in America," 129.

13. Fox, "Mass Shootings Not Trending."

14. Fox and Delateur, "Mass Shootings in America," 132.

15. Holly J. Bowen, and Julia Spaniol, "Chronic Exposure to Violent Video Games Is Not Associated with Alterations of Emotional Memory," *Applied Cognitive Psychology* 25, no. 6 (2011): 906–16.

16. Christopher J. Ferguson, "Sandy Hook Shooting: Video Games Blamed, Again," *Time.com*, December 20, 2012, accessed January 2, 2014, http://ideas.time.com/2012/12/20/sandy-hook-shooting-video-games-blamed-again/.

17. Brooks Brown, and Rob Merritt, *No Easy Answers: The Truth behind Death at Columbine* (New York: Lantern Books, 2002),15.

18. Ibid., 16.

19. Ibid.

20. Ibid.

21. Bowen and Spaniol, "Chronic Exposure."

22. Dmitri Williams, and Marko Skoric, "Internet Fantasy Violence: A Test of Aggression in an Online Game," *Communication Monographs* 72, no. 2 (June 2005): 217–33.

23. Christopher J. Ferguson, "Video Games and Youth Violence: A Prospective Analysis in Adolescents," *Journal of Youth and Adolescence* 40, no. 4 (2010), doi: 10.1007/s10964-010-9610-x.

24. Ibid.

25. Ibid.

26. Fox and Delateur, "Mass Shootings in America," 133.

27. Joni R. Bodart, "Young Adult Authors as Trusted Adults for Disconnected Teens," *The ALAN Review* 38, no. 1 (2010): 16–22.

28. Fox and Delateur, "Mass Shootings in America," 133–34.

29. Christopher J. Ferguson, "Sandy Hook Shooting: Why Did Lanza Target a School?" *Time.com*, December 15, 2012, accessed January 2, 2014, http://ideas.time.com/2012/12/15/sandy-hook-shooting-why-did-lanza-target-a-school/.

30. Fox and Delateur, "Mass Shootings in America," 134–35.

31. Benedict Carey and Anemona Hartocollis, "Warning Signs of Violent Acts Often Unclear," *New York Times.com*, January 15, 2013, accessed January 19, 2014, http://www.nytimes.com/2013/01/16/health/breaking-link-of-violence-and-mental-illness.html?_r=0.

32. Fox and Delateur, "Mass Shootings in America," 135–36.

33. Crutcher, "The Outsiders," 55.

34. Ibid., 56.

35. Ibid., 55.

## 1. *I WISH YOU WERE DEAD*
## BY TODD STRASSER

1. Todd Strasser, *I Wish You Were Dead* (New York: Egmont, 2009), 5.

2. Amanda L. Farrell, Robert D. Keppel, and Victoria B. Titterington, "Testing Existing Classifications of Serial Murder Considering Gender: An Exploratory Analysis of Solo Female Serial Murderers," *Journal of Investigative Psychology and Offender Profiling* 10, no. 3 (2013): 268–88.

3. Ibid.

4. Todd Strasser, e-mail message to author, January 6, 2014.

## 2. THE FORENSIC MYSTERY SERIES
## BY ALANE FERGUSON

1. "Interviews," *Alaneferguson.com*, accessed February 10, 2015, http://www.alaneferguson.com/Interviews_1.html.

2. Ibid.

3. Ibid.

4. Ibid.

## 3. *ACCELERATION*
## BY GRAHAM MCNAMEE

1. "*Acceleration* by Graham McNamee—Interview," *BookClubs.ca*. http://www.bookclubs.ca/catalog/display.pperl?isbn=9780307207340& view=auqa (accessed March 29, 2014).

2. Ibid.

3. Ibid.

## 4. IN THE PATH OF FALLING OBJECTS
## BY ANDREW SMITH

1. "The Quintessentially Questionable Query Experiment," Andrew Smith Interview, accessed March 29, 2014, http://theqqqe.blogspot.com/2011/02/andrew-smith-interview.html.

2. "Andrew Smith: Author Bio," Amazon.com, accessed February 17, 2015, http://www.amazon.com/Andrew-Smith/e/B001JS8PRM.

3. "Quintessentially Questionable Query Experiment."

4. Andrew Smith, "Eighteen Days," *Ghost Medicine*, accessed March 30, 2014, http://ghostmedicine.blogspot.com/2009/08/eighteen-days.html.

5. Andrew Smith, "What We Do," *Ghost Medicine*, accessed March 30, 2014, http://ghostmedicine.blogspot.com/2009/10/what-we-do.html.

6. Andrew Smith, *In the Path of Falling Objects* (New York: Feiwel and Friends, 2009), 258.

7. Andrew Smith, e-mail message to author, March 30, 2014.

8. Smith, *In the Path of Falling Objects*, 309.

9. "Meet Andrew Smith," *The Reading Tub*, accessed February 17, 2015, http://thereadingtub.com/displayInterview.php?id=67.

## 5. I HUNT KILLERS SERIES
## BY BARRY LYGA

1. Barry Lyga, "How I Created *I Hunt Killers* by Accident," Mullholland Books, April 2, 2012, accessed February 17, 2015, http://www.mulhollandbooks.com/2012/04/02/2029/.

2. Brandy Schillace, "Fiction Reboot Author Interview: Barry Lyga," *Fiction Reboot, Daily Dose and the Rogue Scholar Salon*, accessed July 9, 2013, http://fictionreboot-dailydose.com/2012/07/19/fiction-reboot-author-interview-barry-lyga/.

3. "Interview: Barry Lyga, author of *I Hunt Killers* and *Game*," *My Bookish Ways*, accessed July 11, 2013, http://www.mybookishways.com/2013/05/interview-barry-lyga-author-of-i-hunt-killers-and-game.html.

4. Lyga, "How I Created *I Hunt Killers*."

5. Schillace, "Fiction Reboot Author Interview: Barry Lyga."

6. "Rage after Columbine," *Booklist* 103, no. 1 (September 2006): 113.

7. Ibid.

8. Ibid.

9. Ibid.; Schillace, "Fiction Reboot Author Interview: Barry Lyga"; Diane Dimond, "Serial Killers—How Many Are There?" *Creators.com*, accessed June 8, 2014, http://www.creators.com/opinion/diane-dimond/serial-killers-how-many-are-there.html.

10. R. J. Morton, and M. A. Hilts, *Serial Murder: Multi-disciplinary Perspectives for Investigator* (Washington, DC: National Criminal Justice Reference Service, 2008), n.p.

11. Ibid., 3.

12. Schillace, "Fiction Reboot Author Interview: Barry Lyga."

13. Ibid.

14. Morton and Hilts, *Serial Murder*, 11.

15. "Fiction Reboot Author Interview: Barry Lyga."

16. Lipkin, Adam. "Q&A with Barry Lyga," *Publishers Weekly*, April 19, 2012 (accessed July 11, 2013)http://www.publishersweekly.com/pw/by-topic/authors/interviews/article/51579-q-a-with-barry-lyga.html. I feel similarly about my own digital profile, since in researching this book, I have done searches on many kinds of crimes and criminals, and occasionally wonder if anyone is putting two and two together and getting six or seven!

17. "Fiction Reboot Author Interview: Barry Lyga."

18. Lipkin, "Q&A with Barry Lyga."

19. *I Hunt Killers* Wiki, accessed February 11, 2015, http://i-hunt-killers.wikia.com/wiki/I_Hunt_Killers_Wiki.

20. Barry Lyga, *I Hunt Killers* (New York: Little, Brown), 12.

21. Lipkin, "Q&A with Barry Lyga."

22. Lipkin, "Q&A with Barry Lyga."

23. *I Hunt Killers* Wiki.

24. Lipkin, "Q&A with Barry Lyga."

25. "Interview," *My Bookish Ways*.

## 6. PROJECT CAIN
## BY GEOFFREY GIRARD

1. Scott Bukti, "An Interview with Geoffrey Girard about His New Books '*Project Cain*' and '*Cain's Blood*,'" *Blogcritics*, accessed January 9, 2014, http://blogcritics.org/an-interview-with-geoffrey-girard-about-his-new-books-project-cain-and-cains-blood/; "Project Cain Blog Tour: Interview with Geoffrey Girard," *Inspiring Insomnia*, accessed January 10, 2014, http://inspiringinsomnia.com/2013/10/project-cain-blog-tour-interview-with-geoffrey-girard-and-giveaway.html.

2. Bukti, "An Interview with Geoffrey Girard."

3. Ibid.

4. Geoffrey Girard, "Cloning Pogo the Clown—TWICE!" *Geoffreygirard.com*. February 7, 2013, accessed February 17, 2015, https://geoffreygirard.wordpress.com/2013/02/07/cloning-pogo-the-clown-twice/.

5. Ibid.

6. Wikimedia Foundation, "Cloning," *Wikipedia*, accessed January 24, 2015, http://en.wikipedia.org/wiki/Cloning.

7. Bukti, "An Interview with Geoffrey Girard."

8. "Project Cain Blog Tour," *Inspiring Insomnia*; "Author R&R—Geoffrey Girard," *In Reference to Murder* accessed January 10, 2014, http://inreferencetomurder.typepad.com/my_weblog/2013/09/author-rr-geoffrey-girard.html.

9. Bukti, "An Interview with Geoffrey Girard."

10. Ibid.

11. Richard Gazala, "Author Spotlight: Geoffrey Girard," *GAZALAPA-LOOZA*, accessed January 10, 2014, http://rgazala.blogspot.com/2013/09/author-spotlight-geoffrey-girard.html.

12. Bukti, "An Interview with Geoffrey Girard."

13. Gazala, "Author Spotlight: Geoffrey Girard."

14. Geoffrey Girard, "The Qwillery," Guest Blog by Geoffrey Girard, author of *Cain's Blood* and *Project Cain*, accessed January 9, 2014, http://qwillery.blogspot.com/2013/08/interview-with-geoffrey-girard-author.html.

15. Girard, "Cloning Pogo the Clown."

16. Bukti, "An Interview with Geoffrey Girard."

17. "Project Cain Blog Tour," *Inspiring Insomnia*.

18. Girard, "The Quillery."

19. R. J. Morton and M. A. Hilts, *Serial Murder: Multi-disciplinary Perspectives for Investigator* (Washington, DC: National Criminal Justice Reference Service, 2008), 3.

20. Girard, "The Quillery."

21. Ibid.

22. Ibid.

23. "Author R&R—Geoffrey Girard."

24. Ibid.

25. Ibid.

## 7. MY FRIEND DAHMER
## BY DERF BACKDERF

1. Derf Backderf, "It All Began with a Sketchbook," *My Friend Dahmer Blog*, February 12, 2012, accessed February 17, 2015, http://myfrienddahmer.blogspot.com/2012/02/official-book-launch-date-is-march-1.html.

2. Svetlana Fedotov, "Q&A: Derf Backderf on His Harrowing, Autobiographical, '*My Friend Dahmer*,' Part One," August 16, 2012, *Fangoria*, accessed September 8, 2013, http://www.fangoria.com/moviestv/fearful-features/7611-qaa-derf-backderf-on-his-harrowing-autobiographical-qmy-friend-dahmerq-part-one.

3. Ibid.

4. Backderf, "It All Began with a Sketchbook."

5. Ibid.

6. "Eisner Award," *Wikipedia*, accessed January 24, 2015, http://en.wikipedia.org/wiki/Eisner_Award.

7. Backderf, "It All Began with a Sketchbook."

8. Derf Backderf, *My Friend Dahmer: A Graphic Novel* (New York: Abrams ComicArts, 2012), 200.

9. Ibid., 200–201.

10. Backderf, "It All Began with a Sketchbook."

11. "An Interview with Derf Backderf," *YALSA: The Hub*, March 28, 2013, accessed February 3, 2015, http://www.yalsa.ala.org/thehub/2013/03/28/an-interview-with-derf-backderf/.

12. Ibid.

13. Fedotov, "Q&A: Derf Backderf, Part One."

14. Backderf, *My Friend Dahmer*, 70–79.

15. "An Interview with Derf Backderf."

16. Svetlana Fedotov, "Q&A: Derf Backderf on His Harrowing, Auto-biographical, '*My Friend Dahmer*,' Part Two," *Fangoria*, August 16, 2012, accessed September 8, 2013, http://www.fangoria.com/moviestv/fearful-features/7611-qaa-derf-backderf-on-his-harrowing-autobiographical-qmy-friend-dahmerq-part-two

17. Derf Backderf, "Recreating the 'Sinister Seventies Adolescent World,'" *My Friend Dahmer Blog*, July 27, 2012, accessed February 17, 2015, http://myfrienddahmer.blogspot.com/2012/07/recreating-sinister-seventies.html; Derf Backderf, *My Friend Dahmer: A Graphic Novel* (Kindle Edition, 2012).

18. Backderf, *My Friend Dahmer*, 33.

19. Backderf, *My Friend Dahmer*, Kindle Edition, appendix.

20. Backderf, *My Friend Dahmer*, 43–47.

21. Ibid., 125, 210.

22. Ibid., 84–85; Derf Backderf, "It Was a Very Different Time," *My Friend Dahmer Blog*, June 27, 2013, accessed February 17, 2015, http://myfrienddahmer.blogspot.com/2013/06/it-was-very-different-time.html.

23. Ibid.

24. Ibid.; Fedotov, "Q&A: Derf Backderf, Part One."

25. Backderf, *My Friend Dahmer*, 208.

26. Backderf, *My Friend Dahmer*, Kindle Edition.

27. Backderf, *My Friend Dahmer*, 97.

28. Ibid., 119.

29. Ibid., 211.

30. Ibid., 113–14, 129–42.

31. Ibid., 132–33, 83, 87.

32. Ibid., 133.

33. Backderf, "It Was a Very Different Time."

34. Backderf, *My Friend Dahmer*, 80; Fedotov, "Q&A: Derf Backderf, Part One."

35. Backderf, *My Friend Dahmer*, 84.

36. Derf Backderf, "It Was a Very Different Time, Part Two"; *My Friend Dahmer* Blog, June 28, 2013.

37. Backderf, *My Friend Dahmer*, 142–43.

38. Ibid., 214–15.

## 8. *GIVE A BOY A GUN*
## BY TODD STRASSER

1. Todd Strasser, e-mail message to author, January 6, 2014.

2. Diane Roback, Jennifer M. Brown, and Jason Britton, "Give a Boy a Gun," *Publishers Weekly* 247 (35): 84.

3. Ibid.

4. Michael Cart, "*Give a Boy a Gun* Review," *Booklist Online*, accessed January 24, 2014, http://www.booklistonline.com/ProductInfo.aspx?pid=5462454&AspxAutoDetectCookieSupport=1

5. Todd Strasser, e-mail message to author, January 6, 2014.

6. Ibid. Until about five years before Columbine, I lived less than five miles from the campus in Littleton, Colorado, and the Columbine branch of Jefferson County Public Library System was my local library. I researched and wrote much of *World's Best Thin Books* there. I knew the area intimately, and had driven past the school many times. In 1999 I still lived in Denver, and had family who lived in Littleton. Columbine was entirely too close to me, and because of that, I had refused to read the book, until I was finishing RR. Even then, it was difficult to read for reasons that had nothing to do with Strasser's writing.

7. Todd Strasser, *Give a Boy a Gun* (New York: Simon & Schuster, 2000), 174.

8. Ibid., 181.

## 9. *THE LAST DOMINO*
## BY ADAM MEYER

1. Joel Shoemaker, "*The Last Domino*," *School Library Journal* 51 (11): 142.

2. Ibid.

3. Francesca Goldsmith, "*The Last Domino*," *Booklist* 102 (1): 63.

## 10. *ENDGAME*
## BY NANCY GARDEN

1.  Barbara Ward, "Hearing Nancy Garden Out," *The ALAN Review* 36, no. 1 (2009): 32.
2.  Ibid., 38.
3.  Ibid., 37–38.
4.  Ibid., 38.
5.  *"Endgame* Review," *Literary Treats*, accessed January 7, 2014, accessed January 7, 2014, http://literarytreats.wordpress.com/2013/01/08/review-endgame-nancy-garden/.
6.  Ward, "Hearing Nancy Garden Out," 39.

## 11. "GUNS FOR GEEKS" BY CHRIS CRUTCHER, FROM *ON THE FRINGE*
## EDITED BY DON GALLO

1.  "Frontier Middle School Shooting," *Wikipedia*, accessed January 24, 2014, http://en.wikipedia.org/wiki/Frontier_Middle_School_shooting; Chris Crutcher, e-mail message to author, January 14, 2014.
2.  Chris Crutcher, e-mail message to author, January 14, 2014.

## 12. *QUAD*
## BY C. G. WATSON

1.  Dwayne Jeffery, "Reaching Reluctant Readers (aka Books for Boys)," *The ALAN Review* 36, no. 2 (2009), accessed January 6, 2014, http://scholar.lib.vt.edu/ejournals/ALAN/v36n2/jeffery.html.
2.  "Interview with C. G. Watson," *Becky's Book Reviews*, accessed January 7, 2014, http://blbooks.blogspot.com/2007/11/interview-with-cg-watson.html.

## 13. HATE LIST
## BY JENNIFER BROWN

1. "Interview with '*Hate List*' author Jennifer Brown," *Old People Writing for Teens*, accessed January 8, 2014, http:// oldpeoplewritingforteens.wordpress.com/2009/12/10/interview-with-hate-list-author-jennifer-brown-and-book-giveaway/.

2. Philip Zimbardo, *The Lucifer Effect: Understanding How Good People Turn Evil* (New York: Random House, 2008).

3. Ibid.

4. Ibid.

5. Ibid.

6. Matthew Weaver, "*Hate List*," *Voice of Youth Advocates* 32, no. 5: 403.

## BULLIES: IN YOUR FACE AND ON YOUR SCREEN

1. Quoted in Donald Spoto, *The Dark Side of Genius: The Life of Alfred Hitchcock* (New York: Da Capo, 1999), 39.

2. John Cloud, "When Bullying Turns Deadly: Can It Be Stopped?" *Time*, accessed July 20, 2014, http://content.time.com/time/magazine/article/0,9171,2024210,00.html#ixzz13ZU70E3j.

3. Emily Bazelon, *Sticks and Stones: Defeating the Culture of Bullying and Rediscovering the Power of Character and Empathy* (New York: Random House, 2013), 15.

4. Alice G. Walton, "Bully Psychology: Where Evolution and Morality Collide," http://www.forbes.com/sites/alicegwalton/2012/07/05/bully-psychology-why-bullying-is-one-of-evolutions-big-snafus/#6b428eb37f22.

5. Adrienne Nishina, Jaana Juvonen, and Melissa R. Witkow, "Sticks and Stones May Break My Bones, but Names Will Make Me Feel Sick: The Psychosocial, Somatic, and Scholastic Consequences of Peer Harassment," *Journal of Clinical Child & Adolescent Psychology* 34, no. 1, 37–48.

6. Amy Malick, "Study: Bullying Common among Teens," *ABC News*, accessed July 31, 2014, http://abcnews.go.com/Health/story?id= 117495.

7. Barbara Coloroso, *The bully, the Bullied, and the Bystander: From Preschool to High School: How Parents and Teachers Can Help Break the Cycle of Violence* (New York: Collins Living, 2008), 17.

8. Judy Lin, "Psychologist's Studies Make Sense of Bullying," *UCLA Newsroom*, May 3, 2012, accessed March 29, 2015, http://newsroom.ucla. edu/stories/bullying-jaana-juvonen-233108.

9. Coloroso, *The Bully, the Bullied, and the Bystander*, 20–21.

10. Alvarez, Lizette. "Felony Counts for 2 in Suicide of Bullied 12-Year-Old," *New York Times*, October 15, 2013, accessed March 13, 2015, http://www.nytimes.com/2013/10/16/us/felony-charges-for-2-girls-in-suicide-of-bullied-12-year-old-rebecca-sedwick.html.

11. Carol Kuruvilla, "Rebecca Sedwick Case: Suicide Victim and Bully Grew Up in 'Disturbing' Family Homes, Cop Says," *New York Daily News*, October 25, 2013, accessed March 29, 2015, http://www. nydailynews.com/news/national/rebecca-sedwick-case-suicide-victim-bully-grew-disturbing-family-homes-article-1.1496991.

12. Ibid.

13. Carrie Goldman, *Bullied: What Every Parent, Teacher, and Kid Needs to Know about Ending the Cycle of Fear* (New York: HarperOne, 2012), xiii.

14. Coloroso, *The Bully, the Bullied, and the Bystander*, 14.

15. Sally Black, "Evaluation of the Olweus Bullying Program: How the Program Can Work for Inner City Youth," paper presented at the 2007 National Conference on Safe Schools, Washington, DC, October 29–31, 2007, http://www.goccp.maryland.gov/msac/documents/gang-studies/ OLWEUS/Black-2007.pdf

16. Manuela Velasco, "Community Problem Report," *The End Bullying Project*, accessed March 9, 2015, http://theendbullyingproject.weebly. com/community-problem-report-annotated-bib.html.

17. Gay, Lesbian Straight Education Network, *The 2009 National School Climate Survey: The Experiences of Lesbian, Gay, Bisexual and Transgender Youth in Our Nation's Schools* (New York: Gay, Lesbian Straight Education Network, 2010).

18. Michelle Brikett, Dorothy Espelage, and Brian Koenig, "LGB and Questioning Students in Schools: The Moderating Effects of Homophobic

Bullying and School Climate on Negative Outcomes," *Journal of Youth and Adolescence*: 37, no. 7; 989–1000.

19. C. Ryan, D. Huebner, R. M. Diaz, and J. Sanchez, "Family Rejection as a Predictor of Negative Health Outcomes in White and Latino Lesbian, Gay, and Bisexual Young Adults," *Pediatrics* 123: 346–52.

20. Ibid.

21. Dani McClain, "If You Read That 'NYT' Story about Two Teens in Oakland, Keep This in Mind," *Nation*, January 30, 2015, accessed January 29, 2015, http://www.thenation.com/blog/196617/if-you-read-nyt-story-about-two-teens-oakland-keep-mind.

22. Curtis Wong, "Sasha Fleischman, Agender California Teen, Speaks Out after Having Skirt Set on Fire on Bus," *Huffington Post*, December 2, 2013, accessed February 21, 2015, http://www.huffingtonpost.com/2013/12/02/sasha-fleischman-attack-interview-_n_4373237.html.

23. Caleb Pershan, "Family of Sasha Fleischman Has 'Mixed Emotions' after Teen Is Sentenced in Skirt Fire Attack," *SFist*, November 14, 2014, accessed March 26, 2015, http://sfist.com/2014/11/14/oakland_teen_sentenced_in_attack_on.php.

24. Dashka Slater, "The Fire on the 57 Bus in Oakland," *New York Times*, January 31, 2015, accessed April 9, 2015, http://www.nytimes.com/2015/02/01/magazine/the-fire-on-the-57-bus-in-oakland.html.

25. Pershan, "Family of Sasha Fleischman Has 'Mixed Emotions.'"

26. Centers for Disease Control (CDC), "Electronic Media and Youth Violence: A CDC Issue Brief for Educators and Caregivers," 2008, accessed July 31, 2014, http://www.cdc.gov/violenceprevention/pdf/ea-brief-a.pdf.

27. Sameer Hinduja and Justin W. Patchin, "High-Tech Cruelty," *Educational Leadership* 68, no. 5, 48–52.

28. CDC, "Electronic Media and Youth Violence."

29. Meredith Melnick, "A Glimmer of Hope in a Bad-News Survey about Bullying," *Time*, October 27, 2010, accessed July 11, 2014, http://healthland.time.com/2010/10/27/a-glimmer-of-hope-in-a-bad-news-survey-about-bullying/.

30. Hinduja and Patchin, "High-Tech Cruelty."

31. Ibid.

32. Young Shin Kim, and Bennett Leventhal, "Bullying and Suicide: A Review," *International Journal of Adolescent Medicine and Health* 20, no. 2 (2008): 133–34.

33. Hinduja and Patchin, "High-Tech Cruelty."

34. "Bullying-Suicide Link Explored in New Study by Researchers at Yale," *Yale News*, July 16, 2008, accessed July 22, 2014, http://news.yale.edu/2008/07/16/bullying-suicide-link-explored-new-study-researchers-yale.

35. Eve Sturges, "The Cruelty of Children," *Rookie*, October 14, 2013, accessed March 18, 2015, http://www.rookiemag.com/2013/10/the-cruelty-of-children/.

36. Kim and Leventhal, "Bullying and Suicide," 134.

37. Ibid., 135; Black, "Evaluation of the Olweus Bullying Program."

38. Malick, "Bullying Common among Teens."

39. Black, "Evaluation of the Olweus Bullying Program."

40. Cloud, "When Bullying Turns Deadly."

41. Brett J. Litwiller, and Amy M. Brausch, "Cyber Bullying and Physical Bullying in Adolescent Suicide: The Role of Violent Behavior and Substance Use," *Journal of Youth and Adolescence* 42, no. 5 (2013): 675.

42. Cloud, "When Bullying Turns Deadly."

43. Bazelon, *Sticks and Stones*, 220.

44. CDC, "Electronic Media and Youth Violence."

45. Black, "Evaluation of the Olweus Bullying Program."

46. Bazelon, *Sticks and Stones*, 210, 232.

47. Ibid., 234.

48. Ibid., 297–98.

49. Taylor Mali, "What Teachers Make," *TaylorMali.com*, accessed July 31, 2014, http://www.taylormali.com/poems-online/what-teachers-make/.

50. Bazelon, *Sticks and Stones*, 290.

## 14. *SHATTERING GLASS*
## BY GAIL GILES

1. Gail Giles, "How I Wrote It—*Shattering Glass*," *Gailgiles.com*, accessed November 20, 2015, http://www.gailgiles.com.

2. Ibid.

3. Ibid.

4. Cynthia Leitich Smith, "Interview with Young Adult Author Gail Giles," *Cynthia Leitich Smith.com*, accessed November 20, 2015, http://

www.cynthialeitichsmith.com/lit_resources/authors/interviews/GailGiles.
html

   5. Giles, "How I Wrote It—*Shattering Glass*."

   6. "Interview with Gail Giles," *YARN*, October 3, 2011, accessed November 20, 2015, http://yareview.net/2011/10/interview-with-gail-giles/.

   7. Smith, "Interview with Young Adult Author Gail Giles."

   8. Giles, "How I Wrote It—*Shattering Glass*."

   9. Ibid.

   10. Smith, "Interview with Young Adult Author Gail Giles."

   11. Beverly Rowe, "Author of the Month: Gail Giles," *Myshelf.com*, accessed November 20, 2015, http://myshelf.com/aom/07/giles.htm.

   12. Ibid.

   13. Gail Giles, *Shattering Glass* (Brookfield, CT: Roaring Brook Press, 2002), p. 1.

   14. Giles, "How I Wrote It—*Shattering Glass*."

   15. "Interview with Gail Giles."

   16. Giles, "How I Wrote It—*Shattering Glass*."

   17. "Interview with Gail Giles."

   18. Giles, "How I Wrote It—*Shattering Glass*."

   19. Smith, "Interview with Gail Giles."

## 15. *TEASE*
## BY AMANDA MACIEL

   1. "Q&A with Amanda Maciel, Author of *Tease*," *BookPeople Teen Press Corps*, May 5, 2014, accessed December 2, 2015, https://bookpeopleteens.wordpress.com/2014/05/05/qa-with-amanda-maciel-author-of-tease/.

   2. Ibid.

   3. "What Amanda Maciel Learned While Writing a Novel," *What I Learned While Writing a Novel*, August 29, 2013, accessed December 2, 2015, https://whatilearnedwhilewritinganovel.wordpress.com/2013/08/29/what-amanda-maciel-learned-while-writing-a-novel/.

   4. "Exclusive Interview with Amanda Maciel," *Dazzled by Books*, June 17, 2014, accessed December 2, 2015, http://dazzledbybooks.com/2014/06/exclusive-interview-with-amanda-maciel-and-giveaway/.

   5. Ibid.

6. *"Tease* by Amanda Maciel—Review," *Guardian*, September 14, 2014, accessed December 2, 2015, http://www.theguardian.com/childrens-books-site/2014/sep/18/review-tease-amanda-maciel.

## 16. *SHINE*
## BY LAUREN MYRACLE

1. "Interview with Lauren Myracle," *Matthew's Place*, accessed December 2, 2015, http://www.matthewsplace.com/voice/interview-with-lauren-myracle/.

2. "Matthew Shepard," *Wikipedia*, accessed December 2, 2015, https://en.wikipedia.org/wiki/Matthew_Shepard.

3. "Interview with Lauren Myracle."

4. Ibid.

5. Ibid.

6. Ibid.

7. Ibid.

8. American Library Association, "Top Ten Frequently Challenged Books Lists of the 21st Century," accessed December 2, 2015, http://www.ala.org/bbooks/frequentlychallengedbooks/top10.

9. Abigail Pesta, "Should This Woman's Books Be Banned?" *Daily Beast*, April 11, 2012, http://www.thedailybeast.com/articles/2012/04/11/lauren-myracle-on-why-her-books-top-list-that-america-wants-banned.html.

10. Debra Lau Whelan, "Interview: Why Lauren Myracle's Proud to Top ALA's List of Most Challenged Books," *School Library Journal*, October 2, 2012.

## 17. *BY THE TIME YOU READ THIS,*
## *I'LL BE DEAD*
## BY JULIE ANNE PETERS

1. Julie Ann Peters, "The Story behind the Story of *By the Time You Read This, I'll Be Dead*," *Julieannpeters.com*, accessed December 2, 2015, http://www.julieannepeters.com/files/InspirationBTT.htm.

2. "Interview: February 2010—Julie Ann Peters," *Teenreads.com*, accessed December 2, 2015, http://www.teenreads.com/authors/julie-anne-peters/news/interview-020110.

3. Julie Ann Peters, "Frequently Asked Questions," *Julieannepeters.com*, accessed December 2, 2015, http://www.julieannepeters.com/files/JPFAQ.htm.

4. Peters, "The Story Behind the Story."

5. Ibid.

6. Ibid.

7. Ibid.

8. Ibid.

9. Ibid.

10. Brigida Alexandra Marcella, "Interview with Julie Anne Peters," *The Interesting Stranger*, June 12, 2011, accessed December 2, 2015, http://brigida-alexandra.blogspot.com/2011/06/interview-with-julie-anne-peters-author.html#.VteW5vkrKUk.

11. Martina Boone, "Julie Anne Peters on LGBTQ and Controversial YA," *Adventures in YA Publishing*, June 24, 2012, accessed December 2, 2015, http://www.adventuresinyapublishing.com/2012/07/julie-anne-peters-on-lgbtq-and.html#.VteXdvkrKUk.

12. Peters, "The Story Behind the Story."

13. "Interview: February 2010—Julie Ann Peters."

## MONSTERS AT SCHOOL: TEACHERS, COACHES, ATHLETES, AND OTHERS

1. "No More Teacher Bullies Page," last modified October 26, 2015, accessed November 8, 2015, https://www.facebook.com/NoMoreTeacherBullies/

2. Katherine Kam, "Teachers Who Bully," *WebMD*, accessed July 15, 2015, http://www.webmd.com/parenting/features/teachers-who-bully.

3. John Schinnerer, "The Consequences of Verbally Abusive Athletic Coaches," *Psych Central*, accessed July 15, 2015, http://psychcentral.com/lib/the-consequences-of-verbally-abusive-athletic-coaches/.

4. Kam, "Teachers Who Bully."

5. Ibid.

6. Schinnerer, "The Consequences of Verbally Abusive Athletic Coaches."

7. Linda Flanagan, "The Real Bullies at School," *Atlantic*, March 16, 2015, accessed July 15, 2015, http://www.theatlantic.com/education/archive/2015/03/the-real-bullies-at-school/387829/.

8. T. F. Charlton, "Why Do Athletes Tolerate Abusive Coaches?" *Salon*, April 5, 2015, accessed November 9, 2015, http://www.salon.com/2013/04/05/why_do_athletes_tolerate_abusive_coaches/.

9. Mariya A. Yukhymenko, "College Athletes with Abusive Coaches More Willing to Cheat," American Psychological Association, July 7, 2014, accessed November 9, 2015, http://www.apa.org/news/press/releases/2014/07/abusive-coaches.aspx.

10. Yukhymenko, "College Athletes with Abusive Coaches More Willing to Cheat."

11. Robert Lipsyte, "Jocks vs. Pukes," *Nation*, July 27, 2011, accessed November 9, 2015, http://www.thenation.com/article/jocks-vs-pukes/.

12. Ibid.

13. Schinnerer, "The Consequences of Verbally Abusive Athletic Coaches."

14. N. L. Swigonski, B. A. Enneking, and K. S. Hendrix, "Bullying Behavior by Athletic Coaches," *Pediatrics* 133, no. 2 (February 2014).

15. Jan Hoffman, "My Coach, the Bully," Well Blog, *New York Times*, January 29, 2014, accessed July 15, 2015, http://well.blogs.nytimes.com/2014/01/29/my-coach-the-bully/.

16. Ibid.

17. Schinnerer, "The Consequences of Verbally Abusive Athletic Coaches."

18. Flanagan, "The Real Bullies at School."

19. Ibid.

20. John Amaechi, "Opinion: Rutgers Coach and Sports' Bully Culture," CNN.com, accessed July 15, 2015, http://www.cnn.com/2013/04/03/opinion/amaechi-rutgers-coach/.

21. Flanagan, "The Real Bullies at School."

22. Amaechi, "Rutgers Coach and Sports' Bully Culture."

23. Hoffman, "My Coach, the Bully."

24. Ibid.

25. Flanagan, "The Real Bullies at School."

26. Ibid.

27. David J. Mitchell, "Former High School Powerlifting Coach Gets Suspended Sentence for Giving Steroids to Unsuspecting Student," *Advocate*, April 2, 2015, accessed November 9, 2015, http://theadvocate.com/news/12007958-123/former-high-school-powerlifting-coach.

28. John Whyte, "Are Student Athletes Taking Steroids?" *Huffington Post*, April 20, 2011, accessed November 9, 2015, http://www.huffingtonpost.com/john-whyte-md-mph/student-athletes-steroids_b_850952.html.

29. Jeff Beckham, "Growth Hormone Usage Rises among Teens," *Wired*, December 4, 2014, accessed November 9, 2015, http://www.wired.com/2014/12/growth-hormone-usage-up-among-teens/.

30. Ron Kroichick and Mitch Stephens, "More High School Athletes Risking Steroid Use / Coaches Fear BALCO Probe May Boost Consumption," *SFGate*. November 2, 2003, accessed November 9, 2015, http://www.sfgate.com/health/article/More-high-school-athletes-risking-steroid-use-2579604.php.

31. Beckham, "Growth Hormone Usage Rises among Teens."

32. Office of Diversion Control, "Steroid Abuse by School Age Children," U.S. Department of Justice, Drug Enforcement Administration, accessed November 9, 2015, http://www.deadiversion.usdoj.gov/pubs/brochures/steroids/children/.

## 18. *LEVERAGE*
## BY JOSHUA C. COHEN

1. Joshua C. Cohen, "About Joshua C. Cohen, Author of Leverage," *Leveragethebook.com.* accessed December 2, 2015, http://leveragethebook.com/html/about.php.

2. "Interview with Author Joshua Cohen," *Books Obsession*, August 7, 2011, accessed December 2, 2015, http://booksobsession.blogspot.com/2011/08/interview-with-author-joshua-cohen.html.

3. Cohen, "About Joshua C. Cohen."

4. "John Dalberg-Acton, 1st Baron Acton," *Wikipedia.* accessed December 2, 2015, https://en.wikipedia.org/wiki/John_Dalberg-Acton,_1st_Baron_Acton.

5. Kelly, "Leverage by Joshua Cohen," *Stacked*, March 3, 2011, accessed December 2, 2015, http://stackedbooks.org/2011/03/leverage-by-joshua-cohen.html.

6. Ibid.

## 19. *BOOT CAMP*
## BY TODD STRASSER

1. Todd Strasser, "Why I Wrote *Boot Camp*," *Help! You're Trapped in Todd Strasser's Body!* February 11, 2011, accessed December 2, 2015, http://toddstrasser.blogspot.com/2011/02/why-i-wrote-boot-camp.html.

2. Ibid.

3. Jesse Hyde, "Life and Death in a Troubled Teen Boot Camp," *Rolling Stone*, November 12, 2015, accessed December 2, 2015, http://www.rollingstone.com/culture/news/life-and-death-in-a-troubled-teen-boot-camp-20151112.

4. Mark Hennion, "Book Review: '*Boot Camp*' by Todd Strasser," *Shrouded Valley*, August 24, 2015, accessed December 2, 2015, https://markhennion.com/2015/08/24/book-review-boot-camp-by-todd-strasser/; "*Boot Camp* by Todd Strasser," *Young Adult Book Reviews*, May 11, 2010, accessed December 2, 2015, http://youngadultbookreviews.com/2010/05/11/boot-camp-by-todd-strasser/.

5. Strasser, "Why I Wrote *Boot Camp*."

6. Rashid Lynn, "Boot Camp: Review," *School Library Journal* 53, no. 4 (2007): 148.

7. Jeanne Larkins, "Boot Camp: Review," *Publishers Weekly* 254, no. 20 (2007): 55.

## 20. *BOY TOY*
## BY BARRY LYGA

1. "Fiction Reboot Author Interview: Barry Lyga, I Hunt Killers Series," *Medhum Fiction/Daily Dose*, May 29, 2015, accessed December 2, 2015, http://fictionreboot-dailydose.com/2015/05/29/fiction-reboot-author-interview-barry-lyga-i-hunt-killers-series/.

2. "20 Questions with Barry Lyga," *Comics Spotlight*, February 16, 2009, accessed December 2, 2015, http://comicsspotlight.blogspot.com/2009/02/20-questions-with-barry-lyga.html.

3. "Barry Lyga Interview, Part 2," Young Adult Review Network, April 25, 2010, accessed December 2, 2015, http://barrylyga.com/2010/05/interview-yarn-pt-2/.

## MONSTERS YOU LIVE WITH:
## NEAREST, BUT NOT DEAREST

1. "Child Abuse and Neglect Statistics," American Humane Association, accessed January 5, 2016, http://www.americanhumane.org/children/stop-child-abuse/fact-sheets/child-abuse-and-neglect-statistics.html.

2. Ibid.

3. Ibid.

4. "Child Maltreatment Prevention," Centers for Disease Control and Prevention, July 24, 2015, accessed January 5, 2016, http://www.cdc.gov/violenceprevention/childmaltreatment/.

5. American Humane Association, "Child Abuse and Neglect Statistics."

6. Ibid.

7. "Child Abuse Facts," Safe Horizon, accessed January 5, 2016, http://www.safehorizon.org/page/child-abuse-facts-56.html.

8. Ibid.

9. "Effects of Domestic Violence on Children," Domestic Violence Roundtable, accessed January 5, 2016, http://www.domesticviolenceroundtable.org/effect-on-children.html.

10. C. S. Widom, S. J. Czaja, and K. A. Dumont, "Intergenerational Transmission of Child Abuse and Neglect: Real or Detection Bias?" *Science*, 2015, 1480–85, accessed January 5, 2016, http://www.sciencemag.org/content/347/6229/1480.full.

11. Ibid.

12. "Sibling Abuse: The Unspoken Threat," HARO: Homeschool Alumni Reaching Out. November 3, 2014, accessed January 5, 2016, https://hareachingout.wordpress.com/sibling-abuse-the-unspoken-threat/.

13. Anahad O'Connor, "When the Bully Is a Sibling," *New York Times*, June 17, 2013, accessed January 5, 2016, http://well.blogs.nytimes.com/2013/06/17/when-the-bully-is-a-sibling/?_r=0.

14. "Sibling Abuse: The Unspoken Threat."

15. Ibid.

16. Katy Butler, "Beyond Rivalry: A Hidden World of Sibling Violence," *New York Times*, February 27, 2006, accessed January 5, 2016, http://www.nytimes.com/2006/02/28/health/28sibl.html?pagewanted=all.

17. B. H. Frazier, and K. C. Hayes, "Selected Resources on Sibling Abuse: An Annotated Bibliography for Researchers, Educators and Consumers," SRB 94-08, Special Reference Briefs, https://archive.org/details/ERIC_ED381715.

18. "Sibling Abuse," University of Michigan Health System, accessed January 5, 2016, http://www.med.umich.edu/yourchild/topics/sibabusec.htm.

19. Ibid.

20. John W. Fantuzzo, and Rachel A. Fusco, "Children's Direct Exposure to Types of Domestic Violence Crime: A Population-Based Investigation," *Journal of Family Violence* 22, no. 7 (2007): 543–52, accessed January 5, 2016, http://repository.upenn.edu/cgi/viewcontent.cgi?article=1125&context=gse_pubs.

21. Ibid.

22. Ibid.

## 22. *THE RULES OF SURVIVAL* BY NANCY WERLIN

1. Nancy Werlin, E-mail communication with author, 2006.

2. Nancy Werlin, *"Rules of Survival*—Inspiration and Discussion Questions," *Nancy Werlin.com*, accessed January 5, 2016, http://www.nancywerlin.com/.

3. Nancy Werlin, "Safe," *Nancy Werlin.com*, accessed January 5, 2016, archived athttp://web.archive.org/web/20120324051350/http://www.nancywerlin.com/safe.htm.

4. Werlin, *"Rules of Survival*—Inspiration."

5. Nancy Werlin, "Working with Fear: What Makes a Good Thriller?" *The Horn Book*, September 1, 2006, accessed January 5, 2016, http://www.

hbook.com/2006/09/choosing-books/horn-book-magazine/working-fear-
makes-good-thriller/.

    6. Ibid.


## 23. *HOPE IN PATIENCE*
## BY BETH FEHLBAUM


    1. Carolyn Lehman, "*Hope in Patience* Review," *School Library Journal* 57, no. 1 (2011): 104.

    2. Nancy Garden, back cover of Beth Fehlbaum, *Hope in Patience* Lodi, NJ: WestSide Books, 2010.

    3. Shelley Rosenfeld, "*Hope in Patience* Review," *Booklist* 107 nos. 9–10 (2011): 106.

    4. Garden, back cover of *Hope in Patience*.

    5. Adam Appleson, "Courage in Patience—Interview with Author Beth Fehlbaum," *Zen Tactics*, accessed January 5, 2016, http://www.zentactics.com/courage-in-patience.html.

    6. "Meet Beth Fehlbaum, Author of *Hope in Patience*," *The Dark Phantom Review*, October 15, 2010, accessed January 5, 2016, https://thedarkphantom.wordpress.com/2010/10/15/meet-beth-fehlbaum-author-of-hope-in-patience/

    7. Beth Fehlbaum, "The Long Goodbye—Beth Fehlbaum," *Beth Fehlbaum Books.com*, accessed January 5, 2016, http://www.bethfehlbaumbooks.com/about-me/the-long-goodbye/.

    8. Appleson, "Courage in Patience Interview."

    9. Ibid.

    10. Cheryl Rainfield, "Interview with YA Author Beth Fehlbaum," *Cheryl Rainfield.com*, June 12, 2011, accessed January 5, 2016, http://cherylrainfield.com/blog/index.php/2011/06/02/interview-with-ya-author-beth-fehlbaum/#.VttZlfkrKUk.

    11. Ibid.

## 24. *WHAT HAPPENED TO CASS MCBRIDE?*
## BY GAIL GILES

1. Beverly Rowe, "Author of the Month: Gail Giles," *MyShelf.com*, accessed November 2, 2015, http://myshelf.com/aom/07/giles.htm.

2. Gail Giles, "How I Wrote *Cass McBride*," *GailGiles.com*, accessed November 2, 2015, http://www.gailgiles.com/How_I_Wrote_Cass_Mc_ Bride.html.

3. Rowe, "Author of the Month: Gail Giles."

4. Ibid.

5. "Interview with Gail Giles," *YA Review Network*, October 11, 2011, accessed November 2, 2015, http://yareview.net/2011/10/interview-with-gail-giles/.

6. Cynthia Leitich Smith, "Author Update: Gail Giles," *Cynsations*, accessed November 2, 2015, http://cynthialeitichsmith.blogspot.com/2006/ 03/author-update-gail-giles.html.

7. Gail Giles, "Teachers Guide—Cass McBride," *GailGiles.com*, accessed November 2, 2015, http://www.gailgiles.com/How_I_Wrote_Cass_ Mc_Bride.html.

8. Ibid.


## 25. *THE CHOSEN ONE*
## BY CAROL LYNCH WILLIAMS

1. "Author Talk: May 2009—Carol Lynch Williams," *Teenreads*, May 1, 2009, accessed January 3, 2016, http://www.teenreads.com/authors/ carol-lynch-williams/news/talk-050909.

2. Cindy Hudson, "Interview with Carol Lynch Williams, Author of *The Chosen One*," *Mother Daughter Bookclub*. May 12, 2009, accessed January 3, 2016, http://motherdaughterbookclub.com/2009/05/the-chosen-one-book-giveaway-author-interview/.

3. "Author Talk: May 2009—Carol Lynch Williams."

4. Ibid.

5. Cynthia Leitich Smith, "Author Interview: Carol Lynch Williams on *The Chosen One*." *Cynsations*, May 12, 2009, accessed January 3,

2016, http://cynthialeitichsmith.blogspot.com/2009/05/author-interview-carol-lynch-williams.html.

6. Ibid.

## MANIPULATORS: RAPISTS, KIDNAPPERS, AND OTHER PREDATORS

1. "Key Facts," National Center for Missing and Exploited Children, accessed January 15, 2016, http://www.missingkids.com/KeyFacts.

2. Karin A. Bilich, "Child Abduction Facts," *Parents*, accessed January 15, 2016, http://www.parents.com/kids/safety/stranger-safety/child-abduction-facts/.

3. Ibid.

4. "Key Facts."

5. Bilich, "Child Abduction Facts."

6. David Finkelhor, "Five Myths about Missing Children," *Washington Post*, May 10, 2013, accessed January 15, 2016, https://www.washingtonpost.com/opinions/five-myths-about-missing-children/2013/05/10/efee398c-b8b4-11e2-aa9e-a02b765ff0ea_story.html.

7. "Some Basic Concepts Needed to Understand Psychopaths in Our World," *Fried Green Tomatoes and Steel Magnolias*, accessed January 15, 2016, http://www.friedgreentomatoes.org/articles/basic_concepts.php.

8. "Psychological Manipulation," *Wikipedia*, accessed January 15, 2016, https://en.wikipedia.org/wiki/Psychological_manipulation.

9. Diane Wetendorf, "Police Culture, Brotherhood, Code of Silence: Police Officer Involved Domestic Violence," *Police Officer Training*, accessed January 15, 2016, http://www.abuseofpower.info/Culture_Training.htm.

10. "Manipulation Tactics: A Closer Look," *Manipulative People.com*, 2013, accessed January 15, 2016, http://www.manipulative-people.com/manipulation-tactics-a-closer-look/.

11. Erica Tempesta, "Are You Dating an Emotional Manipulator? Relationship Experts Reveal Six Warning Signs That Prove Your Relationship Is Toxic," *Daily Mail Online*, July 31, 2015, accessed January 15, 2016, http://www.dailymail.co.uk/femail/article-3180252/Are-dating-emotional-manipulator-Relationship-experts-reveal-six-warning-signs-prove-relationship-toxic-lead-heartbreak.html.

12.  Harry W. More, W. Fred Wegener, and Larry S. Miller, *Effective Police Supervision* (New York, NY: Routledge, 2010).

## 26. *THIS GORGEOUS GAME*
## BY DONNA FREITAS

1.  "Interview with Author Donna Freitas," The INSPY Awards, 2010, accessed January 15, 2016, http://inspys.com/?p=622.
2.  "Donna Freitas Interview," *Angieville*, June 1, 2010, accessed January 15, 2016, http://www.angie-ville.com/2010/06/donna-freitas-interview-this-gorgeous.html.
3.  Ibid.
4.  Ibid.
5.  "Review #3: *This Gorgeous Game*, by Donna Freitas," Random Library Adventures, 2010, Accessed January 15, 2016, https://randomlibris.wordpress.com/2010/12/28/review-3-this-gorgeous-game-by-donna-freitas/.
6.  Ibid.
7.  "Interview with Donna Freitas."
8.  "*This Gorgeous Game*—Editorial Reviews," Barnes & Noble, accessed January 15, 2016, http://www.barnesandnoble.com/w/this-gorgeous-game-donna-freitas/1100358326.
9.  "Review—*This Gorgeous Game* by Donna Freitas," *Slayground*, accessed January 15, 2016, http://slayground.livejournal.com/589627.html.
10.  "Review #3: *This Gorgeous Game.*"

## 27. *CUT ME FREE*
## BY J. R. JOHANSSON

1.  "*Cut Me Free* by J. R. Johansson," *Forever Bookish*, January 22, 2015, Accessed January 15, 2016, http://foreverbookish.com/2015/01/22/cutmefree/.
2.  Ibid.

3. *"Cut Me Free*—Editorial Reviews," Barnes & Noble, accessed January 15, 2016, http://www.barnesandnoble.com/w/cut-me-free-j-r-johansson/1118931329.

4. "J. R. Johansson, Author of *Insomnia* and *Paranoia*," *Indie & Debut Author Interviews*. September 8, 2014, accessed January 15, 2016, http://interviwingauthors.blogspot.com/2014/09/jr-johansson-author-of-insomnia-and.html.

5. Ibid.

6. Ibid.

7. Ibid.

8. "Teen Author Boot Camp Interview 2015: J. R. Johansson," *Patheos: The Rogue*, accessed January 15, 2016, http://www.patheos.com/blogs/geekgoesrogue/2015/04/teen-author-boot-camp-interview-2015-j-r-johansson/.

9. Ibid.

10. "J. R. Johansson, Author of *Insomnia* and *Paranoia*."

11. "Teen Author Boot Camp Interview 2015: J. R. Johansson."

12. *"Cut Me Free* by J. R. Johansson."

## 28. *RUTHLESS*
## BY CAROLYN LEE ADAMS

1. "Author Interview: *Ruthless* by Carolyn Lee Adams," *Her Book Thoughts*, 2015, accessed January 15, 2016, http://herbookthoughts.reads-it.com/?p=4298.

2. Kristin Halbrook, "YA Highway Query Series: Carolyn Lee Adams and Mandy Hubbard Discuss *Ruthless*," *YA Highway*, accessed January 15, 2016, http://www.yahighway.com/2014/06/query-series-carolyn-lee-and-mandy.html.

3. "Gary Ridgway," *Wikipedia*, accessed January 15, 2016, https://en.wikipedia.org/wiki/Gary_Ridgway.

4. "Author Interview, *Ruthless*."

5. Ibid.

6. *"Ruthless* by Carolyn Lee Adams," *Addicted Readers*, July 11, 2015, accessed January 15, 2016, http://addictreaders.blogspot.com/2015/07/ruthlessby-carolyn-lee-adams-blog-tour.html.

7. "Author Interview, *Ruthless*."

8. Carolyn Lee Adams Author Page, accessed November 11, 2015, https://www.facebook.com/permalink.php?story_fbid= 1494124950884353&id=1411876522442530.

9. Jocelyn Rish, "Carolyn Lee Adams, Author of *Ruthless*, on Taking 'Thinking Showers' When Stuck," *Adventures in YA Publishing*, July 18, 2015, accessed January 15, 2016.

10. Ibid.

11. "Author Interview, *Ruthless*."

12. Rish, "Carolyn Lee Adams."

13. Ibid.

14. "*Ruthless* by Carolyn Lee Adams."

15. "Author Interview, *Ruthless*."

16. Rish, "Carolyn Lee Adams."

17. Ibid.

# BIBLIOGRAPHY

**N**ote to the Reader: This is not a comprehensive bibliography of books on various kinds of human monsters, but rather is limited to the titles in which I saw truly awful, toxic characters, as opposed to people struggling to survive in difficult and horrific situations. I have not included titles in which the characters are struggling to survive mental illness, because I don't consider that process to be monstrous. I have made these decisions based on my knowledge of the content of these titles and the characters that populate them. Of course, any reader is free to disagree. with my selections

## MASS MURDERERS: SERIAL KILLERS AND SCHOOL SHOOTINGS

Backderf, Derf. 2012. *My Friend Dahmer: A Graphic Novel*. New York: Abrams Co-micArts.

Belasen, Amy, and Jacob Osborn. 2008. *Jenny Green's Killer Junior Year*. New York: Simon Pulse.

Brooks, Kevin. 2003. *Lucas*. New York: Chicken House/Scholastic.

Brown, Jennifer. 2009. *Hate List*. New York: Little, Brown.

Cormier, Robert. 1997. *Tenderness: A Novel*. New York: Delacorte Press.

Ewell, Katherine. 2014. *Dear Killer*. New York: HarperCollinsPublishers.

Ferguson, Alane. 2006. *The Angel of Death: A Forensic Mystery*. New York: Sleuth/Viking.

Ferguson, Alane. 2009. *The Dying Breath: A Forensic Mystery*. New York: Viking.

Ferguson, Alane. 2008. *The Circle Of Blood: A Forensic Mystery*. New York: Viking.

Ferguson, Alane. 2006. *The Christopher Killer: A Forensic Mystery*. New York: Viking/Sleuth.
Flinn, Alex. 2002. *Breaking Point*. New York: HarperTempest.
Gallo, Donald R. 2001. *On the Fringe*. New York: Dial Books.
Garden, Nancy. 2006. *Endgame*. Orlando, FL: Harcourt.
Girard, Geoffrey. 2013. *Cain's Blood*. New York: Simon & Schuster.
Girard, Geoffrey. 2013. *Project Cain*. New York: Simon & Schuster.
Green, S. E. 2014. *Killer Instinct*. New York: Simon Pulse.
Halliday, John. 2003. *Shooting Monarchs*. New York: Margaret K. Mcelderry Books.
Johnson, Maureen. 2013. *The Madness Underneath*. New York: G. P. Putnam's Sons.
Johnson, Maureen. 2011. *The Name of the Star*. New York: G. P. Putnam's Sons.
Libby, Alisa M. 2006. *The Blood Confession*. New York: Dutton Books.
Lyga, Barry. 2014. *Blood of My Blood*. New York: Little, Brown.
Lyga, Barry. 2012. *I Hunt Killers*. New York: Little, Brown.
Lyga, Barry. 2013. *Game*. New York: Little, Brown.
McNamee, Graham. 2003. *Acceleration*. New York: Wendy Lamb Books.
Meyer, Adam. 2005. *The Last Domino*. New York: G.P. Putnam's Sons.
Myers, Walter Dean. 2004. *Shooter*. New York: Amistad/Harpertempest.
Ostow, Micol. 2011. *Family*. New York: Egmont USA.
Petrucha, Stefan. 2012. *Ripper*. New York: Philomel Books.
Phillips, Suzanne. 2008. *Burn: A Novel*. New York: Little, Brown and Co.
Reeves, Amy Carol. 2014. *Resurrection*. Woodbury, MN: Flux.
Reeves, Amy Carol. 2013. *Renegade*. Woodbury, MN: Flux.
Reeves, Amy Carol. 2012. *Ripper*. Woodbury, MN: Flux.
Reeves, Dia. 2011. *Slice of Cherry*. New York: Simon Pulse.
Schrefer, Eliot. *School for Dangerous Girls*. 2010. New York: Scholastic.
Smith, Andrew. 2009. *In the Path of Falling Objects*. New York: Feiwel and Friends.
Strasser, Todd. 2000. *Give a Boy a Gun*. New York: Simon & Schuster Books for Young Readers.
Strasser, Todd. 2009. *Wish You Were Dead*. New York: Egmont USA.
Watson, C. G. 2007. *Quad*. New York: Razorbill.

# BULLIES: IN YOUR FACE AND ON YOUR SCREEN

Anderson, M. T. 1999. *Burger Wuss*. Cambridge, MA: Candlewick Press.
Asher, Jay. 2007. *Thirteen Reasons Why: A Novel*. New York: Razorbill.
Benoit, Charles. 2014. *Cold Calls*. New York: Houghton Mifflin Harcourt.
Flinn, Alex. (2002). *Breaking Point*. New York: HarperTempest.
Giles, G. (2002). *Shattering Glass*. Brookfield, CT: Roaring Brook Press.
Hautman, Pete. (2010). *Blank Confession*. New York: Simon & Schuster Books for Young Readers.
Lange, Erin J. 2012. *Butter*. New York: Bloomsbury.
Littman, S. (2011). *Want to Go Private?* New York: Scholastic Press.
Maciel, A. (2014). *Tease*. New York: Balzer + Bray.
McGowan, A. (2010). *The Knife That Killed Me*. New York: Delacorte Press.
Myracle, L. (2011). *Shine*. New York: Amulet Books.
Peters, J. A. (2010). *By the Time You Read This, I'll Be Dead*. New York: Hyperion/ DBG.
Plum-Ucci, C. (2000). *The Body of Christopher Creed*. San Diego: Harcourt.
Plum-Ucci, C. (2002). *What Happened to Lani Garver*. San Diego: Harcourt.

Preller, J. (2009). *Bystander*. New York: Feiwel and Friends.
Prose, F. (2007). *Bullyville*. New York: HarperTeen.
Shulman, M. (2010). *Scrawl: A Novel*. New York: Roaring Brook Press.
Walton, K. M. (2012). *Cracked*. New York: Simon Pulse.

## MONSTERS AT SCHOOL: TEACHERS, COACHES, ATHLETES, AND OTHERS

Brooks, Kevin. 2015. *The Bunker Diary*. Minneapolis, MN: Carolrhoda.
Brown, Chris Carlton. 2009. *Hoppergrass*. New York: Henry Holt.
Burgess, Melvin. 2010. *Nicholas Dane*. New York: Henry Holt and Co.
Cohen, Joshua. 2011. *Leverage*. New York: Dutton Books.
Cormier, Robert. 1974. *The Chocolate War: A Novel*. New York: Pantheon Books.
Coy, John. 2005. *Crackback*. New York: Scholastic Press.
Crutcher, Chris. 2001. *Whale Talk*. New York: Greenwillow Books.
Crutcher, Chris. 1995. *Ironman: A Novel*. New York: Greenwillow Books.
Deuker, Carl. 2007. *Gym Candy*. Boston: Houghton Mifflin Co.
Deuker, Carl. 2013. *Swagger*. New York: Houghton Mifflin Harcourt.
Frank, E. R. 2003. *Friction: A Novel*. New York: Atheneum Books for Young Readers.
Gardner, Graham. (2004). *Inventing Elliot*. New York: Dial Books.
Hartinger, Brent. 2003. *Geography Club*. New York: HarperTempest.
Hartinger, Brent. 2005. *The Order of the Poison Oak*. New York: HarperTempest.
Lipsyte, Robert. 2006. *Raiders Night*. New York: HarperTempest.
Lyga, Barry. 2007. *Boy Toy*. Boston: Graphia.
Nelson, R. A. 2005. *Teach Me: A Novel*. New York: Razorbill.
Rapp, Adam. 1997. *The Buffalo Tree*. Arden, NC: Front Street.
Sleator, William. 1974. *House of Stairs*. New York: E.P. Dutton.
Strasser, Todd. 2007. *Boot Camp*. New York: Simon & Schuster Books for Young Readers.
Summers, C. (2009). *Some Girls Are*. New York: St. Martin's Griffin.
Summers, C. (2009). *Cracked Up to Be*. New York: St. Martin's Griffin.
Thompson, Julian F. 1997. *The Grounding of Group 6*. New York: Henry Holt.
Whitney, D. (2010). *The Mockingbirds*. New York: Little, Brown.

## MONSTERS YOU LIVE WITH: NEAREST, BUT NOT DEAREST

Alphin, Elaine M. 2000. *Counterfeit Son*. San Diego: Harcourt.
Anderson, Laurie H. (2007). *Twisted*. New York: Viking.
Bloor, Edward. (1997). *Tangerine*. San Diego: Harcourt Brace.
Bodeen, S. A. (2008). *The Compound*. New York: Feiwel and Friends.
Bodeen, S. A. (2013). *The Fallout*. New York: Feiwel and Friends.
Caletti, Deb. 2005. *Wild Roses*. New York: Simon & Schuster Books for Young Readers.
Colasanti, S. (2012). *Keep Holding On*. New York: Viking.
Crutcher, C. (1989). *Chinese Handcuffs*. New York: Greenwillow Books.

Crutcher, Chris. 1993. *Staying Fat for Sarah Byrnes*. New York: Greenwillow Books.
Cumbie, P. (2008). *Where People Like Us Live*. New York: Laura Geringer Books/ Harperteen.
Dean, C. (2002). *Comfort*. Boston: Houghton Mifflin.
Fehlbaum, Beth. 2010. *Hope in Patience*. Lodi, NJ: WestSide Books.
Flinn, Alex. (2001). *Breathing Underwater*. New York: HarperCollins Publishers.
Flinn, A. (2004). *Nothing to Lose*. New York: Harpertempest.
Frank, E. R. (2002). *America: A Novel*. New York: Atheneum Books for Young Readers.
Friend, N. (2006). *Lush*. New York: Scholastic Press.
Giles, Gail. 2006. *What Happened to Cass McBride? A Novel*. New York: Little, Brown and Company.
Klass, David. (2010). *You Don't Know Me*. New York: Square Fish.
Lynch, C. (2005). *Inexcusable*. New York: Atheneum Books for Young Readers.
Lyons, C. J. *Broken*. 2014. New York: Sourcebook Fire.
Mazer, Norma Fox. 1997. *When She Was Good*. New York: Arthur A. Levine Books.
Oaks, J. Adams. 2009. *Why I Fight: A Novel*. New York: Atheneum Books for Young Readers.
Quick, M. (2008) *Forgive Me, Leonard Peacock*. New York: Little Brown.
Rapp, A. (2002). *Little Chicago*. Asheville, NC: Front Street.
Shusterman, N. (2007). *Unwind*. New York: Simon & Schuster Books for Young Readers.
Shusterman, N. (2012). *UnWholly*. New York: Simon & Schuster Books for Young Readers.
Suzuma, T. (2011). *Forbidden*. New York: Simon Pulse.
Sweeney, J. (2009). *The Guardian*. New York: Henry Holt.
Voigt, Cynthia. 1994. *When She Hollers*. New York: Scholastic.
Werlin, Nancy. 2006. *The Rules of Survival*. New York: Dial Books.
Williams, Carol Lynch. 2009. *The Chosen One*. New York: St. Martin's Griffin.

## MANIPULATORS: RAPISTS, KIDNAPPERS, AND OTHER PREDATORS

Adams, Carolyn L. 2015. *Ruthless*. New York: Simon Pulse.
Anderson, Laurie H. 1999. *Speak*. New York: Farrar, Straus, and Giroux.
Brooks, Kevin. 2015. *The Bunker Diary*. New York: Scholastic Inc.
Cassidy, Anne. 2007. *Looking for JJ*. Orlando, FL: Harcourt.
Christopher, Lucy. (2010). *Stolen*. New York: Chicken House/Scholastic.
Cole, Brent. (1997). *The Facts Speak for Themselves*. Arden, NC: Front Street.
Cormier, Robert. 2003. *The Rag and Bone Shop*. New York: Random House Children's Books.
De la Pena, Matt. *I Will Save You*. 2011. New York: Ember.
Dessen, S. (2000). *Dreamland: A Novel*. New York: Viking.
Freitas, Donna. 2010. *This Gorgeous Game*. New York: Farrar, Straus, and Giroux.
Johanssen, J. R. 2015. *Cut Me Free*. New York: Farrar, Straus, and Giroux.
Knowles, J. (2007). *Lessons from a Dead Girl*. Cambridge, MA: Candlewick Press.
Marcus, Kimberly. (2011). *Exposed*. New York: Random House.
McCormick, Patricia. 2006. *Sold*. New York: Hyperion.
Rainfield, C. A. (2010). *Scars*. New York: Westside Books.

Rapp, Adam, and Timothy B. Ering. (2003). *33 Snowfish*. Cambridge, MA: Candlewick Press.

Rapp, A. (2012). *The Children and the Wolves*. Asheville, NC: Front Street.

Sáenz, B. A. (2009). *Last Night I Sang to the Monster: A Novel*. El Paso, TX: Cinco Puntos Press.

Scott, Elizabeth. (2009). *Living Dead Girl*. New York: Simon & Schuster Children's Pub.

Shaw, S. (2007). *Safe*. New York: Dutton Books.

Silvey, C. (2011). *Jasper Jones: A Novel*. New York: Alfred A. Knopf.

Stratton, A. (2000). *Leslie's Journal: A Novel*. Toronto: Annick Press.

Turner, Ann. *Learning to Swim*. 2000. New York: Scholastic.

Williams, Carol Lynch. (2009). *The Chosen One*. New York: St. Martin's Griffin.

Wittlinger, E. (2005). *Sandpiper*. New York: Simon & Schuster Books for Young Readers.

# INDEX

abuse of teens and children: "boot camps", 147–149; effects of, 205–206, 207, 209–210; recovery from, 207–208; statistics, xxii; survival, 208, 209. *See also* coaches, abusive; family violence; parental abuse; peers, abuse by; teachers

*Acceleration*, 2, 23–26

Adams, Carolyn Lee, 211–219

adolescent brain, development of, xix–xxi, xxxi, 115

alcohol abuse by teens, 57–58, 59–60; statistics, xxv

ambiguous endings, 91, 108, 109, 110, 112, 125–126, 131–132, 149, 184, 190, 222, 224–225, 229

*And Then There Were Four*, 171

anger, prevalence of, xv; in teens, xx–xxi

animal mutilation, 23–24

Aronson, Marc, 233

Backderf, Derf, 2, 48, 53–60

*Beyond the Chocolate War*, 225

bisexual teens. *See* LGBTQ teens

*The Body of Christopher Creed*, 134

bookmobile, 186, 188–189

books as therapy, xvi, 107–108, 121, 125, 127, 128, 132, 167–168, 171, 182, 186–187, 188, 198, 208, 231

*Boot Camp*, 134, 147–149

Boston Marathon shooting, xiv

*Boy Toy*, 133, 151–153

brain, development of. *See* adolescent brain, development of

*Breaking Point*, 134

*Breaking Rank*, 134

*Breathing Underwater*, xviii

Brown, Jennifer, 2, 11, 85–89

*The Buffalo Tree*, 134

bullies, 94, 101, 113, 114, 115–116; statistics, 102

bullying, xiii, 13–17, 71–74, 82, 83, 86, 91–92, 113–117, 126–132, 133–141, 212; biological origins of, 93; bystanders, effects on, 101; physical behaviors, 93; physical effects of, xxiii–xxiv, 7, 63, 95, 100, 101; psychological effects of, 100, 101; solutions, 103–104; statistics, xxiii, 102; suicide as an effect of, 101, 114, 116–117. *See also* coaches, abusive; cyberbullying; LGBTQ teens, bullying of; teachers

*The Bunker Diary*, 134

# ABOUT THE AUTHOR

**Joni Richards Bodart** is an associate professor at the San Jose State University School of Information (iSchool). She received her PhD in library science from Texas Woman's University and also holds an MLS and a MA in psychology. She has taught for SJSU since 2003, and has also taught for Emporia State University and the University of Denver. Dr. Bodart also speaks regularly at school and public library workshops and conferences.

In addition to controversial literature and monster literature, her research interests include the need in LIS education for youth librarianship coursework on the culture of adolescents and their developmental psychosocial needs and how to create a "third place" for them at public libraries, and how the changes in technology (i.e., websites, blogs, social networking) have impacted the ways YA authors communicate with their readers, and the impact that has on their writing.

Dr. Bodart has published more than twenty books on young adult literature, including two series on booktalking, which are considered to be the standard for the field. Her books for Scarecrow include *The World's Best Thin Books: What to Read When Your Book Report Is Due Tomorrow* (2000) and *Radical Reads: 101 YA Novels on the Edge* (2002). *Radical Reads 2: Working with the Newest Edgy Titles for Teens* (2009), which focuses on the newest and most controversial fiction titles for teens, is designed to help librarians and teachers use and defend these important titles. She has contributed one previous title to the Studies in Young Adult Literature series, *They Suck, They Bite, They Eat, They Kill: The Psychological Meaning of Supernatural Monsters in Young Adult Fiction* (2012). Her next book will be *World's Best Thin Books for Twenty-First-Century Teens: What to Read When Your Book Report Is Due Tomorrow!*

Dr. Bodart is the winner of the 2010 Scholastic Library Publishing Award, formerly the Grolier Award, given annually to a librarian whose "extraordinary contributions to promoting access to books and encouraging a love of reading for lifelong learning exemplifies outstanding achievement in the profession."